Aging in Rural Places

Kristina M. Hash, PhD, LICSW, is an associate professor in the School of Social Work and director of the Gerontology Certificate Program at West Virginia University. She holds a PhD in social work from Virginia Commonwealth University, a master's degree in social work and a graduate gerontology certificate from West Virginia University, and a bachelor of arts degree from St. Catherine University. Her research interests include geriatric education, rural gerontology, LGBT (lesbian, gay, bisexual, and transgender) issues, and the use of technology in teaching and research. Her work has been published in the *Journal of Gerontological Social Work, Journal of Gay and Lesbian Social Services, Clinical Social Work Journal,* and *Geriatric and Gerontology Education* as well as in edited books. She has taught courses on diversity, health and aging, rural gerontology, social work practice, social work research, and human behavior in the social environment. Dr. Hash is an expert trainer and consultant for the Council on Social Work Education's National Center for Gerontological Social Work Education; was one of 15 participants chosen nationally for the National Institute of Aging (NIA) First Annual Institute on Aging and Social Work; and has been an investigator for four geriatric education grants funded by the John A. Hartford Foundation and the U.S. Department of Health and Human Services (HHS), Health Resources and Services Administration (HRSA), and Bureau of Health Professions (BHPR).

Dr. Hash is a recipient of the Outstanding Principal Investigator Award from the New York Academy of Medicine's Social Work Leadership Institute; the David Z. Morgan Award for Excellence in Geriatric Education from the West Virginia Geriatric Education Center and West Virginia Geriatrics Society; and the Judith Gold Stitzel Award for teaching and leadership from the West Virginia University Center for Women's Studies. Her practice background includes positions in home health care, social work continuing education, and research and program evaluation. Additionally, she has been involved in several volunteer activities with community-based agencies serving older adults. Her experience as a caregiver for her grandmother was the driving force behind her interest in social work and aging.

Elaine T. Jurkowski, PhD, MSW, is a professor and interim director at Southern Illinois University Carbondale's School of Social Work, where she teaches courses in health and aging policy, research, and program evaluation and also holds a joint appointment with the Department of Health Education. Dr. Jurkowski earned her bachelor's and master's degrees in social work from the University of Manitoba in Winnipeg, Manitoba, Canada, and her PhD from the University of Illinois, Chicago. Dr. Jurkowski's early career experience working as a social worker in a community public health interdisciplinary setting in Manitoba, Canada, exposed her to mental health, disability, vocational rehabilitation, and aging programs. These early experiences, coupled with her training in community health sciences and epidemiology, have shaped Dr. Jurkowski's research and practice interests. Dr. Jurkowski's research has been funded by the National Institutes of Health (NIH), the John A. Hartford Foundation, the Health and Human Services Administration, the Administration on Aging (AoA), and the Illinois Department on Aging. Her published research articles have focused on the topics of health disparities, access to mental health and health care services, aging, and disability issues. She has held elected offices in the American Public Health Association (APHA), National Association of Social Workers (NASW), the Gerontological Society of America (GSA), and the Illinois Rural Health Association (IRHA).

Her work experiences have included consultation within settings in Niger (West Africa), Hong Kong, India, China, Russia, and Egypt. She is the author of *Policy and Program Planning for Older Adults* (2008, Springer Publishing Company) and *Implementing Culture Change in Long-Term Care: Benchmarks and Strategies for Management and Practice* (2013, Springer Publishing Company), was managing coeditor of *Handbook for Public Health Social Work* (2013, Springer Publishing Company), and has written numerous book chapters and professional articles. Dr. Jurkowski's community service includes serving as a member of the board of directors for various not-for-profit health care agencies within the southern Illinois area. Dr. Jurkowski also serves as an advisor to the Southern Illinois Pioneer Coalition Advisory Board.

John A. Krout, PhD, is a professor emeritus of gerontology at Ithaca College, where he served as professor of gerontology and director of the Gerontology Institute from 1993 to 2011. He received degrees in sociology from Denison University (BA), Bowling Green State University (MA), and Pennsylvania State University (PhD). The author of six other books, he has also written some 75 book chapters and journal articles and has made more than 125 presentations at national and state conferences. Dr. Krout has received some 20 grants to support a research program on rural aging, community-based services, relocation and housing, and service learning. While heading the Gerontology Institute at Ithaca, he initiated the college's intergenerational partnership with Longview, a multilevel residential care facility for older adults; received more than $2 million in external funding to support faculty and student research; initiated and headed the Linden Center for Creativity and Aging; and developed Ithaca's partnership with the federally funded Finger Lakes Geriatric Education Center,

as well as other programs to provide education and training to practitioners across upstate New York. A dedicated scholar and teacher, he was (and
remains) passionate about developing academic programs and supporting
student and faculty research that embraces interdisciplinary and multidisciplinary approaches to studying aging and improving the lives of older adults.

Dr. Krout is a past president of the State Society on Aging (SSA) of New
York; a fellow of the Gerontological Society of America (GSA), where he was
the founding chair of the Rural Aging Interest Group at GSA; and a charter fellow of the Association of Gerontology in Higher Education (AGHE). He served
on the board of AGHE where he also worked on the Public Policy, Program of
Merit, and K–12 committees. Dr. Krout has received several awards from the
National Council on the Aging (NCOA) for his work on rural aging and senior
centers. Other honors include the Walter M. Beattie Jr. Award from SSA and the
Mildred Seltzer Distinguished Service Recognition from AGHE.

Aging in Rural Places

Policies, Programs, and Professional Practice

Kristina M. Hash, PhD, LICSW
Elaine T. Jurkowski, PhD, MSW
John A. Krout, PhD

Editors

SPRINGER PUBLISHING COMPANY
NEW YORK

Springer Publishing Company, LLC
11 West 42nd Street
New York, NY 10036
www.springerpub.com

Acquisitions Editor: Sheri W. Sussman
Production Editor: Shelby Peak
Composition: Amnet

Photo Acknowledgments
Cover: Ms. Barb, by Kristina Hash, PhD, LICSW
Part I: Buster and Friend, by Neal A. Newfield, PhD
Part II: Lowell: Born and Raised in Rural WV, by Sherry K. Kuhl, MSW, MS
Part III: Family Ties, by Neal A. Newfield, PhD
Part IV: Health Care, by Neal A. Newfield, PhD
Part V: Shenandoah Sunset, by Sueann F. Schwille, MSW, LMHP-E

ISBN: 978-0-8261-9809-9
e-book ISBN: 978-0-8261-9811-2
Instructor's Manual ISBN: 978-0-8261-9602-6
Instructor's PowerPoint Slides ISBN: 978-0-8261-9601-9

Instructor's Materials: Instructors may request supplements by emailing textbook@springerpub.com

14 15 16 17 / 5 4 3 2 1

The author and the publisher of this Work have made every effort to use sources believed to be reliable to provide information that is accurate and compatible with the standards generally accepted at the time of publication. The author and publisher shall not be liable for any special, consequential, or exemplary damages resulting, in whole or in part, from the readers' use of, or reliance on, the information contained in this book. The publisher has no responsibility for the persistence or accuracy of URLs for external or third-party Internet websites referred to in this publication and does not guarantee that any content on such websites is, or will remain, accurate or appropriate.

Library of Congress Cataloging-in-Publication Data
Hash, Kristina Michelle, author.
 Aging in rural places : policies, programs, and professional practice / Kristina Michelle Hash, Elaine Theresa Jurkowski, John A. Krout.
     p. ; cm.
 Includes bibliographical references and index.
 ISBN 978-0-8261-9809-9 (alk. paper) — ISBN 978-0-8261-9811-2 (e-book)   I. Jurkowski, Elaine Theresa, author. II. Krout, John A., author. III. Title.
 [DNLM: 1. Health Services for the Aged. 2. Rural Health Services. 3. Aged. 4. Health Policy. 5. Rural Population. 6. Socioeconomic Factors. WT 31]
 RA564.8
 362.1084'6—dc23
                                                                              2014011221

Printed in the United States of America by McNaughton & Gunn.

To older adults residing in rural settings and communities
—Kris, Elaine, and John

To my gals, Sarah and Alyssa—Kris

To Bill and our families residing in rural communities—Elaine

In memory of John E. Krout, Patricia Kehr, and Sidney E. Nobbs—John

CONTENTS

CONTRIBUTORS

Anwer U. Azim, MBA
Elder Law Clinic
School of Law
School of Social Work
Southern Illinois University
Carbondale, Illinois

JoAnn Damron-Rodriguez, PhD
Luskin School of Public Affairs
University of California, Los Angeles
Los Angeles, California

Sarah R. DeWolfe, MSW
Boalsburg, PA

David P. Elliott, PharmD
School of Pharmacy
West Virginia University
Charleston, West Virginia

Denise Gammonley, PhD
School of Social Work
University of Central Florida
Orlando, Florida

Sarah A. Harvey, MSW
Center on Aging
University of Maine
Bangor, Maine

Kristina M. Hash, PhD, LICSW
School of Social Work
West Virginia University
Morgantown, West Virginia

M. Helen Hogue, MSW
School of Social Work
Department of Health Education and Recreation
Southern Illinois University
Carbondale, Illinois

Elaine T. Jurkowski, PhD, MSW
School of Social Work
Southern Illinois University
Carbondale, Illinois

Lenard W. Kaye, PhD, DSW
Center on Aging
University of Maine
Bangor, Maine

Lindsay Knaus, MSW
Paul Simon Public Policy Institute
Southern Illinois University
Carbondale, Illinois

John A. Krout, PhD
Professor Emeritus
Gerontology Institute
Ithaca College
Ithaca, New York

Janice Elich Monroe, PhD
Department of Recreation and Leisure Studies
Ithaca College
Ithaca, New York

Shirley M. Neitch, MD
School of Medicine
Marshall University
Huntington, West Virginia

Barbara L. Nunley, PhD
School of Nursing
West Virginia University
Morgantown, West Virginia

Maor Rubinstein, BSW
School of Social Work
Southern Illinois University
Carbondale, Illinois

Loriann Sonntag, MA, MSW
Alzheimer's Association–West Virginia Chapter
Morgantown, West Virginia

S. Melinda Spencer, PhD
Department of Health Promotion, Education, and Behavior
Arnold School of Public Health
University of South Carolina
Columbia, South Carolina

Hanna Thurman, MSW, MPA
West Virginia Geriatric Education Center
Charleston, West Virginia

Rebecca Wells, BA
Department of Health Promotion, Education, and Behavior
Arnold School of Public Health
University of South Carolina
Columbia, South Carolina

R. Constance Wiener, PhD
School of Dentistry
West Virginia University
Morgantown, West Virginia

FOREWORD

Over several decades of studying the lived experience of older adults in rural settings, I have on a number of occasions come across the adage, "When you have seen one rural community, you have seen one rural community," that appears in the opening chapter of this book. And yet, when I make presentations at conferences and community forums on my field research in Colton (a pseudonym), a rural Appalachian community, a member of the audience invariably comes up to me after my talk to wryly let me know that, of course, he or she is familiar with Colton and is pleased that I have been able to capture the essence of life in his or her community. That person is always wrong. The place I studied is not the one that has been identified. At the same time, I am flattered by repeated confirmation that my research has been able to capture and portray something of life in rural Appalachia that is recognizable and has meaning to all local residents.

When you have seen one rural community, you have *not* just seen one rural community, but rather have been privileged to enter a world that is very different from the urban settings within which most people reside. Although this world is diversely manifest, it has elements of consistent identity and ambiance that resonate regardless of whether the setting is rural North Carolina, rural Kansas, or rural California. Since 1967, when E. Grant Youmans published his pioneering book *Older Rural Americans: A Sociological Perspective,* there have been a plethora of sometimes anguished writings trying to define what we mean when we use the term *rural*. These have included formal demographic definitions, Calvin Beale's rural–urban continuum codes, and my own attempt in 1988 to answer the question "What is rural about rural aging?" by distinguishing among aging in rural environments, the environment of rural aging, and the rural environment of the aging. There are also the cultural perspectives of scholars who have tried to identify the distinguishing features of rural lifestyles, culture, and values. Rather than continuing to immerse ourselves in this definitional quagmire, I have come to believe that the most useful way to think about aging in rural places is to utilize the basic distinction that geographers have made for more than a century between functional and formal regions. Functional regions are defined by their core, while formal regions are defined by their boundaries. Thus, in considering notions of "rurality," the focus is on the indisputable core of the concept rather than on the ambiguity of its periphery and transitions to urbanity.

Space and time, geography and history are intimately interwoven; indeed, a dominant motif of contemporary rural settings is change. Rural environments are no longer solely the stable, dispersed, and bucolic farm communities of the popularly imagined past. Few people in rural settings now make their livelihood exclusively from farming. Rather, the contemporary rural environments in which people grow old are often characterized by increasing residential mobility and population turnover, new forms of economic activity, intensified economic and social ties to urban settings, and the concentration of resources within targeted small-town growth centers. Associated with these changes have been the demise of service outlets in the smallest settlements, and a redefinition of the very idea of rural community. Even amid such change, the essence of rurality remains a part of public consciousness. It finds expression in images of low population–density communities with room to breathe, a slower pace of life, and intimate ways of life lived on a small scale within the rhythm and routine of a simple culture of care. There remains a wistful longing for an imagined agrarian past that nurtures enduring images of everything that is the antithesis of an urban way of life and culture.

It is within this context that we must consider the present volume a successor to a series of edited volumes over almost five decades that have endeavored to distill the primary characteristics of growing old in rural America and explore the service delivery and policy issues resulting from these characteristics. These include Raymond Coward and Gary Lee's *The Elderly in Rural Society* (1985), C. Neil Bull's *Aging in Rural America* (1993), Raymond Coward and John A. Krout's *Aging in Rural Settings* (1998), R. Turner Goins and John A. Krout's *Service Delivery to Rural Adults* (2006), Nora Keating's *Rural Ageing: A Good Place to Grow Old* (2008), and, most recently, Nina Glasgow and Helen Berry's *Rural Aging in 21st Century America* (2013). It seems that every few years one of these contributions updates our information on a litany of persistent disadvantages for rural older adults: high rates of poverty, inadequate housing, limited or non-existent transportation, poor physical health, untreated mental illness, geographical isolation, and limited access to services and service providers. Beyond an updated compendium of demographic, economic, and social statistics, each successive anthology has provided additional insight by adding new themes. Clearly apparent trends include growing acknowledgment over the years of more refined distinctions among the life histories and demographic characteristics of different subpopulations and cohorts of rural older adults; progressive advancement in considering the complex dilemmas of service delivery to this population; and increasing sophistication in exploring the role of the personal, social, and cultural meaning of rural places in shaping the aging experience.

Kristina M. Hash, Elaine T. Jurkowski and John A. Krout's latest addition to this genre is no exception. The breadth of discourse is expanded and enriched by material on the civic and cultural engagement of well elders in rural communities and the constraints of limited resources, infrastructure, appropriate services, and volunteer opportunities for this population. This issue becomes increasingly problematic as frailty increases.

A key addition is consideration of new technologies in supporting rural older adults' ability to age in place, including the Internet, telehealth monitoring devices, motion sensors, assistive robots, and systems guided by artificial intelligence. Such devices are likely to become increasingly common features of life for future generations of older adults who will have grown up with these technologies. The potential for technology to overcome the constraints of distance and isolation is especially significant in rural areas.

There is welcome inclusion of social and gender minority populations: Lesbian, gay, bisexual, and transgender individuals (the LGBT population) are increasingly recognized as a component of rural communities. The reader is also introduced to the often neglected dark side of rural residence for many rural older adults: elder mistreatment, untreated mental illness, and associated themes of prejudice and stigma that have been hidden from view by the resilience and stoicism of victims who see no way out amid a lingering cultural ethic of concealment and denial.

Each of these directions is a significant addition to the literature, but the most important contribution of this book is its strong orientation toward practice and the role of service professionals in rural areas. As the editors note, for some time there has been a critical need to focus directly on the people who provide hands-on service to older adults in rural areas. In seeking to address this need, Hash, Jurkowski, and Krout have succeeded admirably in their aspiration to provide a resource that will explore "the challenges faced by, and best practices for, the health and human services professionals that work with or aspire to work with this population" (p. xix). Practice-oriented chapters focusing on the roles of physicians, dentists, nurse practitioners, and pharmacists working in rural areas provide critical insight into the challenges involved in working with older adults in these settings and useful commentary on difficulties in recruiting and retaining health professionals. Reflecting the unique circumstances of rural practice, detailed explication of the operation and importance of multi-, inter-, and transdisciplinary teams of appropriately trained health providers who are sensitive to local conditions and rural cultural expectations represents an important advance in our thinking about health care provision. These chapters provide a set of innovative contemporary models and guidelines for developing interprofessional collaborative practice approaches that are both economically and culturally viable and sorely needed in health professional–deficient rural communities.

Moving to an even more detailed perspective, a chapter by Kristina M. Hash provides fresh ideas on the role of the human service professional. The complex expectations of rural social workers in facilitating transitions between levels of care and in bridging health and human services is revealed in an exposition that identifies the need for generalists—persons attuned to local mores and values who understand rural culture. To be effective, such persons need to become integrated within and committed to the community. They must be adept at accommodating an environment of resource deficiency and acutely aware of community factions and relationships. Most important, they must be able to live comfortably within the "fishbowl" of community scrutiny while reconciling dual but overlapping worlds in their personal and professional lives.

One of the real problems in addressing the challenges faced by both medical and human services professionals in America's rural communities is the apparent estrangement of what occurs on the ground from the policies that evolve in state capitals and in Washington, DC. There is a long and sad history of policies for rural service delivery and practice that were modeled on successful urban-based programs but lacked practicality, relevance, and, in many cases, even credence in rural areas. Especially useful in this context is a clearly articulated penultimate chapter of this book in which Elaine Jurkowski traces the link between policies conceived at the national level and the translation of those policies into action on the local level. Her concise account of the historical development of national policies of relevance to rural older adults (including the Affordable Care Act) provides a long-needed attempt to consider policy not only as something that is translated down from the corridors of power to the level of community practitioners, but also as something that originates, or should originate, from rural communities as their needs are articulated and translated up the food chain. This is something that is potentially empowering to practitioners who usually are unable to see the link between what they deal with on an everyday basis and the laws and policies that supposedly are designed to enable them to achieve their goals. This chapter emphasizes the importance of understanding how the evolution of policy as a reflection of "bottom-up" evidence-based best practice adds a new dimension to a process that has for too long been implicit and relatively ineffective. Jurkowski's discussion provides the perfect context for her framing of a series of policy recommendations. If pursued, such policies would enable rural practitioners to enhance the quality of care they provide, improve the economic viability of services, increase access, recruit and retain more appropriately trained providers, and promote innovative, locally relevant service models and practices consistent with rural culture.

Primary themes in the experience of growing old in rural America are brought to life through a series of case study vignettes. These set a human context for each chapter. Early in the book, there is the story of 73-year-old Gladys Miller, an African American woman, and 77-year-old Mack Harrison, her friend since childhood, both residents of a rural county in South Carolina. At the end, we are introduced to Vernita Simonz, a 96-year-old woman who lives alone in a community of 850 people in northern California. In between, we encounter an array of older rural people who are dealing with a variety of challenges. These windows into the lives of individual older people not only enliven the book and give the reader much to ponder, but also add a frequently poignant human dimension. Too often, with notable exceptions such as Eva Salber's *Don't Send Me Flowers When I'm Dead: Voices of Rural Elderly* (1983) and Dena Shenk's *Someone to Lend a Helping Hand: Women Growing Old in Rural America* (1998), we have been denied access to the voices of rural older adults. As a result, our understanding is sterile and impoverished.

The book you are about to read includes new directions and emphases in expanding understanding of what it means to grow old in a rural community, the challenges faced by older adults, and the resources and services available to them. It also provides frequent glimpses into the contributors' visions of what this experience can become with creative and sensitive intervention through informed evidence-based practice. Against the backdrop of deeper and more comprehensive understanding of the culture of rural life, these visions provide hope that we can nurture rural environments that become increasingly elder friendly— supportive and wonderful places in which to grow old.

When that day arrives, we will no longer need to rue the challenges of growing old in rural America. Rather, we will be able to report that we have effectively responded to these challenges and to celebrate this accomplishment. In the interim, we have this volume in which two relatively new voices join John A. Krout, a seminal thinker in the field, in providing us with the latest step along the pathway. We have come a long way since E. Grant Youmans started us on this journey so long ago.

Graham D. Rowles, PhD
University of Kentucky

PREFACE

In the fall of 2011, I had a passing conversation with Elaine Jurkowski at a conference about my need to find an updated textbook for my rural gerontology course. Her response to my asking for suggested titles was "Why don't you write one?" Once I sat down and looked at the other options in this area of study, I realized that there was a critical need for a book that not only describes rural areas, their older residents, and their unique issues, but that also discusses challenges faced by, and best practices for, the health and human service professionals who work with, or aspire to work with, this population. Students, educators, researchers, professionals, policy makers, and community and program planners could use such a text. A year later, Elaine and I had contacted a renowned rural gerontologist named John Krout and the three of us had developed and submitted a book proposal to Springer Publishing Company. The end result is a work that we believe meets this critical need and can be useful to a wide variety of readers.

This book contains 13 chapters, organized into five parts. Part I provides an introduction to aging in rural places, with Chapter 1 including the overwhelming task of defining what is meant by "rural" and presenting demographics, descriptions, and the diversity of rural communities. Chapter 2 offers a picture of persons aging in rural areas, including their challenges and strengths, with special consideration for social and ethnic minorities within this population. With the foundation provided in Part I, Part II moves the focus to the health status and the specific health and human service needs and opportunities of rural older adults and their families. Chapter 3 examines the health status of persons aging in small towns and rural areas, and the common health and mental health conditions that they must manage. Chapter 4 sheds light on the interconnected issues and challenges of housing, poverty, and transportation for older adults in these communities. Chapter 5 concludes the section and moves from challenges to opportunities, including employment, retirement, and volunteerism for this population.

Whereas Part II focuses on needs and opportunities, Part III moves toward addressing these issues with health and human services available to rural older adults and their families. Chapter 6 provides an overview of these services, with special attention to the aging services network and area agencies on aging, and introduces them in the framework of the Older Adult Services Matrix. Chapter 7 relates the services available to well older adults, including those geared toward socialization and recreation; Chapter 8 offers a picture of care targeting rural older adults who are frailer, such as community-based and institutional long-term care services. Best practices for programs and services are highlighted in each of the chapters of Part III. Part IV examines the role of health and human service professionals who work with rural older adults and their families in these programs and services, with attention to interdisciplinary practice and professional competency. Chapter 9 begins the section, looking at the larger function of professional roles of interdisciplinary teams in providing effective services to rural older adults and their families, as well as the challenge of recruiting and maintaining a sufficient and competent workforce in rural communities. Chapter 10 focuses on the health disciplines of medicine, nursing, pharmacy, and dentistry and their roles in serving older adults in rural communities and their rural residents. Chapter 11 examines the role of the human service professional, such as the social worker, in meeting the needs of rural older adults. Each chapter in this section puts forward unique professional roles and issues, professional competencies, and practice and educational principles that pertain to working in this special context.

Building on the previous sections that introduce the rural environment and the challenges and opportunities facing its residents, and examine programs and services designed and professionals trained to meet these needs and advance these opportunities, Part V concludes this book with a look forward to future directions in research, policy and programming, education, and practice. Chapter 12 details current policies relevant to aging in rural communities, including health care, mental health, long-term care, caregiver support, housing, transportation, and income. Finally, Chapter 13 summarizes the five sections of the book and outlines recommendations for policy, future research, and the recruitment, retention, and training of professionals in this area.

In addition to the aforementioned content, this book offers several unique features, including the following:

- Case examples
- Professional competencies
- Useful websites
- Suggested activities and exercises
- Discussion questions
- PowerPoint slides
- Instructors Manual with test question bank

As a truly unusual feature, audio podcasts are provided to supplement the text's written chapters. These podcasts are available online at http://www.springerpub.com/Aging-in-Rural-America-podcast and include interviews with scholars and professionals working in the field, representing timely topics such as health issues facing older adults in rural communities, rural transportation services, and the service network for rural older adults.

To obtain an electronic copy of the instructors' materials, faculty should contact Springer Publishing Company at textbook@springer pub.com.

I have had the great fortune to meet and work with many rural older adults and their caregivers, as well as students and professionals who are committed to working in rural communities. This book acknowledges and honors these and other rural individuals and communities— the challenges they face and the strengths and resilience they embody and share.

Kristina M. Hash
Morgantown, West Virginia

ACKNOWLEDGMENTS

There are many individuals who are owed a world of gratitude for their support of this book and contribution to its publication. The authors especially thank Executive Editor Sheri W. Sussman and the staff at Springer Publishing Company for having a vision well beyond our own and for their tireless hours of direction and support. The contributing authors, who spent countless hours writing and revising their chapters, also deserve our greatest appreciation. Master of Social Work student at West Virginia University Kristin White spent numerous hours searching through the professional literature, creating tables, and proofreading chapters. A few talented and generous social workers contributed compelling photographs for inclusion in the text. Our families are owed a mountain of thanks for their support of our work and understanding of its time commitment.

Kristina Hash acknowledges the support of the administration, faculty, staff, and students at the West Virginia University School of Social Work and the Eberly College of Arts and Sciences, as well as her amazing mentors in rural practice and geriatrics, Drs. Roger and Nancy Lohmann, Dr. F. Ellen Netting, Dr. Barry Locke, Dr. Karen Harper-Dorton, and Dr. Rick Briggs. In addition, the John A. Hartford Foundation, the National Center for Gerontological Social Work Education, the Social Work Leadership Institute, and the West Virginia Geriatric Education Center are recognized and applauded for their support as well as their tireless work in professional education and competency in geriatrics.

Elaine Jurkowski expresses her gratitude for the strong support of Dr. Mizan Miah, former director of the School of Social Work at Southern Illinois University Carbondale (SIUC), in encouraging her engagement in this project. She also thanks the faculty, staff, and students within the

School of Social Work for their insights, encouragement, and support. The Illinois Rural Health Association (IRHA), Dr. Sandra Beebe, and Dr. Charla Lautar have played central roles in the support of the importance and value of understanding older adults living in rural settings. John Smith at the Egyptian Area Agency on Aging deserves acknowledgment for helping to keep Dr. Jurkowski grounded in the realities of older adults living in rural communities. Rimina Azad, Anwer Azim, Erick Kittange, and Maor Rubinstein all deserve thanks for their roles in proofreading, providing feedback, and helping secure resources in the developmental stages of this book. Kent Mattox, Chris Corzine, Brittany Oullette, and Eric Eblin from Caring Counseling Ministries and the Dare to Care radio program, as well as the staff at radio station WGGH in Marion, Illinois, all have earned recognition for their help with the podcast series associated with this book. The Certificate in Gerontology Program, housed within the College of Education and Human Services at Southern Illinois University, is accorded special appreciation for its many bright students who keep us honest about the nature of living in rural communities with people who are advancing in age.

Introduction

1

What Is Rural? Introduction to Aging in Rural Places

JOHN A. KROUT

KRISTINA M. HASH

AN AGING WORLD

The United States and the world are rapidly aging. In 2010, 40.4 million Americans were age 65 or older comprising 13.1% of the population (Administration on Aging, 2011). Worldwide, that number stood at 506 million in 2007, with some nations (i.e., Italy, Germany, and Japan) already counting 20% or more of their populations in the age 65 and older category (Jacobson, Kent, Lee, & Mather, 2011; Kinsella & Wan, 2008). With the aging of the baby boomers, the U.S. older population is projected to double to 89 million by 2050 (20%; Jacobson et al., 2011), and the number of older adults worldwide is expected to hit 1.3 billion (13%) by 2040 (Kinsella & Wan, 2008). The increase in the size of the older population will be greatest in the developing regions of Africa, Latin America, and Asia and especially in the most populous of the world's nations such as China and India. Developing nations will likely see a fivefold increase in older adults, placing strains on families as well as formal systems of care. China alone is expected to have more than 300 million older adults by 2050 (Kinsella & Wan, 2008).

The growth in the number of older adults is due to historical trends of greater life expectancy at all ages. The increase in the percentage of the population that is old is largely due to the decline in fertility rates that started in the 1900s and less to increasing life expectancy in old age (Hooyman & Kiyak, 2008). Concomitantly, the world's population has urbanized rapidly since the mid-20th century. In 1950, 30% of the world's population lived in urban areas. Today that number is 50%, with projections of 60% by 2030. Nations in regions defined as more developed (e.g., North America and Europe) are more urban (about 75%). Increased urbanization in developing regions (e.g., parts of South America, Africa, and Southeast Asia) has raised their percentage of urban dwellers from less than 20% to almost 40% today, with projections of 60% by 2030 (Weeks, 2012). Although rapidly urbanizing, developing nations have a greater percentage of their older populations living in rural areas rather than more developed nations; thus, issues of rural aging are particularly salient for them. The out-migration of younger adults from rural to urban areas is a significant component of an urbanization phenomenon that not only impacts the age structures of both areas but a wide range of other aging issues such as the availability of kin for caregiving (Longino & Mannheimer, 2006).

Many positive outcomes are associated with aging at the individual and societal level. Advanced aging can bring an increase in the time available for leisure activity and creative pursuits (Cohen, 2000) as well as community volunteerism (Freedman, 1999). Society can benefit from these as well as the wisdom that older adults bring to understanding and addressing community challenges (Thomas, 2004). An increasing number of older adults living longer than in previous generations also create business opportunities in many sectors of the economy (Furlong, 2007). However, these contributions tend to be overshadowed in our public discourse by the concerns of families as well as of program and policy experts about the costs associated with supporting the economic, health, and social needs of older adults—especially as they live into their 80s and beyond (Buckley, 2007). In fact, the aging of populations is often characterized as a *tsunami* that may overwhelm society's ability to provide services to older persons and may soak up resources required to confront other issues and the needs of younger adults and children.

Although the subject of the global aging boom is quite popular, most discussions of aging fail to consider that people do not age in a spatial vacuum. They all age somewhere, and the *place* of aging has impacts on people, just as population aging impacts those places. People age in the open country, in small towns, in medium-sized cities, and in mega-metropolises. They age in big and small, rich and poor, largely urban or more rural nations. In the United States, the large majority of older people do not live in rural places; however, older adults represent a higher percentage of the rural population. Indeed, this older rural age structure is also found in other nations, making this phenomenon international in scope (Glasgow & Berry, 2013a). In 2011, 16.2% of the nonmetropolitan versus 12.6% of the metropolitan population in the United States was age 65 or older (U.S. Bureau of the Census, 2012). For the age 85 or older group, the nonmetropolitan figure was 2.2% versus 1.7% for metropolitan counties (U.S. Bureau of the Census, 2012). Despite this demographic reality, the study of aging has generally focused on increases in the numbers and percentages of older adults and their implications for social institutions, and has not looked at the relationship between residence and aging. This chapter and book shed much-needed light on the topic of rural aging and its implications for older adults, health and social services, and service professionals.

This chapter begins with an examination of the importance of and reasons for focusing on older people who reside in rural parts of the country, and identifies the salient dimensions of rural communities that shape the experience of aging. Next, a detailed investigation is provided of the definitions and meanings of the term *rural*, with special attention to explanations of rural versus urban and nonmetropolitan versus metropolitan. This is followed by an exploration of historical changes in the spatial distribution of the U.S. population from rural to urban places; a consideration of the regional distribution of rural people and older adults; and an overview of recent rural population change. The chapter concludes by identifying six underlying premises that guide the text's examination of rural aging and providing an overview of the book's content.

THE IMPORTANCE OF RURAL AGING

The growth of the older population in rural areas has been influenced by the same forces that underlie the growth of the older population in the United States and the world. Thus, an increased understanding of rural aging contributes to the knowledge of the causes and impacts of aging in general. In fact, during the last 40 years, the study of aging and older people in rural places has emerged as an important specialty area within gerontology (Bull, 1993; Coward & Krout, 1998; Coward & Lee, 1985; Glasgow & Berry, 2013b; Goins & Krout, 2006a; Krout, 1983, 1986, 1994; Youmans, 1967). Overall, however, the attention given to rural older persons and their needs within gerontology and other disciplines has been relatively minor, as has the attention given at the national level by program and policy makers. So, we ask, why is it important to know more about rural aging? As Goins and Krout (2006b) have noted, the reasons are many and varied and include the following facts:

- Almost two thirds of U.S. counties are classified as rural (i.e., nonmetropolitan).
- One in five older adults live in rural America.
- Rural areas have greater proportions of population that are ages 65 or older and 85 and older.
- Rural areas are rapidly becoming more diverse ethnically/ racially.
- Many myths exist about rural older adults that affect the efficacy of programs and policies.
- Rural compared to urban older adults have lower incomes and higher poverty rates and are more likely to live in substandard housing.
- Rural older people have higher rates of chronic and acute disease, and health and social services are less available and accessible to them.
- Rural diversity or the differences among older populations found in various rural areas has not been well documented.
- Certain aspects of rural environments and living are uniquely rural and are not found in urban places.
- Understanding more about rural aging contributes to the understanding of aging in general.

Despite these observations, a paucity of data are available to practitioners and policy makers on the problems facing rural older adults and effective practice and program responses to them. Conceptually, the study of rural aging fits within the tradition of "person–environment" theories based on the work on Lewin (1951), who posited that behavior is a function of the interplay between the individual and the environment. In gerontology, this approach has been used by architects

(Eshelman, Evans, & Utamura, 2003; Scheidt & Windley, 1998), designers (Bakker, 1997), planners (AARP, 2005; Stafford, 2009), and others to investigate how features of the natural and built environments influence older persons' behaviors, attitudes, and quality of life. Perhaps the most accomplished scholar in the area of environmental gerontology is M. Powell Lawton (1980; Lawton, Windley, & Byerts, 1982). He and colleague Lucille Nahemow developed the competence-press model that suggests an individual's response (psychological and/or behavioral) to an environmental stimulus (press) is determined by that person's competencies (biological, sensorimotor, perceptual, and cognitive; Lawton & Nahemow, 1973). Although there has been a dearth of research based on this perspective, it reinforces the contention that aspects of where older people live are important and should be considered in examinations of their well-being (Krout & Wethington, 2003; Rowles, 1984).

The most common approach to studying rural aging and older persons is to compare rural quality-of-life (QOL) measures, including health, housing, and economic resources with urban (or nonrural) QOL measures. This approach provides important insights into the situations of rural older adults and is of particular interest to policy makers. However, there is much to be learned about rural aging by focusing on rural circumstances alone and realizing rural experiences are worthy of study in their own right, without urban comparisons. Much more can be learned about a wide range of gerontological topics by investigating how rural family and community systems work within a diverse set of environments whose major commonalities are smaller population size and greater distance to large cities. This holds true even though many communication and other technologies are not bounded by geography, making rural and urban areas more similar in some ways than in past years. Looking at rural without urban comparisons reduces the variation in a variable (where one lives) that can impact and interact with a wide array of other factors known to relate to aging.

This perspective leads to a central question about the impact of rural environments on aging that was perhaps most succinctly stated by Graham Rowles, when he asked, "What is rural about rural aging?" (Rowles, 1988, p. 115). It is also fair for gerontologists to ask, "How does rural matter?" As these fundamental questions are explored, it must be kept in mind that considerable variation exists among rural places and their populations. Chuck Fluharty from the Rural Policy Institute noted, "If you've seen one rural community, you've seen . . . one rural community" (Lohmann & Lohmann, 2005, p. xxii). Rural communities also vary on a number of economic and social factors at the regional, state, and local levels.

DEFINTIONS OF RURAL

One of the most important questions underlying the examination of the experiences of aging and being older in rural America is how to conceptualize or define rural. It should be noted that rural people come to older age with differences based on ethnicity, race, gender, income, education, culture, and health, to name just a few factors. Residence interacts with these variables to produce different impacts based on community type and resources. The environment can be viewed in both *micro* and *macro* terms. Micro generally refers to the immediate space in which individuals live, such as their housing and its characteristics, whereas macro generally refers to the larger community. Discussions of how rural affects aging have historically focused on macro factors, but they can impact the micro level. Continuing the macro theme, it is instructive to look at rural more broadly and consider what have been called salient characteristics or critical dimensions of rural environments that impact aging (Goins & Krout, 2006b) The experience of rural aging can be better understood by paying attention to the following dimensions:

- *Behavioral:* Normative behavior around health such as exercise, diet, and drug and alcohol use; social relationships including family and friends; and service utilization
- *Compositional:* Sociodemographic characteristics of the younger and older population in areas such as age, gender, education, race, ethnicity, and economic status
- *Cultural:* Generally shared values and beliefs that influence attitudes and behaviors of a population. These can impact interpersonal relationships, expectations of kin care, and health- and service-seeking behaviors.
- *Ecological:* A place's population size and density, natural environment, and location vis-à-vis other communities (e.g., proximity to a larger city)
- *Organizational:* Structure of formal activities related to government, economics, health and social services, recreation, and religion

- *Social and Economic Resources:* Economic, physical, and organizational infrastructure available to sustain and improve a population's health and social needs

It is beyond the scope of this chapter to examine each of these dimensions in detail; however, they are embedded in the chapters that follow. For example, the compositional characteristics of rural older adults and, to a lesser extent, communities are considered carefully in Chapter 2. Certain aspects of rural behavior and culture that affect health and wellness are included in Chapter 3. Reviews of the economic, lifestyle, and living circumstances available to rural older adults are provided in Chapters 4 and 5. Considerations of the impact of organizational resources of rural communities on service provision to rural older adults are found in Chapters 6, 7, and 8, as well as in the discussions of competent rural practice throughout this book. Many of these dimensions are factored into the discussions of effective practices and professional competencies examined in Chapters 9, 10, and 11.

The ecological dimension is the one most commonly used to define rural and in rural versus urban comparisons of older adults. Although this dimension seems easily quantifiable by variables such as population size and density and proximity of large urban places, a consistent definition of rural has not been used by researchers over the years. Further, investigators who do not focus on rural issues often include an ecological measure of residence as a variable in their data sets with virtually no consideration of its meaning. Studies of different aspects of rural QOL such as health, housing, or income are often not comparable, complicating the overall understanding of rural aging and the development of effective programs, practice, and policy.

No standard definition of rural is used by federal agencies. Various government agencies use different definitions of rural, confusing the use of research findings on policy decisions. In addition, definitions with very different empirical bases, meanings, and utilities are often used interchangeably. Perhaps the best example of this is the interchangeable use of the terms rural and nonmetropolitan and, conversely, urban and metropolitan. These are based on very different units of measurement and can result in very diverse answers to seemingly straightforward questions such as how many people or older people live in the rural United States. For future reference and to aid readers in assessing other works on rural aging, a detailed compilation of contrasting ecological definitions of rural is presented in Table 1.1.

TABLE 1.1 Common Terminology and Descriptions of Rural

Terminology	Agency	Description
Metropolitan statistical area (MSA) and Nonmetropolitan statistical area (NonMSA)	U.S. Office of Management and Budget	MSAs contain (a) at least one central county with either a place with a population of 50,000 or more, or an urbanized area and total MSA of 100,000 or more population; or (b) one or more MSAs and more outlying counties that have close economic and social relationships (i.e., commuting) with the central county. A NonMSA is any area that does not fit these criteria.
Core-based statistical areas (CBSAs) and outside CBSAs[a]	U.S. Bureau of the Census	The 2000 revision to the previous system that defines CBSAs comprising two categories: metropolitan areas, based around at least one defined urbanized area of 50,000 or more population, and micropolitan areas, based around at least one urban cluster of 10,000–49,000 population. A metropolitan area with a single core of at least 2,500,000 population can be subdivided into component metropolitan divisions. Counties that are not included in a CBSA are referred to as outside CBSAs.
Rural and urban[b]	U.S. Bureau of the Census	Defines urban as all territory, population, and housing units in places of population 2,500 or more incorporated as cities, villages, boroughs (except in Alaska and New York), and towns (except in the six New England states, New York, and Wisconsin). This excludes rural portions of "extended cities," in the U.S. Bureau of the Census–designated places of 2,500 or more, or in other territory included in urbanized areas. Territory, population, and housing units not classified as urban are classified as rural. These can be further divided into farm areas, defined as any place from which $1,000 or more of agricultural products were sold or normally would have been sold during the year under consideration, and nonfarm areas.
Rural-urban continuum codes[b]	U.S. Department of Agriculture, Economic Research Service	Categorizes counties on a scale of 0–9 by degree of urbanization and nearness to a metropolitan area. For nonmetropolitan counties, this classification system indicates the size of the urban population in a county and the county's proximity to a metropolitan area.

Urban influence codes[b]	U.S. Department of Agriculture, Economic Research Service	Categorizes counties on a scale of 0–9 based on the size of the MSA in the case of metropolitan counties, and adjacency to MSAs and the size of the largest city in the nonmetropolitan counties. The counties are classified by the population of the cities within each county, rather than the degree of urbanization.
1989 county typology codes[b]	U.S. Department of Agriculture, Economic Research Service	Classifies nonmetropolitan counties based on economic policy traits. Primary economic activity includes the following nonoverlapping types: farming-dependent, mining-dependent, manufacturing-dependent, government-dependent, services-dependent, and nonspecialized. The five overlapping policy types include retirement-destination, federal lands, commuting, persistent poverty, and transfer-dependent.
Census tracts[b]	U.S. Bureau of the Census	Uses the census tract, the smallest geographic building block for which reliable commuting data are available, to classify areas as rural. The census tract is used instead of the county level of analysis.
Isolated rural areas[b]	H. F. Goldsmith, U.S. Office of Management and Budget	Also known as the Goldsmith modification, this uses census tracts to identify rural areas in large metropolitan counties (LMCs), or counties with at least 1,225 sq mi. Rural areas in LMCs are census tracts with (a) no persons living in central areas (i.e., urbanized areas) or (b) no persons living in cities of population 25,000 or more. Isolated rural areas are defined as areas in which less than 15% of the population commuted to work in the central area, or rural areas in which greater than 15% commuted to work in the central area, if 45% of the labor force commuted 30 min or more to work.
Frontier areas[b]	Frontier Education Center	Describes an area (county or census tract) with extremely low population density, usually fewer than six people per sq mi. Frontier areas are isolated rural areas characterized by considerable distances from central places, poor access to market areas, and relative isolation between people in large geographic areas.

(continued)

11

TABLE 1.1 Common Terminology and Descriptions of Rural (*continued*)

Terminology	Agency	Description
Nonmetro commuting zones (CZs) and labor market areas (LMAs)[c]	U.S. Department of Agriculture, Economic Research Service	CZs and LMAs are based on economic and labor force activities. Nonmetro CZs and LMAs do not contain a metropolitan area and are ranked based on the size of the largest city, town, or census-designated place. Three subcategories are used: small town/rural, small urban center, and large urban center. Three subcategories are also used to describe metro CZs and LMAs: small metro center, medium metro center, and major metro center.
Rural-urban commuting area codes[d]	U.S. Department of Agriculture, Economic Research Service	The 2000 codes are based on the theoretical concepts used by the U.S. Office of Management and Budget to define county-level metropolitan and micropolitan areas (density, urbanization, and daily commuting). These 10 codes use U.S. Bureau of the Census tracts instead of counties to provide a different and more detailed delineation of metropolitan and nonmetropolitan settlement based on the size and direction of the primary commuting flows.

[a]U.S. Office of Management and Budget (2000).
[b]Rural Policy Research Institute (n.d.).
[c]U.S. Department of Agriculture. Economic Research Service (2003).
[d]U.S. Department of Agriculture. Economic Research Service (2005).
Reprinted with permission from Goins and Krout (2006b).

The nonmetropolitan versus metropolitan distinction as defined by the U.S. Office of Management and Budget is the most commonly used residence distinction and utilizes counties as the unit of analysis (Glasgow & Berry, 2013a). Metropolitan core areas are defined as having one or more cities with at least 50,000 people or containing a total county population of 100,000 people called an urbanized area. Further, an urbanized area has a central place and surrounding area that total at least 50,000 people. Counties can also be designated as metropolitan if they are adjacent to a core metropolitan area and have a high degree of social and economic integration with that area, even if they do not meet the metropolitan population size criteria (U.S. Bureau of the Census, 1992). Nonmetropolitan categories are a residual category of counties that do not meet the metropolitan or metropolitan fringe criteria and include small cities, villages, and open country. Nonmetropolitan counties are also divided into *micropolitan* (those with at least 10,000 persons) or non–core nonmetropolitan counties (those with no place of 10,000 people or more). All micropolitan nonmetropolitan counties are considered nonmetropolitan. To summarize, any county that is not metropolitan is considered nonmetropolitan. About two thirds of the nation's counties are nonmetropolitan (2,053 out of a total 3,140 counties; Colello, 2007).

A second frequently used distinction is also based on population size but does not use the county as a unit of analysis. In the rural–urban dichotomy, urban residents are defined as those living in an urbanized area plus those outside an urbanized area but in a place with a population of at least 2,500 people. Rural, like nonmetropolitan, is a residual category including all those people not living in an urbanized area or urban place of at least 2,500 people (U.S. Bureau of the Census, 1992). Rural farm residence is an occupational not a geographic designation and is determined by the amount of sales that can be classified as agricultural (at least $1,000), and a very small percentage of older adults nationally live on farms.

One can see that both the nonmetropolitan–metropolitan and rural–urban dichotomies result in categories that include a diversity of communities. The urban category includes very small places of several thousand people to huge central cities of millions in population. Likewise, rural residents could live in extremely sparsely populated open country areas or in a small village near a city. Typically, a wide variety of places are lumped into the residual category of nonmetropolitan and are often then talked about broadly as being rural.

Further complicating the usefulness of these residence categories is the fact that living in a rural place and living in a metropolitan area are not mutually exclusive. Data from the census of 1990, although dated, demonstrate this point dramatically. In 1990, 37% of rural older adults lived in metropolitan counties (Coward & Krout, 1998), leading to the argument that the U.S. Office of Management and Budget metropolitan/ nonmetropolitan dichotomy undercounts the rural population. Recognizing the problems inherent in using dichotomies such as rural versus urban and nonmetropolitan versus metropolitan, researchers have developed a number of multicategory classifications based on a variety of indicators such as population size, density, and proximity to central cities. One example is the typology developed by demographer Calvin Beale that classifies counties on a 10-point scale varying from completely rural counties not adjacent to a metropolitan county to counties that are coterminous with central cities (Economic Research Service, 1993). Continuums such as these have the advantage of allowing finer residential distinctions and not reducing variation in their measures by collapsing multiple categories into dichotomies.

These definitional variations and ambiguities require that researchers, policy makers, and others pay close attention as to how rural is being measured, when they look at data on QOL indicators. Unfortunately, this problem is generally only given lip service when seemingly inevitable rural versus urban comparisons are made or data for different states and regions are compared. Because of the large variety in the residence categories by which data on older people are gathered and reported, the authors in this book utilize a range of terms when referring to rural. Every effort is made to use them accurately and to make the reader aware of the definitions and data being used. For an overview of 2010 census data, go to the U.S. Bureau of the Census website (quickfacts.census.gov/qfd/ index.html) and check for the state, county, and/or city in which you live.

SPATIAL DISTRIBUTION OF THE OLDER POPULATION

The primary determinant of population aging variation found below the national level (among different regions and states) is rural to urban migration, a factor that was the primary cause of changes in population distribution in the United States and the world in the 19th and 20th centuries. In the United States, migration and immigration patterns underlie the variation found in the population experiences of states and regions, and are the dominant cause of the growth of the South and West at the expense of the Northeast and Midwest since World War II (Glasgow & Berry, 2013a).

Nationwide, the most populous states have the largest numbers of older persons, with just 5 states (in descending order of number of older adults: California, Florida, New York, Texas, and Pennsylvania) accounting for 37% and the top 10 states including 54% of the older population. It follows then that states with smaller populations have fewer older persons. The regional distribution of the older population is also unequal. In 2005, 36% of older people lived in the South, with 24% in the Midwest, 21% in the Northeast, and 20% in the West. The growth of the older population in the Northeast and Midwest was almost flat between 2000 and 2005, whereas it grew 7% in the South and 9.5% in the West. Although the South has a greater percentage of the nation's older adults than does any other region, a larger percentage of nonmetropolitan older adults live in the Midwest and Northeast. In addition, the nonmetropolitan Midwest has the highest percentage of population in the age 85 or older group (Colello, 2007).

States with the largest numbers of older people typically do not have the highest percentages of their populations in the age 65 or older group. That is because a state's or local area's percentage of population that is older is significantly affected by migration. For more rural states and areas, this usually involves the out-migration of young adults and sometimes the in-migration of older adults. Some of this older in-migration is actually the return of previous cohorts of younger out-migrants. For decades, the out-migration of younger adults has been more prevalent in the Midwest and Northeast, leading the age structures of those regions to be proportionately older than in other regions (Colello, 2007).

RURAL POPULATION CHANGE AND VARIATION

Regardless of the definition or indicator used, the number and proportion of U.S. population that is rural have been declining for decades. According to the U.S. Bureau of the Census, in 2010 some 3,573 urban areas contained 81% (71% in urban areas and 10% in urban clusters) of the population, up from 79% in 2000, leaving 19% of the total population as rural. Using the metropolitan/nonmetropolitan distinction, 51 million or 16% of the population was rural in 2010 (Economic Research Service, 2012).

For most of the last 75 years, metropolitan growth has outstripped nonmetropolitan growth, due largely to the out-migration of younger adults. Between 1930 and 1970, rural growth was entirely due to natural increase offsetting migration losses. People left rural America largely due to economic *push–pull* factors that heavily favored urban and suburban areas over rural areas. These economic pressures trumped a long-standing preference in the country for small-town life and an agrarian myth that rural life was better (Longino & Smith, 1998). The 1970s saw a net increase in migration to nonmetropolitan counties for the first time in decades, a condition that reversed in the 1980s but has returned since 1990. Nonetheless, nonmetropolitan growth in the last 20 years has been considerably less than metropolitan growth (10% vs. 14% in the 1990s and 6% vs. 11% in the last decade; Johnson, 2012).

Rural population change has not been even nationwide. Historically, rural population has declined the most in the Great Plains, the Corn Belt, the Mississippi delta, parts of Appalachia, and the industrial and mining belts in New York and Pennsylvania. Over the last 20 years, nonmetropolitan counties in the West and Southeast and in areas adjacent to large urban areas in the Midwest and Northeast plus some recreation areas in the Great Lakes, the Ozarks, and the Northeast have fared better than others. But rural trends are fickle. Between 2010 and 2011, more than half of nonmetropolitan counties lost population, with one notable exception being areas of the West and Midwest more heavily involved in energy and mining (Economic Research Service, 2012).

Nonmetropolitan counties vary considerably on a large number of characteristics in addition to population change (Economic Research Service, 1993). Nationally, for example, although farming and mining have declined over the years as the primary economic activity in rural areas, farming still dominates in 403 counties and mining in another 113 counties. Until very recently, these areas have been very slow growing. Almost 600 nonmetropolitan counties are classified as dependent on manufacturing, and they have grown at a much greater pace in the last 20 years, mostly from in-migration. Rural counties noted for natural amenities, QOL advantages, and recreational opportunities have far outpaced the other categories in population growth since 1990. Some 277 rural counties are considered retiree destination areas and have benefited greatly from in-migration when labor-force participants are attracted by the jobs that follow retirees as well as the same QOL factors that older adults value (Johnson, 2012).

The historical trend of lower population growth in nonmetropolitan versus metropolitan areas changed suddenly in the 1970s, only to return in the 1980s and abate again for part of the 1990s (Johnson, 2012). Older adults were an important part of this brief *rural renaissance* and are generally acknowledged to view rural destinations positively. Individual-level data from the census of 2000 revealed that older migrants were more likely to select less urbanized/more rural places than metropolitan centers and did so to a greater degree than migrants aged 25 to 59 (Bradley & Longino, 2006).

PLAN OF THE BOOK

Aging in a variety of residential contexts needs to be studied because residence, in this case rural residence, matters. A significant amount of research shows that the life circumstances of rural older adults do not generally compare favorably to their urban counterparts. Despite these demonstrated disadvantages, there is a scarcity of detailed and current research and information on the scope and complexity of the problems facing rural older people and their families and on professional practices that effectively serve this population. In addition, not enough attention has been paid to the benefits and advantages of rural living for older adults. Thus, a compelling need exists for research that examines the underlying causes and correlates of the QOL of rural older adults. This book responds to this need by presenting current data on the characteristics and status of rural older adults for a number of substantive topics. Based on a review of the existing rural aging literature and data on rural populations and population change, six premises underlie and guide the chapters that follow:

- The impact of population aging is proportionately greater in rural than in urban areas because rural area populations are older.
- The study of rural aging contributes to the larger academic enterprise that is gerontology.
- It is important to compare rural and urban older populations and to study rural older people without reference to urban older adults.
- Considerable variation is found in the characteristics and circumstances of rural older citizens across the United States.

- Rural older people are disadvantaged on most QOL measures when compared to urban older adults.
- Rural places and populations have unique characteristics and needs that require different approaches for effective programs, policies, and practices.

This book provides an application of research findings to professional practice and programs, and policies designed to meet the needs of rural older adults. Unlike previous examinations of rural aging, specific competencies for the health and human service professionals who work with rural residents are identified and defined. This work adopts a state-of-the-art, multidisciplinary, research-driven, and competency-based approach to the topics of rural gerontology and geriatrics. It is designed for students, faculty, and researchers in health disciplines as well as health and human service professionals. The following content and learning tools are presented:

- Contemporary topics and current data
- Best practices, interventions, and policy derived from evidence-based research in the field
- Rural and urban differences and the interfaces between the two
- Multidisciplinary perspectives
- Applied content
- Professional competencies
- Case examples
- Suggested activities and exercises
- Discussion questions
- PowerPoint slides
- Test questions

As a truly unique feature, the book also offers audio podcasts to supplement the content of the print chapters. These podcasts are available online at http://www.springerpub.com/Aging-in-Rural-America-podcast and include interviews with scholars and professionals working in the field, representing timely topics such as health issues facing older adults in rural communities, rural transportation services, and the service network for rural older adults.

Finally, the word *rural* can be defined in many ways. As discussed earlier in this chapter, it can refer to population size, values, organizational traits, or lived experiences. The word is used generically in this book as an umbrella term to refer to all of these things and to contrast rural living environments with those that are more populated, typically faster paced, and that generally have more services and resources for older adults. The data presented for residential differences are typically for nonmetropolitan versus metropolitan areas; however, wherever possible, chapter authors specify the definition of rural used when presenting data on older adults or services.

CONCLUSION

The United States, like the world, is rapidly aging. By 2050, some 90 million older people will make up 20% of its population. Although the large majority of the nation's older population lives in urban and suburban communities, issues associated with aging are of great importance in rural areas. Older adults make up a greater percentage of rural populations, and, compared to their urban counterparts, they are disadvantaged on QOL indicators such as health and nutrition, income, housing, and access to health and social services. Many aspects of rural communities and populations, including low population size and density, lack of organizational and economic resources, and fewer community-based service options, create unique challenges to providing services to older people. Many rural areas have experienced population loss even as they are becoming more ethnically diverse. National trends in economic growth (or lack thereof), health care, and government spending are leaving large parts of rural America and its older citizens more vulnerable to the challenges that can accompany aging.

Over the years, researchers and policy makers have not paid adequate attention to the unique challenges inherent in developing and providing health and human services to rural older adults. Little information is available on effective program approaches and on the knowledge and skills professionals require to successfully address the needs of rural older adults. This chapter presented a state-of-the art review of the geographic and demographic realities of rural America and provided an important context for the understanding of what is rural and why it is important to study aging in this context.

USEFUL WEBSITES

Population Reference Bureau
www.prb.org

Rural Assistance Center (RAC)
www.raconline.org
United Nations
www.un.org/en
U.S. Bureau of the Census
www.census.gov
U.S. Department of Agriculture (USDA), Rural Population and Economy
www.ers.usda.gov/topics/rural-economy-population.aspx#.Ujdo4FSnX5g

REFERENCES

AARP. (2005). *Livable communities: An evaluation guide.* Washington, DC: Author.
Administration on Aging. (2011). *A profile of older Americans.* Washington, DC: U.S. Department of Health and Human Services.
Bakker, R. (1997). *Elder design: Designing and furnishing a home for your later years.* New York, NY: Penguin Books.
Bradley, D. E., & Longino, C. F. (2006). Demographic resettlement impacts on rural services. In R. T. Goins & J. A. Krout (Eds.), *Service delivery to rural older adults: Research, policy and practice* (pp. 37–53). New York, NY: Springer Publishing Company.
Buckley, C. (2007). Boomsday. In H. R. Moody (Ed.), *Aging: Concepts and controversies* (pp. 438–439). Los Angeles, CA: Pine Forge Press.
Bull, C. N. (1993). *Aging in rural America.* Thousand Oaks, CA: Sage.
Cohen, G. D. (2000). *The creative age: Awakening human potential in the second half of life.* New York, NY: Avon Books.
Colello, K. J. (2007). *Where do older Americans live? Geographic distribution of the older population.* Washington, DC: Congressional Research Service.
Coward, R. T., & Krout, J. A. (Eds.). (1998). *Aging in rural settings: Life circumstances and distinctive features.* New York, NY: Springer Publishing Company.
Coward, R. T., & Lee, G. R. (Eds.). (1985). *The elderly in rural society.* New York, NY: Springer Publishing Company.
Economic Research Service. (1993). *Rural conditions and trends.* Washington, DC: U.S. Department of Agriculture.
Economic Research Service. (2012). *Rural America at a glance: 2012 edition* (Economic Brief No. 21). Washington, DC: U.S. Department of Agriculture.
Eshelman, P. E., Evans, G. W., & Utamura, S. (2003). Housing satisfaction: Design lessons from the community. In J. A. Krout & E. Wethington (Eds.), *Residential choices and experiences of older adults: Pathways to life quality* (pp. 49–68). New York, NY: Springer Publishing Company.

Freedman, M. (1999). *Prime time. How baby boomers will revolutionize retirement and transform America.* New York, NY: Public Affairs.

Furlong, M. S. (2007). *Turning silver into gold: How to profit in the new boomer market place.* Upper Saddle River, NJ: FT Press.

Glasgow, N., & Berry, E. H. (2013a). Introduction to rural aging in twenty-first century America. In N. Glasgow & E. H. Berry (Eds.), *Rural aging in twenty first century America* (pp. 1–16). Dordrecht, Netherlands: Springer Science+Business Media.

Glasgow, N., & Berry, E. H. (Eds.). (2013b). *Rural aging in twenty first century America.* Dordrecht, Netherlands: Springer Science+Business Media.

Goins, R. T., & Krout, J. A. (Eds.). (2006a). *Service delivery to rural older adults: Research, policy and practice.* New York, NY: Springer Publishing Company.

Goins, R. T., & Krout, J. A. (2006b). Aging in rural America. In R. T. Goins & J. A. Krout (Eds.), *Service delivery to rural older adults: Research, policy and practice* (pp. 3–20). New York, NY: Springer Publishing Company.

Hooyman, N. R., & Kiyak, H. A. (2008). *Social gerontology: A multidisciplinary perspective* (8th ed.). Boston, MA: Allyn & Bacon.

Jacobson, L. A., Kent, M., Lee, M., & Mather, M. (2011). *America's aging population* (Population Bulletin No. 66[1]). Washington, DC: Population Reference Bureau.

Johnson, K. (2012). *Rural demographic change in the new century: Slower growth, increased diversity* (Carsey Institute Issue Brief No. 44). Durham, NH: Carsey Institute.

Kinsella, K., & Wan, H. (2008). *U.S. Census Bureau international population reports P95/09-1, an aging world: 2008.* Washington, DC: U.S. Government Printing Office.

Krout, J. A. (1983). *The rural elderly: An annotated bibliography of social science research.* Westport, CT: Greenwood Press.

Krout, J. A. (1986). *The aged in rural America.* Westport, CT: Greenwood Press.

Krout, J. A. (Ed.). (1994). *Providing community-based services to the rural elderly.* Thousand Oaks, CA: Sage.

Krout, J. A., & Wethington, E. (Eds.). (2003). *Residential choices and experiences of older adults: Pathways to life quality.* New York, NY: Springer Publishing Company.

Lawton, M. P. (1980). *Environment and aging.* Belmont, CA: Wadsworth.

Lawton, M. P., & Nahemow, L. (1973). Ecology and the aging process. In C. Eisdorfer & M. P. Lawton (Eds.), *Psychology of adult development and aging* (pp. 619–674). Washington, DC: American Psychological Association.

Lawton, M. P., Windley, P. G., & Byerts, T. O. (1982). *Aging and the environment: Theoretical approaches.* New York, NY: Springer Publishing Company.

Lewin, K. (1951). *Field theory in social sciences.* New York, NY: Harper & Row.

Lohmann, R. A., & Lohmann, N. (2005). Introduction. In N. Lohmann & R. A. Lohmann (Eds.), *Rural social work practice* (pp. xi–xxvii). New York, NY: Columbia University Press.

Longino, C. F., & Mannheimer, R. F. (Eds.). (2006). *Retirement migration in America.* Houston, TX: Vacations.

Longino, C. F., & Smith, M. H. (1998). The impact of elderly migration on rural communities. In R. T. Coward & J. A. Krout (Eds.), *Aging in rural settings: Life circumstances and distinctive features,* (pp. 209–226). New York, NY: Springer Publishing Company.

Rowles, G. D. (1984). Aging in rural environments. In I. Altman, M. P. Lawton, & J. F. Wohlwill (Eds.), *Elderly people and the environment* (pp. 129–157). New York, NY: Plenum Press.

Rowles, G. D. (1988). What's rural about rural aging? An Appalachian perspective. *Journal of Rural Studies, 4,* 115–124.

Rural Policy Research Institute. (n.d.). *Defining rural: Definitions of rural areas in the U.S.* Retrieved November 10, 2005, from http://www.rupri.org/resources/context/rural.html

Scheidt, R. J., & Windley, P. G. (Eds.). (1998). *Environment and aging theory: A focus on housing.* Westport, CT: Greenwood Press.

Stafford, P. (2009). *Elderburbia: Aging with a sense of place in America.* Santa Barbara, CA: Praeger.

Thomas, W. H. (2004). *What are old people for: How elders will save the world.* Acton, MA: VanderWyk & Burnham.

U.S. Bureau of the Census. (1992). *Census of population and housing, 1990: Public use microdata sample U.S. technical documentation.* Washington, DC: Author.

U.S. Bureau of the Census. (2012). *American Community Survey 2007–2011.* Retrieved from Census.gov/acs/www/data_documentation/2011_release

U.S. Department of Agriculture. Economic Research Service. (2003). *Measuring rurality: Commuting zones and labor market areas.* Retrieved November 10, 2005, from http://www.ers.usda.gov/briefing/rurality/lmacz

U.S. Department of Agriculture. Economic Research Service. (2005). *Measuring rurality: Rural-urban commuting area codes.* Retrieved November 10, 2005, from http://www.ers.gov/briefing/Rurality/RuralUrbanCommutingAreas

U.S. Office of Management and Budget. (2000). *Final report and recommendations from the Metropolitan Area Standards Review Committee to the Office of Management and Budget concerning changes to the standards for defining metropolitan areas.* Retrieved November 10, 2005, from http://www.whitehouse.gov/omb/inforeg/merto2000.pdf

Weeks, J. R. (2012). *Population: An introduction to concepts and issues* (11th ed.). Belmont, CA: Wadsworth.

Youmans, E. G. (1967). *Older rural Americans: A sociological perspective.* Lexington: University of Kentucky Press.

Who Are Rural Older Adults?

KRISTINA M. HASH

REBECCA WELLS

S. MELINDA SPENCER

Gladys Miller is a 73-year-old, widowed African American woman who lives in a rural county in South Carolina. Within the last year, the only hospital in her county closed, leaving residents without a nearby source of emergency care. She recently told Rachel, a graduate student doing a research project about the hospital's closure, about her experiences. Like many residents, Gladys has had to access care at the nearest hospital in another county. She had mashed her finger in the car door; thankfully, the incident was not serious. Recently, however, Gladys had to visit that same out-of-county hospital for her friend Mack Harrison.

Mack is a 77-year-old African American man who lives alone and has several chronic health conditions, including diabetes. His wife died last year, and his nearest child lives in Virginia. Mack was a former high school classmate of Gladys's husband, and Gladys checks on him frequently to see how he is doing. She also brings him home-cooked meals because she knows he does not cook for himself and has a hard time paying for groceries by the end of the month. She is always telling him that he needs to take better care of himself by eating healthy, exercising, and going to the doctor. Gladys phoned Mack several times one day to arrange to take him to church; when there was no answer, she drove over to his house. When she arrived at 11 a.m., Mack was unconscious and appeared to have been lying on the living room floor for several hours. Gladys immediately called 911, and Mack was rushed to the nearest hospital—25 miles away.

Gladys followed the ambulance in her car. Round-trip, she would have to drive close to 50 miles to the hospital, but she knew Mack had no other family or friends nearby to go with him. She also knew that he did not like filling out forms and talking to doctors. She waited with him at the hospital for hours. Since it was nearing 10 p.m., Gladys asked the nurse on call if they were planning to keep her friend. She had not planned to be at the hospital so long and was not prepared to stay the night. She needed to know something soon because her children were worried about her traveling back home so late at night.

Finally, the doctor came into the room and shared that Mack's blood sugar was extremely high (700 mg/dL) and that they would be keeping him overnight. She worried about leaving her friend alone at the hospital, but she knew with the dark drive ahead that she needed to get on the road.

The experiences of Gladys and Mack are not uncommon for individuals aging in small towns and rural communities. The rural environment has long been recognized as a unique context where geographic isolation and a low population density converge to create both challenges and opportunities for rural populations. Rural America[1] is home to approximately 50 million people, an estimated 16% of the total U.S. population. According to 5-year estimates from the 2008–2012 American Community Survey (ACS), adults age 65 years and older represent 16.2% of the rural population versus 12.6% of the urban population and the U.S. population as a whole. The 85 years and older age group comprises 2.1% of the rural population compared to 1.7% of the urban population and 1.8% of the U.S. population. Rural areas have a higher median age of 40.3 years compared to 36.6 years for urban areas and for the nation (U.S. Bureau of the Census, 2008–2012a). This age difference reflects the out-migration

of young adults to metropolitan areas, the greater decline of rural versus urban birthrates, and older adult in-migration to rural amenity areas
(Kirschner, Berry, & Glasgow, 2006). One consequence of these trends
has been the aging in place (AIP) of rural older populations—a phenomenon of considerable interest and concern to gerontologists and policy
makers (Colello, 2007).

As is true for the nation as a whole, women age 65 years and
older represent a larger proportion of the total rural population than
do their male counterparts (18.0% vs. 14.1%). Women account for a
slightly lower percentage of rural older adults (55.5%) compared to
the older U.S. population as a whole (56.0%) and those in urban areas
(57.1%; U.S. Bureau of the Census, 2008–2012b). Rural older adults
are also more likely to be married than are urban older adults and
the aging population nationally (31% vs. 29% and 29%, respectively).
Rural older adults, however, are just as likely to be widowed as their
urban and national counterparts (28.6% are widowed; U.S. Bureau
of the Census, 2008–2012c). Data on same-sex marriages or domestic
partnerships are not readily available for this population. Figures for
the educational attainment of older rural residents show 12.5% having less than a 9th-grade education; 38.6% completing high school or
reporting a GED as their highest level; 8.7% completing a bachelor's
degree, and 6.5% having a graduate or professional degree. Older
adults in urban areas and nationally have higher levels of education,
with only 11.0% having less than a 9th-grade education and 23.1%
attaining a bachelor's degree or higher (U.S. Bureau of the Census,
2006–2012d). Finally, rural communities are home to a slightly higher
proportion of older veterans (23.7% of those age 65 or older in these
areas, compared to 22.5% in urban areas and 22.8% nationally; U.S.
Bureau of the Census, 2006–2012e).

It is often said that rural individuals compared to urban people are
more "traditional" on social issues, less accepting and trusting of "government" programs, more independent and self-reliant, more religious,
and generally more politically conservative (Kellogg Foundation, 2001;
Krout, 1986). For example, although regional and other variations exist,
the Carsey Institute reports that data from the government's General
Social Survey (GSS) show rural Americans to be more religious and
more likely to be opposed to abortion and same-sex marriage (Dillon
& Savage, 2006). The 2012 presidential election clearly showed a rural
versus urban divide on support for the Democratic president, with 61%
of voters in rural areas nationwide voting Republican (Associated Press,

2012). This more conservative/traditional outlook has been linked by a number of rural observers to a reluctance of rural dwellers to participate in public programs (Goins & Krout, 2006).

The other chapters in this book explore various aspects of this aging, rural environment in great detail, ranging from the many definitions of rural and nonmetropolitan to evidence-based practice recommendations for service providers in rural areas. The purpose of this chapter is to provide an overview of the issues faced by rural residents, such as Gladys and her friend Mack, as they age in place, including both the challenges and the positive aspects of rural aging. It also dispels the myth that rural older adults are a homogenous group; in fact, rural areas of the country often reflect the increasing diversity of the United States, including racial and ethnic minorities; immigrants; and lesbian, gay, bisexual, and transgender (LGBT) persons. The term *rural* conjures a number of images and stereotypes; however, researchers and practitioners must work to build an understanding of rural aging that is firmly grounded in reality— if they are to adequately meet the needs of the rural older population.

CHALLENGES FOR RURAL OLDER ADULTS

Although rural areas include communities and regions as diverse as any in the United States, the rural environment itself can have a particularly strong impact on older adults. In general, an older adult's social environment—or life space—tends to constrict over the life course (Cagney, Browning, & Wen, 2005). Older adults are also less likely to travel than younger adults, making them more dependent on the interactions within their physical and social environments. Moreover, older adults are less likely to relocate when compared with other age groups. The Administration on Aging (AoA) reported that between 2011 and 2012, only 3% of adults age 65 and older moved residences, whereas 14% of adults under the age of 65 moved during that year. Of those 3% who did move, 61% remained in their same county, and 83% continued to live in the same state (Administration on Aging, 2012). A more restricted life space, coupled with a higher physical and social dependency, make the rural context particularly salient in older adulthood and cause rural older adults to be at greater risk for the intersecting challenges of poverty, health disparities, and the lack of access to health and social services. These challenges and needs are briefly discussed in the following paragraphs and further detailed in subsequent chapters.

Poverty

Although every rural community is different, older adults in these areas face similar challenges related to aging in place, including higher rates of community- and individual-level poverty than urban areas, diminished access to health care, and a lack of community resources (U.S. Department of Health and Human Services [HHS], 2008). Many of the challenges faced by rural older adults can be attributed to low population density and fragile local economies. The availability of local resources is inextricably tied to the financial well-being of a region and, over time, economic shifts from industries like manufacturing and farming to the service sector have left many rural communities economically vulnerable. When jobs and younger workers leave rural communities for urban and suburban areas, older adults are often left behind in communities with shrinking resources (Bull, Krout, Rathbone-McCuan, & Shreffler-McCuan, 2001). A combination of higher unemployment and lower paying jobs in rural areas has also led to a persistent poverty gap between nonmetropolitan and metropolitan areas, a gap that widened from 2006 to 2011 (U.S. Department of Agriculture [USDA], 2012). These lower earnings across the life span translate to lower Social Security (SS) and retirement benefits in older adulthood (Dorfman, 1998). Related to poverty, rural older adults are more likely to experience food insecurity than older adults in urban areas, putting them at a greater risk for hunger (Ziliak & Gundersen, 2009). Rural older adults are also more likely to be uninsured and more likely to report having deferred care due to costs than their urban counterparts (Bennett, Olatosi, & Probst, 2008). Like many other nonurban older adults, Mack appears to have problems with affording and preparing food. It is also possible that the health episode described in the earlier case study occurred because financial difficulties caused Mack to postpone or avoid seeking care to help manage his chronic conditions or because the options for care in his area are limited.

Health Disparities

Despite romanticized notions of a robust and healthy rural population, the reality is that nonurban residents are, in general, characterized by poorer health and less healthy behaviors than their urban counterparts. Defined as "a particular type of health difference that is closely linked with social, economic, and/or environmental disadvantage" (HHS, 2010), rural residents experience significant *health disparities* when compared with individuals in more urban areas (Gamm, Hutchison, Dabney, & Dorsey, 2003). According to a summary report from the South Carolina Rural Health Research Center (SCRHRC), nonurban adults have a higher prevalence of obesity, more activity limitations, and a greater prevalence of chronic conditions when compared with urban adults. Rural residents are also comparatively more likely to report fair or poor health and are less likely to engage in healthy behaviors (i.e., physical activity) than their urban counterparts. They are also less likely than urban residents to seek and receive preventive health services (Bennett et al., 2008). In addition, disability in older adulthood also seems to have a strong regional component. Research has indicated that when compared to urban older adults, nonurban older adults live more years with physical impairment and are impaired for a greater overall proportion of their lives (Laditka, Laditka, Olatosi, & Elder, 2007).

Mack lives with many of the indicators of health disparities, including poor health behaviors, disability, chronic health conditions, and barriers to accessing needed care and services. Current studies have not consistently shown that persons aging in rural areas have prevalence rates for mental health disorders that differ from their urban counterparts. It is possible that the stigma of mental health problems is greater in rural areas and prevents persons from seeking help and being counted (Larson, Corrigan, & Cothran, 2012). Suicide rates, however, are thought to be higher for rural residents of all ages (Hirsh, 2006). In addition, if geography impacts mental health, rural people may be more vulnerable to isolation and loneliness (Rainer & Martin, 2012). Mack is at risk for isolation because he is widowed and does not live near family. Fortunately, he has his friend Gladys to provide support, which was particularly important during his recent health crisis.

Access to Care and Services

As mentioned, poverty and health disparities can adversely affect the health and functional status of rural older adults. Compounding these disadvantages is the sparseness of health and human services and professionals to provide needed preventative and management care. Rural areas have a shortage of primary care physicians and dental providers; additionally, very few specialists practice in rural areas, forcing non-urban older adults to seek specialty care in larger cities (Hartman & Weierbach, 2013). Areas are designated as Health Professional Shortage Areas (HPSAs) if there are not enough health professionals available to meet the health needs of the population. According to the most recent data from the Health Resources and Services Administration (HRSA), a greater percentage of HPSAs are in nonmetropolitan areas. Specifically, 63% of primary medical, 57% of dental, and 53% of mental health HPSAs are in nonmetropolitan areas (HHS, 2013). In terms of communicating with professionals who are accessible and understanding health-related information, nonurban older adults also have the disadvantage of lower health literacy levels (the ability to read and understand health information) than their urban counterparts (Zahnd, Scaife, & Francis, 2009).

In addition to limited access to health care and communication barriers, rural older adults can experience difficulty acquiring other services that would help facilitate aging in place. These include respite care and homemaker services (Li, 2006; Li, Kyrouac, McManus, Cranston, & Hughes, 2012); hospice care (Virnig, Haijun, Hartman, Moscovice, & Carlin, 2006); transportation (Kershner, 2006; Li, 2006; Li et al., 2012); and affordable, accessible housing (Housing Assistance Council, 2013). Rural older adults who are raising their grandchildren may face additional challenges including poverty and fewer community-based resources, such as transportation, health care and mental health care, support groups, food pantries, and child care services (King et al., 2009; Robinson, Kropf, & Myers, 2000).

Living in a small rural community, Mack most likely faces the challenge of limited access to health care and mental health care as well as transportation and other social services that he may need. It is also possible that his "dislike" of filling out forms and talking to doctors may stem from problems with literacy, health literacy, or negative prior experiences with insensitive service providers.

OPPORTUNITIES AND STRENGTHS

The rural environment also offers many strengths and opportunities for those aging within its context. Such communities are often praised for being very tight-knit in terms of social networks and supports. These networks can consist of family, friends, neighbors, church members, and so forth. For older adults who have lived the majority of their lives in one rural community, such networks can be long-standing and very strong. The research in this area is very limited, and it is unclear whether nonurban older adults have significantly larger social support networks than their urban counterparts. A few studies have shown, however, that support from family and friends can have a positive influence on life satisfaction for rural aging residents (Yoon & Lee, 2007) and that strong, informal ties tend to benefit nonurban older adults more than their urban or suburban counterparts in terms of an increased sense of well-being (Mair & Thivierge-Rikard, 2010).

It is a commonly held belief that rural communities and their older populations benefit from strong church participation and faith-based ties. Again, there is a paucity of research to confirm this. One study, however, found that rural older adults were more likely to experience greater life satisfaction and less depression when they used a religious or spiritual source as a means of coping with health and other difficulties (e.g., God or a higher power) or utilized support from spiritual sources or faith-based networks (Yoon & Lee, 2007). Given his current situation, Mack is likely experiencing a lower sense of overall well-being. Fortunately, the presence of and assistance from his longtime friend might serve as a buffer to the stress of his hospitalization. It also seems from his church participation that he has a connection to a higher power from which he can gain strength in coping. Other persons from his faith community may also be available to provide emotional or instrumental support to Mack.

DIVERSITY AMONG RURAL OLDER ADULTS

Racial/Ethnic Minority and Immigrant Populations

According to U.S. Bureau of the Census (2008–2012b) estimates, 85% of the population of rural communities identify as White, compared with 72% of urban areas and 74% of the overall U.S. population. These statistics may lead one to believe that rural residents represent a homogenous group in terms of their racial and ethnic composition. In reality, however, it depends on the specific community because members of racial/ethnic minorities are not evenly distributed throughout rural America. Many of these racial/ethnic groups cluster together geographically and, depending on the state, one can find significant percentages of these "minority" populations in rural towns and communities.

African Americans comprise about 8% of the population of rural areas and the majority live in the southern states of Alabama, Georgia, North Carolina, South Carolina, and Virginia, as well as states in the Lower Mississippi Delta region including Arkansas, Louisiana, and Mississippi. Nearly half of all Native Americans live in rural areas and the majority resides in the plains of the Midwest, the Southwest, and Alaska; more than half of all rural Hispanics live in Arizona, California, New Mexico, or Texas. Rural Hispanics, who comprise individuals from many different national backgrounds, are heavily concentrated in the Southwest. As of the 2010 census, Hispanics are now the largest ethnic minority group in rural areas, making up more than 9% of the population. Although racial/ethnic minorities in general account for the largest gains in population in rural areas, Hispanics accounted for more than half of the growth in small towns and rural areas between 2000 and 2010. Similarly, although representing less than 2% of the population of rural areas, both Asian Americans and Pacific Islanders experienced more than 30% growth in these areas in that 10-year period (Hartman & Weierbach, 2013; Housing Assistance Council, 2012a).

Growing in number and concentrated in specific areas of the United States, racial/ethnic minority older adults who are aging in the rural environment, such as Mack and Gladys, are at an increased risk for poverty and poor health outcomes when compared with their urban counterparts. Rural racial/ethnic minorities of all ages are more likely to be poor and live in substandard housing (Housing Assistance Council, 2013). One can imagine that this is even more of a problem for older minorities living in these areas. In addition, many of the transportation and distance barriers experienced by rural older adults are even more problematic for racial/ethnic minority groups. For example, in one study comparing African American and White older adults in Alabama, African Americans were twice as likely as Whites to report difficulty in acquiring transportation (Park et al., 2010). Racial/ethnic minority adults in rural areas were also more likely than same-age rural Whites to report that they deferred health care due to cost (Bennett et al., 2008). Poverty and limited resources provide two partial explanations for these differences in health-related outcomes among rural minority aging populations.

The health disadvantages of rural racial/ethnic minorities stem from both their minority status and rural residence, and accumulate over the life span. Coward and Krout (1998) argue that rural residence compounds other risk factors leading to "double jeopardy" for rural older adults and "triple jeopardy" for older rural minorities. For instance, when compared with Whites in rural areas American Indians and African Americans were more likely to have diabetes and African Americans were at a particularly high risk for obesity and sedentary behavior (Bennett et al., 2008). African Americans were also found to have higher rates of disability than Caucasians in both metro and non-metro areas (Lee & Singelmann, 2013). Health disparities can also occur when the community as a whole does not receive the same resources as majority White communities. This is illustrated by the finding that rural areas with high racial/ethnic minority populations are more likely to have the HPSA designation. An overwhelming 92% of rural counties with a majority American Indian/Alaskan Native population are HPSAs, followed by 83% of counties with African American majority populations and 81% of Hispanic majority counties (Probst, Moore, Glover, & Samuels, 2004).

Closely related to the topic of racial/ethnic minorities, the face of the American immigrant has shifted from being largely European to being of either Asian or Latin American descent. Although the majority of immigrants are concentrated in urban areas, some have migrated to other parts of the country including rural areas (Lichter & Johnson, 2006). It is difficult to make generalizations about the lives of rural immigrant older adults because they constitute such a small proportion of recent immigrants and have not been discussed in the extant literature. In fact, for those immigrants who came to the United States after 1990 and who live in rural areas, fewer than 5% are adults aged 65 and older. It is known that, in general, immigrants who live in rural communities have lower levels of education than their urban counterparts and are at greater risk for poverty and for experiencing barriers to services such as food stamps and health care. As positives, rural immigrants are more likely to be employed (although often underemployed), married, in good health, and homeowners (Jensen, 2006). Depending on their countries of origin, rural immigrants may also have the additional challenge of limited English proficiency. The unique health issues experienced by racial/ethnic minority populations and immigrants will become even more relevant as the United States sees an increase in the absolute number and proportion of minority residents and more immigrants dispersing to rural areas, particularly if these residents age in place.

Social and Gender Minority Populations

Social minority older adults such as LGBT persons and women are also at risk for experiencing disadvantages while living in rural communities. Gender identity and sexual orientation have been largely ignored in the gerontological literature, and research on rural LGBT older adults is even sparser. What is known from the general LGBT aging literature is that this population may experience higher rates of disability and certain conditions such as obesity, HIV, substance abuse, depression, loneliness, and suicide than their heterosexual counterparts. Older adults who identify as transgender are thought to be at an even greater risk for experiencing health and mental health problems (Fredriksen-Goldsen et al., 2011). In addition, older LGBT people have faced lifelong stigma, discrimination, and even harassment from family members, employers, and professionals. They have also dealt with governmental and organizational policies during most of their lifetimes that have not been sensitive to or supportive of their identities and relationships (Cahill & South, 2002; Hash, 2006). Past negative experiences with professionals, organizations, and policies, and the fear that they may not be understood and supported, may prevent older LGBT adults from seeking needed care and services (McFarland & Sanders, 2003). As an advantage in older age and as a protective factor in the face of lifelong discrimination by family and society, many LGBT individuals have built strong alternative support networks that consist of friends, former partners, and some family members (Grossman, D'Augelli, & Hershberger, 2000; Metlife Mature Market Institute, 2010).

As mentioned earlier, very little research has been done to understand the experience of LGBT older adults in rural areas. In one of the few large-scale surveys on the rural LGBT experience, Oswald and Culton (2003) interviewed 527 LGBT people, ranging in age from 17 to 77, about their experiences living in rural areas. Results suggested that the worst aspects of living in a rural area included weak/fragmented resources for LGBT residents, homophobia, and a lack of equal rights. A small study conducted by Comerford, Henson-Stroud, Sionainn, and Wheeler (2004) of a group of older rural lesbians found that their challenges included social isolation, lack of support from family of origin, and coming out to formal support networks. Many of these women had developed a strong informal support network made up of mostly lesbian friends. They also found support and a sense of community by traveling to larger communities that had gay bars, specialized bookstores, and other groups and services (Comerford et al., 2004). A more recent study using secondary data found that when compared with urban LGBT older adults, individuals in rural areas tended to have lower levels of "outness" and were more guarded about their sexual or gender identity, especially with siblings, neighbors, friends, coworkers, and church members. Interestingly, levels of support from family and friends were not found to be different among rural and urban residents (Lee & Quam, 2013). King and Dabelko-Schoeny's (2009) qualitative study of 20 midlife and older LGB persons in rural areas found a sense of isolation and lack of community among this population, as well as a fear of disclosing sexual orientation to professionals. Another significant concern for this group was finding health care and mental health care professionals who were sensitive to and supportive of their sexual orientation.

Although not considered a minority in terms of number, older women residing in rural areas also face many unique challenges. They are more likely, in general, to be poorer than their male counterparts, and rural residents are at greater risk for poverty than are urban and suburban residents (Housing Assistance Council, 2012b). Older Hispanic and African American women are at particular risk for being poor (HHS, 2013). According to the National Rural Health Association (NRHA), adult women living in rural areas face significant health disparities such as barriers to accessing health care (especially gynecologic care) and higher rates of some health conditions including obesity, cervical cancer, and mobility-reducing chronic conditions—when compared to their urban counterparts (Bennett, Lopes, Spencer, & van Hecke, 2013). Older rural women may also experience greater health risks such as problems with mobility, stroke, and depression (Alkadry & Tower, 2010; Ziembroski & Breiding, 2006).

Because of isolation and lack of services and personal resources, older women in rural areas may be at special risk for intimate-partner violence. It is also thought that the nature of the rural culture—traditional gender roles that may be strengthened by religious beliefs, acceptance of relationship violence as a part of life, possession of weapons by men, and an abuser's close connections with law enforcement and others in power in the community—may contribute to women staying in abusive relationships (Teaster, Roberto, & Dugar, 2006). To compound this problem, women of all ages in rural areas may suffer more from physical abuse and have less access to domestic violence help and resources (Peek-Asa et al., 2011). Despite being at special risk for intimate-partner violence and other health and mental health challenges, women aging in rural areas may also exhibit unique strength and resilience from facing and overcoming these and other challenges (Dorfman, Mendez, & Osterhaus, 2009).

CONCLUSION

The introductory chapters of this book lay the groundwork for understanding the basic population trends and characteristics of rural areas. This chapter asks the fundamental question, "Who are rural older adults?" and provides a general picture of this population and its special issues, challenges, and strengths. It also examines the added disadvantages faced by racial/ethnic and social minorities who are aging in these areas. This examination illustrates the paucity of data available to comprehensively describe persons who age in small towns and rural areas. Increasing the visibility of this population in terms of research and education would make it easier to advocate for policies and programs to address the unique needs of rural residents and their communities. Shedding more light on the experiences and disparities of minorities in these communities is especially warranted.

The statement in Chapter 1 that "when you see one rural community, you have seen one rural community" applies not only to the communities but also to their diverse residents. Rural areas and populations do, however, have characteristics and common experiences that lead to important health disadvantages, and impact the availability of formal and informal supports that can help people like Gladys and Mack age in place. Factors such as poverty, less formal education, and a lack of community resources are issues that disadvantage rural residents and their communities, and impact access to health care and mental health care, transportation, and nutrition services. These disadvantages can be even more pronounced for racial/ethnic and social minorities in these communities. The chapters that follow further detail specific barriers to care and service provision for rural older adults as well as offer possible solutions to remedy these disadvantages in terms of policy and programming, and the education of health and human service professionals.

USEFUL WEBSITES

Administration on Aging–Aging Statistics
www.aoa.gov/Aging_Statistics
Administration on Aging–Minority Aging Statistics
www.aoa.gov/Aging_Statistics/minority_aging
Center for Rural Affairs
www.cfra.org
Indian Health Service
www.ihs.gov
National Asian and Pacific Center on Aging
www.napca.org
National Association for Hispanic Elderly
anppm.org
National Center and Caucus on the Black Aging, Inc.
www.ncba-aged.org
National Hispanic Council on Aging
www.nhcoa.org
National Institute on Minority Health and Health Disparities
www.nimhd.nih.gov
National Resource Center for Native American Aging
www.nrcnaa.org
National Resource Center on LGBT Aging
www.lgbtagingcenter.org
Older Women's League (OWL)
www.owl-national.org
Rural Assistance Center–Aging
www.raconline.org/topics/aging
Services and Advocacy for Gay, Lesbian, Bisexual and Transgender Elders (SAGE)
www.sageusa.org

NOTE

1. Data used from the U.S. Bureau of the Census 2008–2012 American Community Survey (ACS) are based on the definition of rural as nonmetro and urban as metro.

REFERENCES

Alkadry, M. G., & Tower, L. E. (2010). The effect of rurality and gender on stroke awareness of adults in West Virginia. *Journal of Health & Human Services Administration, 33*(1), 63–93.

Associated Press. (2012, November 6). 2012 election polls show voter demographics. *The Sacramento Bee.* Retrieved October 10, 2013, from http://www .sacbee.com/2012/11/06/4966431/2012-election-exit-poll-shows.html

Bennett, K. J., Lopes, J. E., Spencer, K., & van Hecke, S. (2013). *Women's rural health: National Rural Health Association policy brief.* Retrieved July 10, 2013, from http://www.ruralhealthweb.org/index.cfm?objectid=F5A503E1-3048- 651A- FE066957562D3AC7

Bennett, K. J., Olatosi, B., & Probst, J. C. (2008). *Health disparities: A rural-urban chartbook.* Retrieved August 12, 2013, from http://rhr.sph.sc.edu/report/ (73)%20Health%20Disparities%20A%20Rural%20Urban%20Chartbook%20- %20Distribution%20Copy.pdf

Bull, C., Krout, J., Rathbone-McCuan, E., & Shreffler-McCuan, M. (2001). Access and issues of equity in remote/rural areas. *The Journal of Rural Health, 17*(4), 356–359.

Cagney, K. A., Browning, C. R., & Wen, M. (2005). Racial disparities in self-rated health at older ages: What difference does the neighborhood make? *Journal of Gerontology, 60B*(4), S181–S190.

Cahill, S., & South, K. (2002). Policy issues affecting lesbian, gay, bisexual, and transgender people in retirement. *Generations, 26*(2), 49–54.

Colello, K. J. (2007). *Where do older Americans live? Geographic distribution of the older population.* Washington, DC: Congressional Research Service.

Comerford, S. A., Henson-Stroud, M., Sionainn, C., & Wheeler, E. (2004). Crone songs: Voices of lesbian elders on aging in a rural environment. *Affilia, 19*(4), 418–436.

Coward, R. T., & Krout, J. A. (Eds.). (1998). *Aging in rural settings: Life circumstances and distinctive features.* New York, NY: Springer Publishing Company.

Dillon, M., & Savage, S. (2006). *Values and religion in rural America: Attitudes toward abortion and same-sex relations* (Issue Brief No. 1). Durham, NH: Carsey Institute. Retrieved from http://www.carseyinstitute.unh.edu/publications/ IB_ruralvalues_06.pdf

Dorfman, L. T. (1998). Economic status, work, and retirement among the rural elderly. In R. T. Coward & J. A. Krout (Eds.), *Aging in rural settings: Life circumstances and distinctive features* (pp. 47–66). New York, NY: Springer Publishing Company.

Dorfman, L. T., Mendez, E. C., & Osterhaus, J. K. (2009). Stress and resilience in the oral histories of rural older women. *Journal of Women & Aging, 21*(4), 303–316.

Fredriksen-Goldsen, K. I., Kim, H. J., Emlet, C. A., Muraco, A., Erosheva, E. A., Hoy-Ellis, C. P., . . . Petry, H. (2011). *The aging and health report: Disparities and resilience among lesbian, gay, bisexual, and transgender older adults.* Seattle, WA: Institute for Multigenerational Health.

Gamm, L. D., Hutchison, L. L., Dabney, B. J., & Dorsey, A. M. (Eds.). (2003). *Rural healthy people 2010: A companion document to healthy people 2010* (Vol. 1). College Station, TX: The Texas A&M University System Health Science Center, School of Rural Public Health, Southwest Rural Health Research Center.

Goins, R. T., & Krout, J. A. (2006). Introduction: Aging in rural America. In R. T. Goins & J. A. Krout (Eds.), *Service delivery to rural older adults: Research, policy, and practice* (pp. 1–36). New York, NY: Springer Publishing Company.

Grossman, A. H., D'Augelli, A. R., & Hershberger, S. L. (2000). Social support networks of lesbian, gay, and bisexual adults 60 years of age and older. *Journals of Gerontology: Series B: Psychological Sciences and Social Sciences, 55B*(3), P171–P179.

Hartman, R. M., & Weierbach, F. M. (2013, February). *Elder health in rural America* (National Rural Health Association Policy Brief). Retrieved July 10, 2013, from http://www.ruralhealthweb.org/go/left/policy-and-advocacy/policy-documents-and-statements/official-nrha-policy-positions

Hash, K. M. (2006). Caregiving and post-caregiving experiences of midlife and older gay men and lesbians. *Journal of Gerontological Social Work, 47*(3/4), 121–138.

Hirsh, J. K. (2006). A review of the literature on rural suicide: Risk and protective factors, incidence, and prevention. *Crisis, 27*(4), 189–199.

Housing Assistance Council. (2012a, April). *Race & ethnicity in rural America: Research note.* Retrieved July 7, 2013, from http://www.ruralhome.org/storage/research_notes/rrn-race-and-ethnicity-web.pdf

Housing Assistance Council. (2012b, June). *Poverty in rural America: Research note.* Retrieved August 27, 2013, from http://www.ruralhome.org/storage/research_notes/rrn_poverty.pdf

Housing Assistance Council. (2013, August). *Rural seniors and their homes.* Retrieved August 27, 2013, from http://www.ruralhome.org/storage/documents/elderly.pdf

Jensen, L. (2006). *New immigrant settlements in rural America: Problems, prospects, and policies* (Reports on Rural America, Vol. 1, No. 1). Durham, NH: Carsey Institute, University of New Hampshire Press.

Kellogg Foundation. (2001). *Perceptions of rural America.* Battle Creek, MI: Author.

Kerschner, H. (2006). *Transportation innovations for seniors: A report from rural America.* Pasadena, CA: Beverly Foundation; Washington, DC: Community Transportation Association of America.

King, S., & Dabelko-Schoeny, H. (2009). "Quite frankly, I have doubts about remaining": Aging-in-place and health care access for rural midlife and older lesbian, gay, and bisexual individuals. *Journal of LGBT Health Research, 5*(1/2), 10–21.

King, S., Kropf, N. P., Perkins, M., Sessley, L., Burt, C., & Lepore, M. (2009). Kinship care in rural Georgia communities: Responding to needs and challenges of grandparent caregivers. *Journal of Intergenerational Relationships,* 7(2/3), 225–242.

Kirschner, A., Berry, E. H., & Glasgow, N. (2006). The changing faces of rural America. In W. A. Kandel & D. L. Brown (Eds.), *Population change and rural society* (pp. 53–74). New York, NY: Springer.

Krout, J. A. (1986). *The aged in rural America.* Westport, CT: Greenwood Press.

Laditka, J. N., Laditka, S. B., Olatosi, B., & Elder, K. T. (2007). The health trade-off of rural residence for impaired older adults: Longer life, more impairment. *The Journal of Rural Health, 23*(2), 124–132.

Larson, J. E., Corrigan, P. W., & Cothran, T. P. (2012). The impact of mental health stigma on clients from rural settings. In K. B. Smalley, J. C. Warren, & J. P. Rainer (Eds.), *Rural mental health: Issues, policies and best practices* (pp. 49–64). New York, NY: Springer Publishing Company.

Lee, M. G., & Quam, J. K. (2013). Comparing supports for LGBT aging in rural versus urban areas. *Journal of Gerontological Social Work, 56*(2), 112–126.

Lee, M. L., & Singelmann, J. (2013). Place and race: Health of African Americans in nonmetropolitan areas. In N. Glascow & H. Berry (Eds.), *Rural aging in 21st century America* (pp. 99–113). New York, NY: Springer Publishing Company.

Li, H. (2006). Rural older adults' access barriers to in-home and community-based services. *Social Work Research, 30*(2), 109–118.

Li, H., Kyrouac, G. A., McManus, D. Q., Cranston, R. E., & Hughes, S. (2012). Unmet home care service needs of rural older adults with Alzheimer's Disease: A perspective of informal caregivers. *Journal of Gerontological Social Work, 55*(5), 409–425.

Lichter, D. T., & Johnson, K. M. (2006). Emerging rural settlement patterns and the geographic redistribution of America's new immigrants. *Rural Sociology, 71*(1), 109–131.

Mair, C. A., & Thivierge-Rikard, R. V. (2010). The strength of strong ties for older rural adults: Regional distinctions in the relationship between social ties and subjective well-being. *The International Journal of Aging & Human Development, 70*(2), 119–143.

McFarland, P. L., & Sanders, S. (2003). Pilot study about the needs of older gays and lesbians: What social workers need to know. *Journal of Gerontological Social Work, 40*(3), 67–80.

Metlife Mature Market Institute. (2010). *Still out, still aging: The Metlife study of lesbian, gay, bisexual, and transgendered baby boomers.* Westport, CT: Author.

Oswald, R., & Culton, L. (2003). Under the rainbow: Rural gay life and its relevance for family providers. *Family Relations, 52*(1), 72–81.

Park, N. S., Roff, L. L., Sun, F., Parker, M. W., Klemmack, D. L., Sawyer, P., & Allman, R. M. (2010). Transportation difficulty of Black and White rural older adults. *Journal of Applied Gerontology, 29*(1), 70–88.

Peek-Asa, C., Wallis, A., Harland, K., Beyer, K., Dickey, P., & Saftlas, A. (2011). Rural disparity in domestic violence prevalence and access to resources. *Journal of Women's Health, 20*(11), 1743–1749.

Probst, J. C., Moore, C. G., Glover, S. H., & Samuels, M. E. (2004). Person and place: The compounding effects of race/ethnicity and rurality on health. *American Journal of Public Health, 94*(10), 1695–1703.

Rainer, J. P., & Martin, J. C. (2012). Loneliness and isolation in rural areas. In K. B. Smalley, J. C. Warren, & J. P. Rainer (Eds.), *Rural mental health: Issues, policies and best practices* (pp. 65–78). New York, NY: Springer Publishing Company.

Robinson, M. M., Kropf, N. P., & Myers, L. L. (2000). Grandparents raising grandchildren in rural communities. *Journal of Mental Health and Aging, 6*(4), 353–365.

Teaster, P. B., Roberto, K. A., & Dugar, T. A. (2006). Intimate partner violence of rural aging women. *Family Relations, 55*, 636–648.

U.S. Bureau of the Census. (2008–2012a). American Community Survey 5-year estimates. *S0101 Age and sex* [Data]. Retrieved September 1, 2013, from http://factfinder2.census.gov

U.S. Bureau of the Census. (2008–2012b). American Community Survey 5-year estimates. *DP05 Demographic and housing estimates* [Data]. Retrieved September 1, 2013, from http://factfinder2.census.gov

U.S. Bureau of the Census. (2008–2012c). American Community Survey 5-year estimates. *B12002 Sex by marital status by age for the population 15 years and over* [Data]. Retrieved September 1, 2013, from http://factfinder2.census.gov

U.S. Bureau of the Census. (2008–2012d). American Community Survey 5-year estimates. *B15001 Sex by educational attainment for the population 18 years and over* [Data]. Retrieved September 1, 2013, from http://factfinder2.census.gov

U.S. Bureau of the Census. (2008–2012e). American Community Survey 5-year estimates. *B21001 Sex by veteran status for the civilian population 18 years and over* [Data]. Retrieved September 1, 2013, from http://factfinder2.census.gov

U.S. Department of Agriculture (USDA). (2012, December). *Rural America at a glance, 2012 edition* (Economic Brief No. 21). Washington, DC: Author. Retrieved August 27, 2013, from http://www.ers.usda.gov/media/965908/eb-21_single_pages.pdf

U.S. Department of Health and Human Services (2013). *A profile of older Americans 2013.* Retrieved from http://www.aoa.gov/AoARoot/Aging_Statistics/Profile/2013/10.aspx

U.S. Department of Health and Human Services. (2013, September). *Designated health professional shortage area statistics.* Retrieved September 18, 2013, from http://ersrs.hrsa.gov/reportserver/Pages/ReportViewer.aspx?/HGDW_Reports/BCD_HPSA/BCD_HPSA_SCR50_Smry_HTML&rs:Format=HTML4.0

U.S. Department of Health and Human Services, National Advisory Committee on Rural Health and Human Services. (2008). *The 2008 report to the Secretary: Rural health and human services issues.* Rockville, MD: Author. Retrieved March 30, 2013, from ftp://ftp.hrsa.gov/ruralhealth/committee/nacreport2008.pdf

U.S. Department of Health and Human Services, Office of Disease Prevention and Health Promotion. (2010). *Healthy people 2020.* Retrieved August 27,

2013, from http://www.healthypeople.gov/2020/about/disparitiesAbout. aspx#six

Virnig, H., Haijun, M., Hartman, L. K., Moscovice, I., & Carlin, B. (2006). Access to home-based hospice care for rural populations: Identification of areas lacking service. *Journal of Palliative Medicine, 9*(6), 1292–1299.

Yoon, D., & Lee, E. (2007). The impact of religiousness, spirituality, and social support on psychological well-being among older adults in rural areas. *Journal of Gerontological Social Work, 48*(3/4), 281–298.

Zahnd, W. E., Scaife, S. L., & Francis, M. L. (2009). Health literacy skills for rural and urban populations. *American Journal of Health Behavior, 33*(5), 550–557.

Ziembroski, J. S., & Breiding, M. J. (2006). The cumulative effect of rural and regional residence on the health of older adults. *Journal of Aging & Health, 18*(5), 631–659.

Ziliak, J., & Gundersen, C. (2009, September). *Senior hunger in the United States: Differences across states and rural and urban areas* (University of Kentucky Center for Poverty Research Special Reports). Lexington, KY: University of Kentucky Center for Poverty Research. Retrieved July 10, 2013, from http://www.mowaa.org/document.doc?id=193

II

Health and Human Service Needs of Rural Older Adults

3

Health and Wellness Among Rural Older Adults

ELAINE T. JURKOWSKI

SARAH R. DeWOLFE

Carol and Murray live in a community of 300 people in rural Nebraska, and are retired dairy farmers. Although retired, Murray tries to work with his sons and grandsons on the family farm that has been in the family for six generations. Active and in relatively good health, Carol suffers from type 2 diabetes; Murray had emergency bypass surgery last year, while the couple were on vacation in California. There is a small health clinic available to them in a neighboring town about 14 miles from their home; however, the nearest hospital is in Omaha—about 55 miles away.

Carol has participated in a host of classes designed for heart-smart living offered by the Farm Extension Bureau program. Through these classes, she has learned to cook in a manner that provides for low-fat food intake and control both for heart health and her diabetes condition. Despite this, it has been difficult for Carol to adjust her cooking portions for two because she was accustomed to cooking in bulk and for her family of six and multiple farmhands.

Carol and Murray also still have many of their own natural teeth but have been complaining of periodontal disease. The nearest periodontist available is located in Omaha. In fact, most specialists require a day's trip. The couple's daughter-in-law tries to attend medical appointments with them, in an effort to keep all of their specific health care needs straight. Fortunately, Carol worked as a local postmaster during her younger years, and her dozen years of service give the couple access to Medicare and services available through Medicare Parts A and B. When Murray recently underwent his bypass surgery, a major portion of the costs were covered through Medicare Part A. Carol receives many of the supplies for her diabetic condition through Medicare Part B and the prescription drug coverage portion (Part D). They are grateful to have these resources for their health care.

As has been evidenced and articulated throughout this book thus far, older adults are particularly vulnerable to many challenges imposed by living in rural communities. Layered within this phenomenon is the context of rural proximity. How does living within a rural context impact older adults in terms of their health and wellness? How does it contribute to or negate their well-being? This chapter explores the multiple benefits, challenges, and disparities that older adults living in rural communities often encounter. Issues such as individual and collective health disparities are addressed to include behavior, screening, and access to health care. Social/familial ramifications that affect older adults in rural areas—out-migration of children, widowhood, social networks, entrepreneurialism, caregiving, and coping strategies—are described. Environmental and geographical issues, perceptions and stigmas, and the idea of stoicism are also discussed. Also necessary is a detailing of current policies such as Social Security (SS), Medicare, and Medicaid and their effects on rural older adults. Finally, implications for policy development, social welfare planning, and interdisciplinary practice are explained in order to provide a concrete understanding of how to meet the unique health and wellness needs of older adults in rural communities.

HEALTH DISPARITIES

One of the initial areas to examine when considering the status of older adults in rural communities is the notion of health disparities and how such disparities have an impact on both older adults and especially older women. The U.S. Department of Health and Human Services (HHS) published its most recent version of *Healthy People 2020: Health Objectives for the Nation* in December 2010, outlining health objectives for the decade ending in 2020. Its purpose was to offer national health-related goals within the time frame of a decade. As stated in its vision statement, the United States should be "a society in which all people live long, healthy lives" (HHS, 2010). This work outlined many objectives for older adults, generally ages 65 and older, focusing on increasing health care, decreasing disease, reducing hip fractures, increasing screening for cancer to decrease risk, increasing diagnoses of dementias, increasing health literacy, decreasing consumption of incorrect medications, decreasing fall-related deaths, increasing the number of health care professionals and providers in geriatrics, and increasing dental care (HHS, 2010). Although these objectives were designed for the older adult population in general, it is essential to explore how older adults who live in rural communities (in comparison to older adults in urban communities) manage and how these goals may be impacted by virtue of living in rural communities. Some of the specific objectives for older adults (OA) included the following:

OA-1: Increase the proportion of older adults who use the Welcome to Medicare benefit.

OA-2: Increase the proportion of older adults who are up to date on a core set of clinical preventive services.

OA-2.1: Increase the proportion of men ages 65 and older who are up to date on a core set of clinical preventive services.

OA-2.2: Increase the proportion of women ages 65 and older who are up to date on a core set of clinical preventive services.

OA-3: (developmental) Increase the proportion of older adults with one or more chronic health conditions who report confidence in managing their conditions.

OA-4: Increase the proportion of older adults who receive diabetes self-management benefits.

OA-5: Reduce the proportion of older adults who have moderate to severe functional limitations.

OA-6: Increase the proportion of older adults with reduced physical or cognitive function who engage in light, moderate, or vigorous leisure-time physical activities.

OA-7: Increase the proportion of the health care workforce with geriatric certification (Centers for Disease Control and Prevention [CDC], 2014).

These objectives, introduced in the most recent version of Healthy People objectives, raise the expectations for understanding how health disparities impact older adults in rural communities. In this segment, some of these disparities are examined.

Rural older women experience multiple disparities in being female, older, and living in rural areas. These women also have a higher risk of falling than do older men and thus a higher risk of fall-related injury or death. A study performed by Hallrup, Albertsson, Tops, Dahlberg, and Grahn (2009) determined how older women cope with previous fragility fractures and their perspectives on living with fall risk. Thirteen rural-dwelling, independently living women ages 76 to 86 with a history of fragility fractures participated in the study. Hallrup et al. (2009) outlined common risk factors for older adults including age (those older than 65 were at greater risk), being female, history of balance issues, history of cognitive impairment, limited physical exercise, and functional ability. These risk factors were compounded by low body weight, difficulty going from sitting to standing position, and history of fragility factors. Hallrup and colleagues also found that previous literature stated that hip fractures occurred due to falls in more than 90% of instances, and hip fractures were more common in women. This is a particularly important aspect of living with risk and fear of falling. Because *Healthy People 2020* (HHS, 2010) aimed to reduce hip fractures and fall-related deaths, understanding factors that lead to increased fall-risk is necessary.

It is well documented that there are differences in health outcomes in rural communities; however, these are not consistent across all communities and across all ethnic groups. In some cases, depending upon the community, rural people may live longer than their urban counterparts. Rural living has at times been associated with a lower degree of stressful living. Some of the contributors to health disparities (cardiovascular disease [CVD], hypertension [HTN], and diabetes mellitus [DM]) may have controls for these risk factors. However, overall greater rates of chronic disease are found in rural communities than in any other area within the United States (Office of Rural Health Policy, 2014). Lack of access to health care and health care providers, health literacy, and opportunities for preventative care are contributing factors to health disparities in rural communities for older adults (Nelson & Gingerich, 2010).

BEHAVIORAL HEALTH

The literature thoroughly documents the lack of behavioral health care providers within rural regions. In addition to the scarcity of behavioral health services available to older women, there is also a strong stigma against utilizing mental health services. Largely, this may be due to the fact that institutional care for the psychiatrically impaired was often the cornerstone of many rural communities, and thus, older women may fear being linked to "those people." Certainly, rural areas tend to generate less economy and are less populated; nevertheless, there also tend to be serious disparities as compared to urban areas regarding the opportunities for behavioral health care services such as screening, early diagnosis, counseling services, and interventions (Cummings & Kroph, 2011). Service providers also often negate the value and impact of counseling or psychotherapy for older adults; therefore, older women—especially living within rural areas—may not benefit from these services.

To further illustrate this point, Crowther, Scogin, and Johnson (2010) provided detailed information about the changing demographics of older people in the United States, examined psychotherapies for aging rural persons, and then utilized a psychotherapy treatment case of a 65-year-old married man living in a rural area to demonstrate that professionals need to understand older individuals' views on gender and therapy and need to take into account the general lack of resources at the disposal of older adults.

In addition, rural older people also have a higher risk for mental health issues such as depression; however, because they live in areas where there is a lack of psychosocial services, this causes them to rely on family members for long-term care (Crowther et al., 2010). These researchers suggested that, particularly, the biopsychosocial model may serve best when working with rural older adults because it allows professionals to "plan treatment with awareness of interdisciplinary principles and resources." These authors also suggest that cognitive behavioral therapy (CBT) can be adapted for use with rural older adults to treat geriatric depression, particularly because psychoeducation is a large part of CBT (Crowther et al., 2010).

These same concepts can be extended to understand some of the rural conditions globally, as well as in domestic settings in North America. Ferdous, Cederholm, Kabir, Hamadani, and Whalin (2010) performed a cross-sectional study of 457 randomly selected people age 60 and older (55% women) in rural Matlab, Bangladesh, to determine the relationship between nutritional status and cognitive functioning.

The population of older persons in Bangladesh, currently at 6% of the total population, is expected to double in the next 20 years, similar to older populations worldwide (Ferdous et al., 2010). Unlike the North American context, it is common in Bangladesh for older adults to contribute to the households of their families, both in practical and in financial support, a role that requires these people to age well in terms of cognitive and physical functionality (Ferdous et al., 2010). In order for this to occur, proper nutrition is essential; however, Ferdous and colleagues explained that the nutritional status, as well as the health condition, of this population was less than optimal (2010).

In order to collect data, Ferdous et al. employed a modified version of the Mini-Nutritional Assessment (MNA), with a maximum score of 28.0 as the best nutritional status; scores between 15.0 and 22.0 indicating risk of malnutrition; and scores less than 15.0 indicating undernutrition (2010). Trained psychologists performed three types of cognitive tests that examined cognitive processes such as general understanding, processing speed, and semantic memory (Ferdous et al., 2010). The Bangla Adaptation of the Mini-Mental Status Examination (BAMSE) was used to assess general cognition, with a maximum score of 30 and higher meaning better cognitive performance (Ferdous et al., 2010). Processing speed was assessed through two written tests (Ferdous et al., 2010). The two scores from these tests were combined into a summary score, or the processing speed score (Ferdous et al., 2010). A word-synonym test was used to assess semantic memory function; participants were requested to choose the synonym from three other words. The number of correctly identified synonyms formed the score (Ferdous et al., 2010).

These investigators also collected demographic information such as age, gender, and literacy, and obtained data from clinical examinations performed by physicians to determine level of health, vision and hearing acuity, and presence or absence of depressive symptoms (2010).

They found that "significantly more men than women were literate"; the health status of women was lower in all areas as compared to men; "women performed slower than men on all cognitive outcomes"; approximately 25% of the participants were undernourished; and more than 50% were at risk of malnutrition (p. 921). Correlations also showed "that processing speed was inversely related to age, female [gender], vision impairment, severity of disease, and depressive symptoms, and positively associated with literacy and nutritional status [and] a similar pattern was observed for general and semantic cognitive function" (Ferdous et al., 2010, p. 921).

Overall, a "better nutritional status was significantly associated with better cognitive performance in the tests of processing speed and general cognitive function" (Ferdous et al., 2010, p. 921). The work of these researchers supports current research findings that nutritional status directly affects cognitive function, despite different study methods (Ferdous et al., 2010). Ferdous and coworkers addressed the regional and cultural contexts within which these rural women lived, explaining that these factors—plus the realization that the women exhibited more depressive symptoms and worse nutrition than did their male counterparts—most likely affected the data.

Gao and colleagues (2009) attempted to explore the association of risk factors for late-life depression to "demographic characteristics, health conditions, *Apolipoprotein E (APOE)* status, and cognitive function." The researchers found a paucity of information regarding depression in later life in rural older Chinese people—75% of China's older population (Gao et al., 2009). They further stated that risk factors such as being female gender, cognitively impaired, older, and poorly educated had been studied earlier, yet results across studies had remained variable (Gao et al., 2009). Gao et al. performed a cross-sectional study of 1,737 rural Chinese aged 65 and older from four counties, between December 2003 and May 2005 (2009). In order to determine level of cognitive functioning, the study participants were involved in interviews during which information on demographics and medical conditions was also collected (Gao et al., 2009).

A second evaluation of the participants was conducted 2½ years after the first investigation, and involved application by trained interviewers of the Geriatric Depression Scale (GDS) in Chinese translation (Gao et al., 2009). During the second set of interviews, the Community Screening Instrument for Dementia (CSID), a word list for learning and recall, was used to assess cognitive functioning (Gao et al., 2009). The second interview also allowed the researchers to collect demographic and health information (Gao et al., 2009).

According to the study results, the authors found that risk factors such as "age, gender, education, marital status, living situation, BMI [body mass index], alcohol, smoking, history of stroke, heart attack, head injury, and fracture were associated with continuous GDS scores univariately . . . [and] living alone, history of heart attack, head injury, and fracture were associated with higher GDS scores, [whereas] drinking alcohol and higher composite cognitive scores were associated with lower GDS scores" (Gao et al., 2009, p. 1360). Of the total participants, 26.5% were considered mildly depressed, whereas 4.3% were found to be severely depressed

(Gao et al., 2009). These researchers found that there were two constant associations that came out of the three models used: "living alone and low cognitive function were risk factors for higher GDS scores, and for increased probabilities of mild or severe depression" (Gao et al., 2009, p. 1361). Gao and colleagues felt that independent living in rural areas might cause further issues for older people because of the decrease in social support and health care opportunities. Gao et al. cited previous findings that determined a link between cognitive dysfunction and increased risk of depression. Interestingly, Gao and coworkers also found that age and gender were not related to GDS scores, or mild to severe depression. Gao et al. suggested that future studies focus on longitudinal evaluation of rural older Chinese and other older adult populations.

In terms of depression, it has been found that there is a higher incidence of depression in urban areas than rural areas. However, women in rural areas are also more likely to exhibit depressive symptoms than are their urban counterparts—about 44% of rural women as compared to 13% to 20% of urban women (Tudiver, Beckett-Edwards, & Pfortmiller, 2010). Risk factors include female gender, low education, and low income, with the implication that older women in rural areas are more likely to be affected because of group characteristics of low education and income (Tudiver et al., 2010). To compound this, rural women are less likely to be diagnosed with and treated for depression than are urban women, often due to the lack of screening and health care options in such isolated areas (Tudiver et al., 2010).

There have been advances into the use of specific intervention programs to address behavioral health issues for older adults, and these same programs have been utilized in rural settings. Programs that have also been effective interventions to promote emotional well-being for older adults include the IDEAS (Identifying Depression, Empowering Activities for Seniors; Casado et al., 2008; Quijano et al., 2008) and PEARLS (Ciechanowski et al., 2004) intervention programs. These programs were designed to help people network with providers and to teach people how to communicate about their behavioral symptoms with their providers.

SCREENING ISSUES

Screening for health issues and the exploration of health disparities are also important in exploring how these impact older women. Screening procedures are often less prevalent in general within rural communities, and have an impact on the health outcomes of older women residing in rural communities.

Brown, Fitzhugh, Neutens, and Klein (2009) explored the prevalence of the use of screening mammography on women living in rural areas within the state of Tennessee. They used a combination of data from the 2001 and 2003 Tennessee Behavioral Risk Factor Surveillance System (BRFSS) in order to obtain an appropriate sample size of 1,922 non-Hispanic White and non-Hispanic Black women, age 40 and older (Brown et al., 2009). These researchers found that women in rural areas were more likely to be White, to be of lower income and education, to report poor to fair health, and to be less likely to drink alcohol, but more likely to be overweight or obese (Brown et al., 2009). They also found that 76.1% of Tennessee women utilized screening mammography. The data also revealed that there was a small difference in utilization rates between urban (78.3%) and rural (71.3%) women. These authors also found that urban women were more likely to be screened than rural women, when compared on a range of demographic variables. Women under age 50 and women 70 years of age and older reported lower screening rates than women ages 50 to 69. Women with greater income were reported to utilize screening more often than those with less income.

Having health insurance and a health care provider made women three times more likely to utilize screening mammography and, most significantly, a recent clinical breast examination influenced women, regardless of rural or urban residence (Brown et al., 2009, p. 168). Despite the fact that the results for women residing in rural communities were different, the research team found that the arbitrary definition of the term *rural* might impact a clear understanding of how the concept of rural played a role in understanding differences between urban and rural.

Feresu, Zhang, Puumala, Ullrich, and Anderson (2009) stated that screening for coronary vascular disease (CVD) could also be an issue for older women residing in rural communities. CVD, particularly coronary heart disease (CHD), was the leading cause of death in women in the United States, with known risk factors including "cigarette smoking, hypertension, diabetes, high cholesterol, and overweight or obesity," although symptoms tended to go undetected until it was too late (Feresu et al., 2009, p. 607). Minority and low-income women had a higher risk of CVD risk factors, disease, and death, making it extremely important to screen for CVD early for proper prevention (Feresu et al., 2009, p. 608). These researchers examined incidence, prevalence, and changes over time of CVD risk factors in participants of the Nebraskan

WISEWOMAN (Well-Integrated Screening and Evaluation for Women Across the Nation) program from September 2002 to December 2004, as well as any links between CVD risk factors and demographics (Feresu et al., 2009, p. 608). The WISEWOMAN program screens for CVD risk factors for low-income and minority women and offers strategies to include counseling that are designed to reduce the risk of acquiring CVD (Feresu et al., 2009). The research team analyzed data collected through the Nebraskan WISEWOMAN program of 10,739 women that included "age, race, education, place of residence, smoking status, previous history of disease, and medication use and other screening tests" (Feresu et al., 2009, p. 609), and found that socioeconomic status was connected to CVD factors, which confirmed preceding research. According to the data, hyperglycemia, high cholesterol, and overweight/obesity were at highest risk in women ages 60 to 64, and women ages 50 to 59 and 60 to 64 were at highest risk for high blood pressure (Feresu et al., 2009).

Findings also showed that Mexican American women were at higher risk of hyperglycemia than were Caucasian American women and that African American, Mexican American, and Native American women were at lower risk for high cholesterol than were Caucasian American women (Feresu et al., 2009). Caucasian women were also at higher risk than were minority women to have a 10-year CHD risk, and less likely to be overweight/obese (Feresu et al., 2009, p. 612). This study also found that a higher BMI was an important risk factor for "hyperglycemia, high blood pressure, high total cholesterol, and an increased 10-year CHD risk" (Feresu et al., 2009, pp. 612–613). These researchers determined that women with only one screening visit were more likely to have a higher rate of hyperglycemia and lower rates of borderline high cholesterol and LDL-C than were women with two or more screenings, thus equating to higher CVD risks (Feresu et al., 2009, p. 613). Feresu and coworkers' data suggested that minority, rural, less-educated, and older women had an increased risk of being overweight or having obesity; overweight/obese, less-educated, older women had higher rates of high blood pressure and hyperglycemia; and overweight/obese, older women had higher risk of increased 10-year CHD risk and high cholesterol (2009, p. 614). These findings showed that women who participated in the WISEWOMAN program for 1 year tended to be "less educated, more likely to live in urban areas, more likely to be from a minority group, and more likely to smoke" (Feresu et al., 2009, p. 610) than did women who participated for 2 or more years.

In addition, Folta and colleagues (2009) explored an intervention and screening process that focused on reducing CVD risk in midlife and older, overweight or obese, and sedentary women through a community-based intervention design (p. 1271). Folta et al. reviewed the literature available regarding CVD and cited that CVD was the major cause of death and disability in American women (2009, p. 1271). CVD cost the United States more than $430 billion in direct and indirect expenses in 2007 and was estimated to increase as the population of older people grew (Folta et al., 2009, p. 1271). Folta and coworkers argued that changes in lifestyle habits could reduce the risk of CVD in older women; however, according to the 1999–2000 National Health and Nutrition Examination Survey (CDC, 2014), high percentages of midlife and older women were not leading heart-healthy lifestyles. About 50% of women ages 51 to 70 did not eat the recommended five servings of fruits and vegetables per day, almost 40% of women ages 45 to 54 did not perform physical activity during leisure time, and almost 70% of these women were overweight or obese.

Folta et al. (2009) acknowledged the WISEWOMAN program—that screens for CVD in midlife, low-income, and uninsured women and contains a lifestyle intervention component—and a few other community-based programs that focus on preventing CVD in women, but felt that more such programs were necessary to improved heart health in older women (p. 1271). In order to help meet this need, Folta and colleagues (2009) established the StrongWomen–Healthy Hearts program, utilizing a partnership between Tufts University and the Cooperative State Research, Education, and Extension Services (CSREES) of the U.S. Department of Agriculture (USDA). CSREES are knowledgeable about and provide health programs in their counties, and thus supply the framework to distribute heart health interventions, both locally and nationally. For the purpose of their study, Folta and coworkers determined results from StrongWomen–Healthy Hearts interventions in Arkansas and Kansas through a randomized controlled trial (RCT) with eight partially or completely rural counties. Folta et al. stated that more than 90% of the residents of the participating counties were Caucasian and had low to medium incomes and education (2009, p. 1271).

Folta and colleagues recruited counties with CSREES' educators who could follow their research goals and time frames and could provide enough assessment of the intervention strategies. Folta et al. paired the counties in each state by population density and socioeconomic status and "one county from each pair was then randomly assigned to the intervention group; the other four counties (two in each state) served as controls and conducted a delayed intervention" (p. 1272). Folta et al. aimed to have CSREES' educators recruit 10 to 15 women per county through advertisements, flyers, and announcements in each county. The participants in each county were "assessed at baseline," and the intervention group participated in the StrongWomen–Healthy Hearts program, whereas the control group did not (Folta et al., 2009). After the conclusion and assessment of all participants, the control group was given the option of participating in the program and thus receiving intervention (Folta et al., 2009, p. 1272). The researchers targeted women ages 40 and older living sedentary, independent lifestyles, with a BMI of 24 kg/m² or higher (Folta et al., 2009, p. 1272). Many of the participants were required to obtain consent from their primary care physicians to take part in the StrongWomen–Healthy Hearts program (Folta et al., 2009, p. 1272).

Folta and coworkers outlined criteria that excluded participants at the outset of the intervention study: "an unstable medical condition that would preclude participation in an exercise program; . . . current participation in another lifestyle modification program; inability to prepare food; cognitive impairment; and pregnancy" (p. 1272). Folta and colleagues measured height, weight, and waist/hip circumference of each participant, as well as dietary food intake with food journals (2009, p. 1272). In order to evaluate preintervention and postintervention aerobic fitness levels, Folta et al. used President Urho Kaleva Kekkonen Institute of Finland's 2-km walking test, which had been found to be effective with older adults and those with obesity (2009, p. 1272). This test measured "time to complete the walk, ending heart rate, age, and BMI . . . to obtain an estimate of maximal oxygen uptake, a standard measure of fitness" (Folta et al., 2009, p. 1272). Participants also wore pedometers to determine average number of steps per day to measure typical physical activity (Folta et al., 2009, p. 1273). The investigators obtained data regarding demographics, cooking in each participant's household, and personal capability for modifying daily diet (Folta et al., 2009, p. 1273).

Folta and coworkers described the intervention as 2 days a week in a 12-week program, beginning midwinter 2007, with classes lasting about one hour each (Folta et al., 2009, p. 1273). The purpose of these classes was to increase aerobic activity to 30 moderate-to-hearty minutes and to promote lower intensity physical activity outside of class, as well as to teach dietary modifications according to the food pyramid for weight control (Folta et al., 2009, p. 1273). The investigators explained that the social cognitive theory created the theoretical framework of the

StrongWomen–Healthy Hearts program (Folta et al., 2009, p. 1273). Data were analyzed through chi-square analysis and regression models with pre-/postchange using Stata software version 8.0 for Windows (Folta et al., 2009, p. 1273). Total data collected included 14 Arkansas women in the control group, 21 Kansas women in the control group, 28 Arkansas women in the intervention group, and 33 Kansas women in the intervention group, leading to an 88.5% completion rate (Folta et al., 2009, p. 1274). The researchers found that a higher percentage of women in the intervention group were married, all participants except one American Indian woman were Caucasian, and average attendance of intervention classes was about 80% (Folta et al., 2009, p. 1274).

Folta et al. determined that women in the intervention group at the conclusion of the study displayed significant decreases in body weight, waist circumference, and energy intake and significantly increased the number of steps taken per day, physical activity, and personal modification of daily diet when compared with those in the control group (2009, pp. 1274–1275). This was important because blood pressure and risk of diabetes decreased with decreasing weight loss (Folta et al., 2009, p. 1275). Folta and colleagues suggested that new measures be developed to be used with "overweight, sedentary, and unfit populations" (2009, pp. 1275–1276). Folta and coworkers found that their results were similar to then current research and community-based interventions with women, showing "that it is possible to facilitate meaningful behavior change in midlife and older women" (2009, p. 1276). Folta et al. also felt that their results were generalizable to related populations of older women (2009, p. 1276).

Screening and assessment within primary care settings by social workers has proved to be an effective strategy to promote the early identification of mental health issues. Early identification of risk factors for depression and anxiety leads to more effective outcomes (Cummings & Kropf, 2008, 2009; Kropf, 2012). A community-based screening and assessment program known as the Gatekeeper program has also provided promising results for community-dwelling older adults (Bartsch & Rodgers, 2009; Bartsch, Rodgers, & Strong, 2013).

> Carol and Murray have been able to take advantage of working with a social worker at their primary care clinic at the University of Nebraska. During their visits to the primary care physician, a social worker asks them a series of questions on an individual basis. The questions, all part of a series of screening tools for

cognition, memory, and depression, were helpful in identifying Murray's threshold for depression shortly after his bypass surgery. Some education related to the impact of his surgery and the potential for one becoming depressed helped protect Murray from becoming seriously depressed.

ACCESS TO HEALTH CARE

Access to health care has been identified as a major issue that leads to health care disparities for older adults living in rural communities. Limited access can be as a result of limited providers in rural areas, lack of health insurance such as Medicare eligibility, or limited providers who accept Medicare or Medicaid. Some strategies to improve access to health care have included health literacy and telemedicine interventions.

Healthy Literacy

The Centers for Disease Control and Prevention (CDC; 2012) defined health literacy as the capacity to obtain, process, and understand basic health information and services to make appropriate health decisions. Health literacy is the degree to which individuals have the capacity to obtain, process, and understand basic health information and services needed to make appropriate health decisions (HHS, 2000). Health literacy affects people's ability to do the following:

- Understand and negotiate the health care system, including filling out complex forms and locating providers and services
- Communicate personal information such as health history to providers
- Participate in self-care and chronic-disease management

Some of the specific skills involved in the process of health literacy include numeracy skills. For example, calculating cholesterol and blood sugar levels, measuring medications, and understanding nutrition labels all require mathematical skills. Choosing between health plans or comparing prescription drug coverage requires calculating premiums, co-pays, and deductibles.

Zahnd, Schaife, and Francis (2009), in their investigation of differences between urban and rural older adults and health literacy, found that rural older adults had lower health literacy levels in terms of health knowledge than did their rural counterparts. Some of the differences resulted from access to health care providers who placed an emphasis on health education and behavior-change strategies.

> Carol participated in the local Farm Extension Bureau programs on a variety of topics related to her diabetes care. The topics included cooking strategies, testing one's blood sugar, and techniques to stabilize one's blood sugar. Despite her remoteness from the primary care physician in the urban setting, she felt that she had some basics from her classes to improve her overall literacy in dealing with her health condition.

Telemedicine

Telemedicine is a strategy now used to provide access to health care in remote and isolated areas, and offers growing promise to reach older adults living in rural communities. Telemedicine utilizes techniques of telecommunication and information technologies in its provision of clinical health care. The process involves the expert, or physician care team, at a distance and the receiver, who can be located in a rural isolated community. The procedure helps eliminate distance barriers and can improve access to medical services that would often not be consistently available in distant rural communities. These technologies permit communications between patient and medical staff with convenience for both; they also allow for the transmission of medical, imaging, and health information data from one site to another.

> Murray underwent open heart and bypass surgery while visiting California. Upon his return to Nebraska, he was able to access his specialists on the West Coast through the use of telemedicine. When he returned home, he was monitored on a weekly basis by the treatment team in California through Skype and telemedicine options.

HEALTH STATUS

Vagenas, McLaughlin, and Dobson (2009) performed a prospective cohort study of 12,778 randomly selected Australian women ages 70 to 75, in order to identify differences in health and mortality of older women based on socioeconomic and behavioral elements versus the utilization of health services. In their literature review, Vagenas and colleagues offered previous findings that showed that rural populations tended to have higher mortality rates than urban areas, even if mortality rates of specific diseases were decreasing. Vagenas et al. also reported that those who lived in rural areas had less access to health services and less treatment options available to them, as a result, than did their urban counterparts. Rural areas also tended to have smaller hospitals that were "less well equipped," had fewer medical and specialist practitioners, and fewer health care providers, in general, than did urban areas (Vegenas et al., 2009). This research team found that their results echoed those of previous studies that pointed out that people in rural areas visited either general and specialist practitioners than did those in urban areas. Also, the findings cited greater distances in rural areas as a possible barrier to accessing health services, as well as the propensity of rural people toward stoicism.

Studies of specific diseases show that even if the relevant mortality rates are decreasing, rural populations continue to have higher rates than those of urban areas. However, disease-specific studies do not necessarily reflect the health status of the community. Previous studies suggested that rural residents faced a number of barriers to good health including poorer access to health service and fewer options for treatment. Rural areas typically have fewer medical practitioners and other health care providers and smaller hospitals than urban areas have. Furthermore, rural health services may be less well equipped than those in cities, with access to fewer specialist practitioners. However, it is unclear from previous studies whether the excess mortality in rural areas reflected poorer health or differences in health services.

The majority of older adults in the United States receive medical care through Medicare, a universal health insurance plan. Although based upon lifetime earnings (one must have worked 40 three-month quarters to qualify), Medicare coverage provides for the majority of the cost of hospital stays, preventative health care, and medically necessary health care. Chapter 12 gives more details on the benefits and the medical procedure specifics for which coverage is provided.

> Whereas Carol and Murray do not have access to many of the specialty services they need within a 30-mile radius of their home, they do take advantage of the services available at the nearest university hospital system—nearly 55 miles away. They

make a day of their appointments and enjoy the urban center by treating themselves to dinner, a movie, and some shopping.

SOCIAL/FAMILIAL ISSUES

Social/familial issues that affect older adults in rural areas, such as out-migration of children, widowhood, domestic violence, social networks, and entrepreneurialism, play a role in the lives of older women living in rural communities.

Out-Migration of Children

The lack of available jobs within rural communities, shifts from agrarian means of survival, and the concept of social mobility have all had a dramatic effect upon children. These realities have left families and aging women struggling to find local resources to attend to and oversee the caretaking needs of older women who reside in rural communities. An examination of census data in rural communities from 1950 to 2010 (U.S. Bureau of the Census, 2014) shows a steady increase of younger groups out-migrating from home-based rural communities and a steady increase in the population of older women age 60 and older. The additional burden this conveys for older women in rural communities is a general dearth of younger people available to carry out home health-related roles with older adult women.

> Carol and Murray feel blessed that three of their six children remained in the community where the family farm serves as the basis of their livelihood. One son and two daughters left the area to work in a more major urban center due to job opportunities.

Widowhood

Women typically will be widowed far sooner than men; in rural communities, this same rule is also upheld. Statistically, we also see that women will be widows for approximately 7 years to 10 years before they either remarry or expire, which leaves women in rural communities more likely to be forced to take care of situations on their own. Women living within rural contexts may face additional challenges with widowhood, when compared to urban-dwelling women. These challenges may include transportation, access to medical services, isolation, and access to handyman resources. In a cohort of women age 70 and older, it was found that fewer than the average drove their own vehicles; widowhood also may have led to relocation from a family farm or a parcel of land to a larger community where access to community living facilities was available. Despite these challenges, older women who were widows also had the capacity to bond with other women and care for each other as a matter of *necessity*; thus, some of the issues related to loneliness and lack of independence may have been compensated for by women who became self-reliant and supportive of each other.

Domestic Violence

Harbison (2008) based her discussion of issues related to older women in abusive situations on a Canadian study that found that people labeled these women as "stoic." The results were discussed at a conference during which women researchers suggested that these women were "perpetuating a cycle of violence in rural communities, one that prevented younger women from escaping their fate" (Harbison, 2008). This perception led Harbison to ask whether "ageism has led to abused old women in need of assistance being poorly served" (2008, p. 223). Harbison discussed viewpoints introduced in other literature that described old age as a social construction focused on "meeting the needs of employers." This is important because feminist discourse tends to focus on young women to those about age 60, however, often not including women in their 70s, 80s, and 90s, thus precluding the clear differences in life situations and experiences among these ages (Harbison, 2008, p. 223). This means that studies and the formulation of frameworks often do not examine older women's views and beliefs, particularly regarding forms of abuse.

In Canada, however, there has been more headway in this area, particularly due to the grassroots efforts of the Older Women's Network (OWN; Harbison, 2008, p. 225). OWN performed a study involving more than 100 culturally diverse women between ages 50 and 85 and older to determine their ideas of women's shelters and abuse-related services (Harbison, 2008, p. 225). The results of the study found that although some of the older women would use shelters, most indicated that they would not leave "their home and family." Instead, they felt they would like support and protection (Harbison, 2008, p. 225). This clearly contrasts multiple findings that suggested that successful intervention can be measured in the number of women who get out of abusive relationships (Harbison, 2008, p. 225). She pointed out that literature documenting abuse of rural older women was lacking—the author found only two studies focusing specifically on older women and abuse (Harbison, 2008, p. 225). According to one of the studies, women in rural areas were more likely to be physically and emotionally abused due to isolation of region and individual (Harbison, 2008). Older women often do not leave abusive situations for several reasons, including difficulty finding a sympathetic person to hear their story; perpetuation of a still-strong rural value of "having made your bed you should lie on it"; no long-term, practical support for leaving; and positive identification with coping (Harbison, 2008, pp. 228–229). These issues are compounded by the need for barrier-free shelters, and additional accommodations for women who have movement and/ or mobility impairments. This encompassing perspective translates into stoicism, generally because older women in abusive relationships view leaving—opposed to staying—as losing and see no other options (Harbison, 2008, p. 229). Current programs and interventions adapt to the needs of older women in abusive relationships by incorporating an understanding of aging, training, resources, and outreach intervention strategies. The role of social workers in this area is to bring light and attention to the matter during policy agenda planning, focusing on macro-level intervention in order to best benefit individuals on the micro level (Harbison, 2008, p. 230).

Carol and Murray vividly remember their neighbor Mabel, who has since passed away. Mabel often sought refuge at Carol and Murray's home when her husband went on a drinking binge and became physically and mentally abusive. Once, Murray had to drive Mabel to the local hospital emergency room in a community 55 miles away. Mabel's husband had lost control, twisted Mabel's arm, tore the shoulder muscles, and dislocated her shoulder. Despite the abuse, Mabel did not want to leave her husband because there were no resources in the nearby area to help her with domestic violence. Leaving the area would also mean leaving the relationships she had built over the years.

Social Networks

Social networks play a critical role in helping people with developing and maintaining mental vitality and overall health. As one ages, the risk of falls and general insecurity about one's physical stability can threaten these social networks and linkages. Hallrup et al. (2009) determined that older adults, and more specifically women living with fall risk, often reduce their "life space," causing them to become more isolated, and thus creating difficulties in establishing and/or maintaining their social networks and relationships. Hallrup et al. suggested that women as a group "found great value in social contacts combined with regular physical activities" (2009, p. 384). Overall, Hallrup et al. emphasized that older women living with fall risk need "a trust-based dialogue between patient and carer" in order to fully provide for their physical and emotional needs.

Regarding adults with mental health issues, Scheyett and colleagues (2010) focused heavily on individuals living with severe and persistent mental illnesses. They concluded that Assertive Community Treatment (ACT) provides individuals with mental illnesses, and their families, with support necessary to maintain mental health well-being. In communities where ACT teams are heavily utilized, mental health care delivery systems have seen increased collaboration across mental health systems and improved access to services. Consequently, individuals with mental illnesses have been able to live successfully in the community without having to resort to hospitalization. This success, as a result of community-based case management services twinned with ACT, has extended into old age for many people who have lived their lives with severe persistent mental illness (Cummings, 2009; Cummings & Kropf, 2009; Cummings & Kropf, 2011).

Social support is crucial for caregivers and people who are growing older, particularly in later life (McDonough & Davitt, 2011). The stress of transition from one's family home into long-term care settings can also pose adjustment disorders and concerns. Depression and anxiety are not normal states for people as they age, despite some common thought about this issue.

Management of Farm/Leasing Land/Entrepreneurialism

Up to this point, much time has been spent in this chapter discussing many of the negative components that impact the health and well-being of older adults who reside in rural communities. However, some literature suggests that there are also benefits to being an older adult in a rural community, and the relationship between rural living and women's entrepreneurialism is one of these benefits. Given that older women often reside on family farms or farm-based operations, it stands to reason that, upon widowhood, they are left to manage the family farm and assets. The literature suggests that farming is now a diversified operation, and often not a sole family or individual effort. Thus, it is reasonable to assume that older women are more likely to manage the farm operation following their husbands' passing, and this may include leasing of land to local farmers or leasing the care of crops and livestock. In addition to the social benefits, there are also financial benefits to older women in rural communities, in this situation. Revenues can help offset the retirement or pension plans that older women may otherwise be tied to in rural communities. In addition, many women from rural communities may not have pension plans at all to resort to.

Caregiving

Caregiving for older adults living in rural communities can pose benefits and challenges. Given the dearth of long-term care, rehabilitation facilities, and assisted-living services found in rural communities, older adults may value having a loved one at home with them as long as possible, when chronic health conditions set in. On the other side, however, the caregiving role may be more stressful and more isolating, given the limited resources available within the rural community. This, coupled with isolation and limited mobility, can lead to caregiver stress and strain. In addition, older women in rural communities are also more likely to take on the role of being a grandparent raising a grandchild (GRG) due to parental incarceration and abandonment (Jurkowski, 2008). The GRG role can significantly impact the caregiver, leading to financial stress and changes in roles, social relationships, and physical and emotional health and well-being.

Coping Strategies

Dorfman, Mendez, and Osterhaus (2009) performed a qualitative study to determine how rural older women are affected by stresses of major historical events and how they manage those stresses. In order to complete their study, Dorfman et al. collected oral histories from 25 older rural women from the Midwest, a strategy that is infrequently utilized with older rural people (2009). Oral history focuses on reflective meaning-making through investigative histories of life experiences, a technique that Dorfman and colleagues used to identify what types of coping strategies older rural women generated to deal with stress. Dorfman and coworkers referred to both the life-course perspective and the stress-process framework to inform their study and conducted an in-depth literature review relating to stress and resilience that rural older women dealt with (2009). Information obtained through the literature review allowed the researchers to gain a better understanding of the factors affecting rural older women—being females, aging, and rural-residing; having less access to resources due to geographic isolation; being more prone to health issues and disability; being more likely to be of low income; and being more likely than their urban counterparts to be widowed and living alone, all of which further contributed to stress (Dorfman et al., 2009). Resilience in rural older women tends to be a traditional value that allows these women to take strategies formulated earlier in life and apply them in later life (Dorfman et al., 2009). The 25 women interviewed for this study came from a rural community in the Midwest and from four different residential locations within the community, "a congregate meal site (n = 3), a semi-independent living site (n = 8), an assisted-living facility (n = 3), and a nursing home (n = 11)" (Dorfman et al., 2009, p. 306). These women were ages 68 to 98, with 76% being in their 80s or 90s. All of them were Caucasian, aptly indicating racial representation according to their communities (Dorfman et al., 2009). Findings showed emphasis of the oral histories placed on the Great Depression and World Wars I and II (Dorfman et al., 2009). The major stressor related to the Great Depression was economic, leading many of the women to become frugal and save items throughout their lives, as well as to rely on social supports (Dorfman et al., 2009). Stressors related to the two world wars included effects on the women's own families, as well as families within their communities, fears and uncertainties caused by the wars, and economic stress. In order to cope, these women stated acceptance of things they could not change themselves, focused on the importance of social supports, and also extended this concern to those affected by the wars in other countries. Dorfman et al. suggested that recollecting coping strategies used earlier in life to deal with economic stress, along with values such as independence and frugality common to rural peoples, could be beneficial to rural older women coping with the economic stress that often occurs with "bereavement, out-migration of children, and the economic restructuring of many small rural communities" (2009, p. 312). These investigators also found that informal support networks such as immediate family, friends, and neighbors played a significant role as a resource in allowing rural older women to cope with stress (Dorfman et al., 2009). Oral histories can be useful for professionals to employ in order to help empower rural older women, although their full effects aren't entirely known because they have been researched very little (Dorfman et al., 2009). Although this study contained certain limitations—it did not reflect the diversity of region, culture, population, occupation, or race of the whole of the United States—it did offer some insight into the usefulness and effectiveness of using oral histories to understand and identify areas of resilience in rural older women (Dorfman et al., 2009).

ENVIRONMENT

Bird and colleagues (2009) found that physical activity is most important for older people because it helps them avoid a sedentary lifestyle that can lead to physical health issues. Despite this, research points out that physical activity generally decreases with age, and older women are less inclined than older men to be physically active (Bird et al., 2009). In order to help older people remain physically active, or become more so, the factors that help or hinder such activity must be defined, as well as taking into account the fact that ethnic culture influences lifestyle choices such as physical activity (Bird et al., 2009). The researchers used an ecological perspective to assess how multiple factors—environment, society, family, and so forth—influenced the choice to be physically active as one ages. Bird and coworkers reported that living alone was a factor that made women more likely to be active, and fear of injury was a factor that made women less likely to be active (Bird et al., 2009 p. 43). Bird and colleagues' findings counteract current literature by stating that those living alone tend to lead a more sedentary lifestyle. However, the researchers suggested that gender, as well as the selection bias that occurred with their recruitment study, may have accounted for attracting those who were less sedentary. Bird et al. recommended further study with larger sample sizes to fully understand the roles of facilitators, barriers, and ethnic groups in regard to physical activity as women age.

Hughes and her colleagues (2004, 2006, 2010) have had much success with transplanting the Fit and Strong program into rural communities to improve overall fitness levels for older adults, and mobilizing forces to improve overall fitness levels. Currently, many Area Agencies on Aging (AAAs) are trying to implement evidence-based fitness and walking programs in rural communities to improve overall fitness and strength levels (J. Smith, personal communication, November 20, 2013).

STOICISM AND SURVIVAL

Despite the many disparities that older adults may face when dealing with health care access and the needs articulated for older adults, many older adults living in rural communities display an incredible grace, stoicism, and capacity for survival. This resiliency is remarkable. Although limited study has gone into understanding the relationship between stoicism, survival, and resiliency, Harbison (2008) addressed this important concept for older women in general, which can be generalized for older women living in rural communities.

Harbison (2008) based her discussion of issues related to older women in abusive situations on a Canadian study that found that people labeled these women as "stoic" and questioned whether "ageism has led to abused old women in need of assistance being poorly served." She discussed viewpoints introduced in other literature that described old age as a social construction focused on "meeting the needs of employers" (Harbison, 2008, p. 223). This is important because feminist discourse tends to focus on young women to those about age 60, but often not including women in their 70s, 80s, and 90s, thus precluding the clear differences in life situations and experiences among these ages. Therefore, studies and the formulation of frameworks often do not examine older women's views and beliefs, particularly regarding forms of abuse. In Canada, however, there has been more headway in this area, particularly due to the grassroots efforts of the Older Women's Network (OWN). OWN performed a study involving more than 100 culturally diverse women between ages 50 and 85 and older to determine their ideas of women's shelters and abuse-related services. The results of the study found that although some of the older women would use shelters, most indicated that they would not leave "their home and family." Instead, they felt they would like support and protection. This clearly contrasts multiple findings that suggested that successful intervention can be measured in the number of women who get out of abusive relationships. Harbison pointed out that literature documenting abuse of rural older women was lacking—the author found only two studies focusing specifically on older women and abuse. According to one of the studies, women in rural areas were more likely to be physically and emotionally abused due to isolation of region and individual. Harbison found that older women often do not leave abusive situations for several reasons, including difficulty finding a sympathetic person to hear their story; perpetuation of a still-strong rural value of "having made your bed you should lie on it"; no long-term, practical support for leaving; and positive identification with coping. This encompassing perspective translates into stoicism, generally because older women in abusive relationships view leaving—as opposed to staying—as losing, and see no other options. Harbison suggested that current programs and interventions adapt to the needs of older women in abusive relationships by incorporating an understanding of aging, training, resources, and outreach intervention strategies (2008, pp. 229–230). The role of social workers in this area, said Harbison, is to bring light and attention to the matter during policy agenda planning, focusing on macro-level intervention in order to best benefit individuals on the micro level.

According to Vagenas and associates (2009), multiple studies point toward a "self-reliance, individualism, and a reluctance to seek medical care unless seriously impaired by health problems," as "traditional characteristics" of rural dwellers (p. 124). Unfortunately, this type of stoic attitude can lead those in rural areas to later diagnosis and thus a worse prognosis than those in urban areas, whose health issues tend to be identified, diagnosed, and treated earlier in the disease course (Vagenas et al., 2009).

INTERNATIONAL PERSPECTIVES

Gómez, Curcio, and Duque (2009) reviewed the features of the population of older people in Colombia, who make up approximately 6% of the total Colombian population, with a life expectancy of 72.3 years (p. 1692). Currently, Colombia is undergoing changes in "population aging, decreasing fertility, and rapid urbanization," as well as "persistence of communicable diseases and a concomitant increase in incommunicable chronic diseases" (Gómez, et al., 2009, p. 1692). Similar to other countries, there are a greater number of older women than men, with the majority of older Colombians living in the community, not in long-term care (less than 1.2%) facilities (Gómez, et al., 2009, p. 1692). The researchers described the Colombian General System of Social Security in Health (SGSSS), under which all who subscribe "have the right to be covered under a basic plan, which includes emergency care, hospitalization, consultation, and medication" (Gómez et al., 2009, p. 1692). The SGSSS reform focuses on "efficiency, universality, solidarity, comprehensiveness, unity, and social participation," yet only 4% of the gross national product (GNP) is apportioned to the SGSSS, a 5% decrease since the 1970s (Gómez et al., 2009, p. 1693). The economic crisis in Colombia has contributed fully to the lack of funding allocated to the health system, which in turn contributes to the "ultimate disappearance of a functional system of health care for an increasingly impoverished and vulnerable older population" (Gómez et al., 2009, p. 1693). Much of the older population of Colombia work in agriculture as long as health allows, and since most older Colombians do not have access to SS, the majority (64%) live under the national poverty line (Gómez et al., 2009, p. 1693). These investigators outlined the most imminent issues that face Columbians: "unemployment, low income, inequity of access to health care, drug trafficking, and armed conflict," particularly for those living in rural areas (Gómez et al., 2009, p. 1693). Concurrently, there has been a decline in access to health care, and in 2004, almost 10% of Colombian people were not covered, resulting in a 26% infant mortality rate and a 12.5% maternal mortality rate (Gómez et al., 2009, p. 1694). The researchers were especially concerned by the shift in coffee growers to cocaine and coca growers due to decreased coffee prices internationally, which could lead to family issues such as violence and mistreatment (Gómez et al., 2009, p. 1694). Gómez et al. briefly mentioned that the rural areas of Colombia have also experienced almost 40 years of conflict between guerrillas and paramilitary troops; however, to what extent this has affected the older adults has not been determined (2009, p. 1694). Colombia's health care system for older people represents a paucity of health care professionals, resources, facilities, and options for both urban and rural dwellers; this issue is especially magnified in rural areas (Gómez et al., 2009, p. 1694). According to Gómez and coworkers, education of geriatricians in Colombia "should be enhanced quantitatively and qualitatively" to ensure the proper care of older Colombians (2009, p. 1695).

POLICIES

Social Security, Medicare/Medicaid

Policies such as Social Security and Medicare/Medicaid also have some specific impacts and implications for older adults living in rural U.S. communities. Many older adults, particularly women, may not be able to benefit from Social Security or have minimal pension plans. First, these women may not have worked full-time outside their family homes, due to family responsibilities. If farming was the main income of the household, they also may have been integral to the family business and not contributed to Social Security. Second, if these women were widowed, their husbands also may have had a very limited pension benefit due to the nature of employment options within rural communities, thus leaving them with only a modest income. Rural women also may not have worked full-time for 40 3-month quarters throughout their lifetimes, rendering them ineligible for Medicare. If eligible for Medicare, local care providers willing to accept Medicare payments may also be limited. Medicare Part C subsidized insurance packages may also be limited in terms of scope and local providers of services to older adults living in rural communities—if health care providers are in fact available. Last, for older people living near the poverty line and eligible for Medicaid health care benefits, they may not be able to access providers willing to provide Medicaid services. Thus, although the policies are in place to financially and medically assist people who are older, the service providers may not necessarily be available within rural communities (Jurkowski, 2008, 2013).

CONCLUSION

This chapter reviews numerous issues that impact older adults living in rural communities, including health care disparities, health care access, screening and assessment, social/familial issues, and environmental issues. As discussed in the text, greater disparities exist in the health status of older persons living in rural areas than in urban areas. The paucity of health care providers and access to health care resources are factors that impact these health disparities. All these issues lead to the importance of policy development, planning, and practice.

Policy

Currently, social welfare policies that address the needs of older adults are designed as *one size fits all* with no special provision for older adults and older women living in rural communities. Services and resources are also based upon head count, rather than on incidence and prevalence rates. Policies that currently impact the lives of older adults such as the Older Americans Act (OAA), SS, and Medicare/Medicaid were not developed to take into consideration the dynamics of rural living conditions. No provisions were made to help assist with transportation costs for an older adult seeking assistance with medical, financial, or social needs. Often, screening and referral services are not available within local rural communities, and older adults are forced to travel to receive these services. In addition, the workforce may not be available within local rural resources to address the needs of older adults and, if they are available, they may not have specialty training to meet the requirements that aging presents. Thus, policies are also necessary to help cultivate a workforce with the capacity to adequately provide for the care of older adults living in rural communities.

Planning

Planning for services to meet the needs of older adults living in rural communities also needs to be addressed by regional and state-based planning authorities. Resource planning may pose a challenge for service providers because resources are often allocated based on number of cases requiring services, rather than on the proportion of a community that requires services. Too often, services are not provided as a *basic right* but rather on the basis of case counts. Too often, rural communities are neglected due to this planning attitude. Advocates for service development would be more effective in their advocacy to rural communities if an epidemiological approach were undertaken, rather than one based on case counts. Such an approach would take into consideration incidence and prevalence rates and would paint a picture of the service needs based upon population rates and ratios as opposed to case counts. This approach would also create a level playing field to demonstrate the inordinate needs that rural communities present.

Practice

Last, to not discuss some of the specific practice needs that professionals must address when working with older adults living in rural communities would be remiss. First and foremost, professionals working within rural communities should recognize the specialized needs that women present and be prepared to address their consumers differentially, based upon gender. The reality is that within rural communities, practitioners will find that women outnumber men. Second, practitioners also need to be prepared for a role not embedded just in case practice but also involving advocacy to help secure needed resources. Last, practitioners may not be ready to address the unique needs that women from rural areas may present—the strong, stoic individual who is likely to want to remain in command of her destiny and who is more likely to be a partner than a puppet in the process.

In summary, this chapter explored the unique features that older women living in rural communities present. The issues of health disparities, social/familial issues, and environment were addressed. Various options for policy development, planning, and practice were examined. Hopefully, this chapter was enlightening about the unique issues that residents in rural communities face as they age.

USEFUL WEBSITES

American Public Health Association
www.apha.org
Centers for Disease Control and Prevention (CDC)
www.cdc.gov
Centers for Medicare and Medicaid Services
www.cms.gov
Healthy People 2020: Health Objectives for the Nation
healthypeople.gov/2020/topicsobjectives2020/default.aspx
Medicare's official government website
medicare.gov
National Rural Health Association
www.ruralhealthweb.org

Senior Medline Plus: A project from the National Library of Medicine and National Institutes of Health

www.nlm.nih.gov/medlineplus/seniorshealth.html

Substance Abuse and Mental Health Services Administration

www.samhsa.gov

REFERENCES

Bartsch, D. A., & Rodgers, V. K. (2009). Senior reach outcomes in comparison with the Spokane gatekeeper program. *Journal of Case Management, 10*(3), 82–88.

Bartsch, D. A., Rodgers, V. K., & Strong, D. (2013). Outcomes of senior reach and gatekeeper referrals: Comparison of the Spokane gatekeeper program, Colorado Senior Reach and Mid Kansas Senior Outreach. *Case Management Journal. 14*(1), 11–20.

Bird, S., Kurowski, W., Feldman, S., Browning, C., Lau, R., Radermacher, H., . . . Sims, J. (2009). The influence of the built environment and other factors on the physical activity of older women from different ethnic communities. *Journal of Women & Aging, 21*, 33–47. doi:10.1080/08952840802633669

Brown, K. C., Fitzhugh, E. C., Neutens, J. J., & Klein, D. A. (2009). Screening mammography utilization in Tennessee women: The association with residence. *The Journal of Rural Health, 25*(2), 167–172.

Casado, B. L., Quijano, L. M., Stanley, M. L., Cully, J. A., Steinberg, E. H., & Wilson, N. (2008). Healthy IDEAS: Implementation of a depression program through community based case management. *The Gerontologist, 48*(6), 828–838.

Centers for Disease Control and Prevention. (2014). National health and nutrition examination surveys, 1999–2000. Hayetsville, MD. Retrieved from http://wwwn.cdc.gov/nchs/nhanes/search/nhanes99_00.aspx

Centers for Disease Control and Prevention, National Center for Health Statistics. (2012). Health indicators for older adults. Retrieved November 20, 2013, from www.healthindicators.gov

Ciechanowski, P., Wagner, E., Schmaling, K., Schwartz, S., Williams, B., Diehr, J., . . . LoGerfo, J. (2004). Community-integrated home-based depression treatment in older adults: A randomized controlled trial. *Journal of the American Medical Association, 291*(13), 1569–1577.

Crowther, M. R., Scogin, F., & Johnson, N. M. (2010). Treating the aged in rural communities: The application of cognitive-behavioral therapy for depression. *Journal of Clinical Psychology, 66*(5), 502–512. doi:10.1002/jclp.20678

Cummings, S. M. (2009). Treating older persons with severe mental illness in the community: Impact of an interdisciplinary geriatric mental health team. *Journal of Gerontological Social Work, 52*(1), 17–31. doi:10.1080/01634370802561919

Cummings, S. M., & Kropf, N. P. (2008). Overview of evidence-based practice with older adults and their families. *Journal of Gerontological Social Work, 50,* 1–10.

Cummings, S. M., & Kropf, N. P. (2009). Formal and informal support for older adults with severe mental illness. *Aging & Mental Health, 13*(4), 619–627. doi:10.1080/13607860902774451

Cummings, S. M., & Kropf, N. P. (2011). Aging with a severe mental illness: Challenges and treatments. *Journal of Gerontological Social Work, 54*(2), 175–188. doi:10.1080/01634372.2010.538815

Dorfman, L. T., Mendez, E. C., & Osterhaus, J. K. (2009). Stress and resilience in the oral histories of rural older women. *Journal of Women and Aging, 21,* 303–316. doi:10.1080/08952840903285237

Ferdous, T., Cederholm, T., Kabir, Z. N., Hamadani, J. D., & Wahlin, Å. (2010). Nutritional status and cognitive function in community living rural Bangladeshi older adults: Data from the Poverty and Health in Ageing project. *Journal of American Geriatrics Society, 58,* 919–924.

Feresu, S. A., Zhang, W., Puumala, S. E., Ullrich, F., & Anderson, J. R. (2009). The frequency and distribution of cardiovascular disease risk factors among Nebraska women enrolled in the WISEWOMAN screening program. *Journal of Women's Health, 17*(4), 607–617. doi:10.1089/jwh.2007.0438

Folta, S. C., Lichtenstein, A. H., Seguin, R. A., Goldberg, J. P., Kuder, J. F., & Nelson, M. E. (2009). The StrongWomen–Healthy Hearts program: Reducing cardiovascular disease risk factors in rural sedentary, overweight, and obese midlife and older women. *American Journal of Public Health, 99*(7), 1271–1277.

Gao, S., Jin, Y., Unverzagt, F., Liang, C., Hall, K. S., Ma, F., . . . Hendrie, H. C. (2009). Correlates of depressive symptoms in rural elderly Chinese. *International Journal of Geriatric Psychiatry, 24,* 1358–1366. doi:10.1002/gps.2271

Gómez, F., Curcio, C. L., & Duque, G. (2009). Health care for older persons in Colombia: A country profile. *The Journal of the American Geriatric Society, 57,* 1692–1696. doi:10.1111/j.1532-541.5.2009.02341.x

Hallrup, L. B., Albertsson, D., Tops, A. B., Dahlberg, K., & Grahn, B. (2009). Elderly women's experiences of living with fall risk in a fragile body: A reflective lifeworld approach. *Health and Social Care in the Community, 17*(4), 379–387. doi:10.1111/j.1365-2524.2008.00836.x

Harbison, J. (2008). Stoic heroines or collaborators: Ageism, feminism, and the provision of assistance to abused old women. *Journal of Social Work Practice,* 22(2), 221–234. doi:10.1080/02650530802099890

Hughes, S. L., Seymour, R. B., & Campbell, R. T. (2004). Impact of the Fit and Strong! intervention on older adults with osteoarthritis. *Gerontologist, 44,* 217–228.

Hughes, S. L., Seymour, R. B., & Campbell, R. T. (2006). Long-term impact of Fit and Strong! on older adults with osteoarthritis. *Gerontologist, 46,* 801–814.

Hughes, S. L., Seymour, R. B., Campbell, R. T., Desai, P., Huber, G., & Chang, J. (2010). Fit and Strong! Bolstering maintenance of physical activity among older adults with lower-extremity osteoarthritis. *American Journal of Health Behavior, 34*(6), 750–763.

Jurkowski, E. T. (2008). *Policy and program planning for older adults: Realities and visions.* New York, NY: Springer Publishing Company.

Jurkowski, E. T. (2013). Aging and caregiving. In Social Work section of APHA, R. Keefe & E. T. Jurkowski (Eds.), *Handbook for Public Health Social Work.* New York, NY: Springer Publishing Company.

Kropf, N. P. (2012, May). Increasing community capacity for older residents and their families. *Journal of Gerontological Social Work, 55*, 301–303. doi:10.1080/01634372.2012.672075

McDonough, K., & Davitt, J. (2011). It takes a village: Community practice, social work and aging-in-place. *Journal of Gerontological Social Work, 54*(5), 528–541.

Nelson, J. A., & Gingerich, B. S. (2010). Rural health: Access to care and services. *Home Health Care Management & Practice, 22*(5), 339–343.

Office of Rural Health Policy. (2014). Retrieved June 20, 2013, from http://www.hrsa.gov/about/organization/bureaus/orhp

Quijano, L., Stanley, M. A., Peterson, N. J., Cusado, B. L., Steinberg, E. H., Cully, J., & Wilson, N. (2008). Healthy IDEAS: A depression intervention delivered by community based case managers. *Journal of Applied Gerontology, 26*(2), 139–156.

Scheyett, A., Pettus-Davis, C., & Cuddeback, G. (2010). Assertive community treatment as community change intervention. *Journal of Community Practice, 18*, 78–93. doi:10.1080/10705421003761199

Tudiver, F., Beckett-Edwards, J., & Pfortmiller, D. T. (2010). Depression screening patters for women in rural health clinics. *Journal of Rural Health, 26*(1), 44–50.

U.S. Bureau of the Census. (2014). United States Census Bureau. Retrieved February 10, 2014, from www.census.gov

U.S. Department of Health and Human Services. (2000). *Healthy people 2010: Health objectives for the nation.* Washington, DC: U.S. Government Printing Office. (Originally developed for Ratzan, S. C., & Parker, R. M. [2000]. Introduction. In C. R. Selden, M. Zorn, S. C. Ratzan, & R. M. Parker [Eds.], *National Library of Medicine current bibliographies in medicine: Health literacy* [NLM Pub. No. CBM 2000-1]. Bethesda, MD: U.S. Department of Health and Human Services, National Institutes of Health).

U.S. Department of Health and Human Services. (2010). *Healthy people 2020: Health objectives for the nation.* Retrieved from http://www.healthypeople.gov/2020/default.aspx

Vagenas, D., McLaughlin, D., & Dobson, A. (2009). Regional variation in the survival and health of older Australian women: A prospective cohort study. *Australian and New Zealand Journal of Public Health, 33*(2), 119–125.

Zahnd, W. E., Scaife, S. L., & Francis, M. L. (2009). Health literacy skills in rural and urban populations. *American Journal of Health Behavior, 33*(5), 550–557.

4

Housing, Poverty, and Transportation in Rural Places

LINDSAY KNAUS

ELAINE T. JURKOWSKI

ANWER U. AZIM

Glenn and Ruby live in the Midwest in a small farming community of about 800 people. They relocated to this community about 65 years ago, shortly after their marriage. Both are in their late 80s, have had relatively good health until the past year, and up to now have been able to remain in their own home. Their seven children have all moved out of the area in order to find employment, leaving their parents to manage the family home. Glenn and Ruby managed the local junkyard for most of their lives, and this business also merged into a scrap metal and recycling enterprise in their later years. Now it is becoming difficult for them to handle the yard work and keep up with house repairs and maintenance. Glenn's heart condition makes it difficult for him to shovel snow during the winter. He has developed macular degeneration and has had to give up driving his car, although, if necessary, he uses a golf cart to travel around town. Although Ruby has a driver's license, she does not want to drive distances because she worries about what would happen if they were to have a breakdown while on the road.

HOUSING

Housing for older adults, as they transition from their family homes, can be difficult at the best of times, due to the often limited availability of reasonable and affordable options. However, housing in rural communities can pose a particular challenge because of additional factors including affordability and access to resources. All too often, people may need to downsize as a result of their diminished capacity to care for their homes or their reduced ability to be able to pay for maintenance and upkeep. As profiled in the case study with Glenn and Ruby, this couple may not be able to remain in their home because of upkeep costs and their individual needs.

A hallmark of many rural communities is the fact that people have spent their entire lives within a specific rural area. This makes relocation difficult, and, for the most part, people want to remain in their home-based communities. As noted in Chapter 3, children often migrate out of their communities into other locales due to seeking employment. Auh and Cook (2009) examined the relationships among rural residents 65 years and older to identify what factors influenced their wanting to remain within home-based communities as they grew older. They found that among an older adult population, satisfaction with their housing was a predictor for aging in place and a predictor for satisfaction with their community. Satisfaction with services germane to the community such as local services and perceptions of their own housing conditions were not as much predictors of their wanting to remain in the area as was their attachment to the community. These data were representative of nearly 1,000 households ($N = 974$).

In the wake of welfare reform, many poor people have exhausted their benefits and must now live with less government support (Behr et al., 2011). Whereas all of these former welfare recipients are struggling, some are experiencing housing problems that are quite severe. Latimer and Woldoff (2010) used survey data on former welfare recipients who had used up the maximum time limits for receiving welfare to better understand three core explanations for rural housing problems among the poor community, individuals, and family factors. They found that rural location was the most consistent predictor of housing outcomes, predicting home ownership and whether families would reside in low-quality housing. Although this may be true, the reality is that rural communities, compared to urban centers, have limited housing opportunities that address this structured care component with options for older adult care needs (McKee, 2012). If, in fact, the literature is used to guide program development within the housing arena, it may be important to consider that poor oral health and nutritional health are major contributing factors to disease and impact overall mortality. In addition, poor oral health and nutritional status do put people at greater risk for cardiovascular and respiratory diseases, especially as they age (Heuberger, 2011).

If, in fact, people fare better in structured settings, then rural residents may be at a distinct disadvantage because there are far fewer opportunities for older adults living in rural communities to take advantage of specific housing options within the continuum of care options. In urban centers, there are campus living options for older adults that provide a continuum of opportunities including older adult condominium or apartment complexes, assisted living, skilled nursing care, foster care, and nursing home care. In many instances, these opportunities span a complete housing campus; however, due to the nature of trying to build facilities that will be economically feasible, many never see their way into rural communities. The costs of these facilities—coupled with a market or community of older adults with limited incomes—make these options unrealistic in rural communities.

> Glenn and Ruby realized that they were limited in their capacity to maintain their family home. They looked at what options were available to them and were disappointed to learn that the only opportunity within their area was a nursing home for frail older adults located in a town about 16 miles away. They were both much more capable than the average resident within the nursing facility. They also realized that if they downsized and relocated, they would no longer be able to travel back and forth to their own community to remain involved with their local church and service clubs. The couple weighed their options and decided to stay in their own home a while longer; however, as a next step, they wanted to identify some specific housing opportunities in communities closer to where their children lived. Unfortunately, this might mean leaving their rural roots.

A closer review of the dilemmas within housing options leads to wondering what options are available for housing, and how many of these exist within communities that are close to home areas and important people. The next section of this chapter describes some potential housing settings. These range from the most independent to the least independent (i.e., nursing home care) of surroundings.

Housing Options for Older Adults

A range of long-term care settings are available to people advancing in age and people with disabilities. These options include independent living, assisted living, intermediate care facilities, skilled nursing care facilities, rehabilitation facilities, naturally occurring retirement communities (NORCs), continuing care retirement communities (CCRCs), adult foster care facilities, board and care facilities, and subacute care facilities (Jurkowski, 2013). For budding professionals, the list might seem daunting and leave them wondering how to differentiate each option. The following section categorizes the options into three specific arenas: independent living, supportive/shelter care, and nursing home care.

Independent Living Options

Independent Living

Independent living is a general name for any housing arrangement designed exclusively for older adults. Other terms include retirement communities, retirement homes, older adult housing, and older adult apartments. These may be apartment complexes, condominiums, or even freestanding homes. In general, the housing is friendlier to older adults, tends to be compact, and includes help with outside maintenance. Sometimes recreational centers or clubhouses are also available on site. This independent living option is available to people, age 55 and older, who have the capacity to care for themselves. Generally, within older adult-oriented communities, a service coordinator will check in routinely to assure that no needs are unmet, and to help facilitate independence. Some supportive services are offered for a fee in certain retirement communities. This option can be within one's home, apartment, retirement village or community, or older adult village (Jurkowski, 2013).

Assisted Living

In general, assisted living is a housing option for those who need assistance with some activities of daily living (ADLs), including minor help with medications. Costs tend to vary according to the level of daily help required, although staff is generally available 24 hours a day. Some assisted-living facilities provide apartment-style living with scaled-down kitchens, whereas others provide rooms. Most facilities have a group dining area and common areas for social and recreational activities.

Assisted-living facilities in an apartment-style habitat are designed to focus on providing assistance with ADLs. They provide a higher level of service for older adults: preparing meals, housekeeping, medication assistance, and laundry; they also do regular check-ins on the residents. They have been designed to bridge the gap between independent living and nursing home facilities. Often the facilities are equipped with emergency signaling devices. All residents use shared spaces that usually include living rooms, dining rooms, or laundry rooms. Minimal services—ranging from central dining programs to organized recreational activities, health, transportation, housekeeping, nonpersonal laundry, and security—are included in most plans for assisted living. Generally, a licensed care staff and physician are not on duty routinely within these facilities.

There are more than 26 designations that states use to refer to what is commonly known as *assisted living*. There is not a single uniform definition of assisted living, and there are no federal regulations for assisted living. In many states, most assisted living is private pay, although some states such as Illinois have developed a Medicaid waiver program to help with the costs of living in these facilities for people below the poverty line (Administration on Aging, 2012).

The Village Concept

The village solution to aging in place is a relatively new concept, enabling active older adults to remain in their own homes without having to rely on family and friends. Members of a *village* can access specialized programs and services, such as transportation to the grocery store, home health care, or help with household chores, as well as a network of social activities with other village members. As of 2009, there were 50 village organizations. Each offers different services depending on the local needs of the individual communities. The cost of membership varies according to area and the level of services required; however, it is often in excess of $500 a year and out of the reach of many older adults living in rural communities (Jurkowski, 2013).

Naturally Occurring Retirement Communities

Like the village concept, NORCs enable older adults to stay in their own homes and access local services, volunteer programs, and social activities; they tend to exist in lower income areas. A NORC may be as small as a single urban high-rise or spread out over a larger suburban area.

Continuing Care Retirement Communities

CCRCs are facilities that include independent living, assisted living, and nursing home care in one location; thus, older adults can stay in the same general area as their housing needs change over time. There is normally the cost of buying a unit in the community as well as monthly fees that increase as higher levels of care are required. This option is attractive to people who would like to stay in the same general facility, regardless of their care needs. They also allow for spouses to be close to one another even if one requires a higher level of care. Within these communities a number of services, including in-home services, are also available. In-home services allow individuals to continue to live in their residences, while receiving help with activities including meals, shopping, or nursing care. Depending on the circumstances, services provided range from minimal (e.g., housekeeping, shopping, or conversation) to extensive help with the care recipient's ADLs (e.g., bathing, dressing, taking medication, etc.). These continuing care retirement communities, or multilevel care facilities, provide a nice balance between the skilled nursing home, the assisted-living facility, and the independent-living facility or retirement community. They assure the care recipient independent living as long as possible, while providing for nursing assistance if or when it is needed. This type of living arrangement can be particularly useful to couples who are often in need of different levels of care and who wish to maintain a strong relationship.

These facilities offer many services including personal conveniences (e.g., hairdressers/barbers, banks, libraries), organized social and recreational activities, educational programs, exercise classes, craft and woodworking activities, gardening spaces, transportation, and health care. Because these activities can be costly, the entrance fee and monthly charges are often quite high. Additionally, entrance restrictions normally specify a minimum age, as well as minimum levels of health and finances. Entrance lists for such facilities are often months or years long, especially in rural communities (Administration on Aging, 2012).

Supportive/Shelter Care Options

Congregate Care

This is very similar to independent-living complexes. It has the aspects of community environment, with one or more meals per day prepared and served in a community dining hall. Private quarters are allowed; transportation, swimming pools, convenience stores, banks, barbers/beauty shops, resident laundries, housekeeping, and security are all services and amenities that may be provided (FamilyCare America, 2012).

Group Homes

Group homes provide an independent-living environment with only minimal services. These services are much like those offered in an independent-living facility. Group homes differ in that the individual usually co-owns or rents the home with a group of individuals who share the common areas of the living environment (FamilyCare America, 2012).

Residential Care Facilities

Residential care facilities—also called board and care homes, personal care homes, sheltered housing, or domiciliary care homes—offer housing for individuals who need assistance with personal care or medical needs. This means that the facility is normally state-licensed and meets minimum staffing requirements—it is staffed 24 hours a day. To be eligible for residential care facilities, individuals usually must be fairly mentally alert; able to dress, feed, and take themselves to the toilet; able to eat meals in a central dining room; and need no more than moderate assistance with personal care or behavior supervision. Check with the specific facility for any policies concerning walkers or wheelchairs.

These facilities usually feature studio or one-bedroom apartments that lack kitchens but have private bathrooms and storage units. Occasionally, they offer only shared rooms, which can be a difficult adjustment for many. Additional services include meals, social activities, laundry, and housekeeping (Administration on Aging, 2012; FamilyCare America, 2012).

Adult Foster Care

Adult foster care options generally match people who are not capable of living independently or safely on their own with a foster family. The family provides room and board around the clock for 24 hours per day, along with help with personal care activities such as bathing, feeding, and medication management. Foster families generally take one person or a small group of adults into their residences. This option is generally licensed by the state, and the name (i.e., adult foster care) may vary from location, region, or state (Administration on Aging, 2012; FamilyCare America, 2012).

Board and Care Homes

Two main types of board and care homes exist: residential care facilities and group homes. The distinction between the two lies within the number of residents for which the home is licensed. Residential facilities, for example, have 20 or fewer residents; group homes have 6 or fewer residents. The rooms may be shared or private, and generally nursing and medical services are not provided. Both types of facilities provide meals, personal care, and staff around the clock during a 24-hour period. This option is generally licensed by the state, and the name (i.e., board and care) may not be consistent across state lines (Administration on Aging, 2012; FamilyCare America, 2012).

Nursing Home Care Options

A nursing home is normally the highest level of care for older adults outside of a hospital. Whereas they do supply assistance in ADLs, they differ from other older adult housing in that they also provide a high level of medical care. A licensed physician supervises each resident's care and a nurse or other medical professional is almost always on the premises. Skilled nursing care and medical professionals such as occupational or physical therapists are also available.

Nursing home care options and the range of services within this network can vary by the type of facility. Generally, all facilities provide housing and housekeeping services. At the nursing home care level, usually assistance is provided with managing medication, personal care, supervision, and 24-hour nursing care under the administration of a physician. In the case of people with Alzheimer's disease (AD), special programs and options may be available. In addition, the facility is often licensed and the constellation of services offered is regulated by the state in which it is located. For example, some states do not allow some types of facilities to include residents who are wheelchair bound or who cannot exit the facility on their own if there is an emergency. The home also provides, rooms, meals, assistance with ADLs, and recreational activities for residents. Most residents in these homes have physical or mental impairments of such a nature that they cannot safely live alone (Administration on Aging, 2012; FamilyCare America, 2012).

Options for care include intermediate care facilities, skilled nursing care, rehabilitation, subacute care, hospice care, and adult day care.

Intermediate Care

Intermediate care as a nursing home care option is designed for people advancing in age or people with disabilities who are in need of assistance with ADLs but do not have any major or compelling nursing requirements. Intermediate care is given to individuals who require assistance with ADLs and some health services and nursing supervision but not constant nursing care. This type of care is usually requested by a doctor and given by a registered nurse (Administration on Aging, 2012; FamilyCare America, 2012).

Skilled Nursing

Skilled nursing homes or facilities are nursing home facilities that have been traditional nursing facilities. They provide medical nursing services 24 hours a day for older adults with serious illnesses or disabilities. Skilled nursing care is given to individuals who need 24-hour medical supervision, skilled nursing care, or rehabilitation.

This level of care includes help with more complex nursing tasks, such as monitoring medications, giving injections, caring for wounds, and providing nourishment by tube feedings (enteral feeding). It also includes therapies such as occupational, speech, respiratory, and physical therapy. This care can be given in a patient's home or in a care setting. Most insurance plans require at least some level of skilled care need, necessitating the services of a licensed professional (such as a nurse, doctor, or therapist) before they will cover other home-care services.

Rehabilitation services are provided on a time-limited basis for individuals in need of short-term rehabilitation or a bridge between their hospital stay and a return to home. People who have had hip or knee replacements, for example, may fit into this model of care because it is a short-term stay. A request by a physician is generally required for admission. The state and federal governments must license these facilities in order for them to provide RNs, licensed practical nurses (LPNs), and certified nurse aids (CNAs). These rehabilitation services generally are designed to help restore functional abilities (mental and physical) that have been lost due to accident or some form of acute illness. Services generally include physical therapy, occupational and/or speech therapy, social services, and nursing assistance.

Subacute Care

This option for care provides care and/or monitoring after one's hospitalization usually within a less expensive setting than the hospital context. The locations can include rehabilitation services in a nursing home or specialized unit within a hospital setting, and the stay is usually short term (Administration on Aging, 2012; FamilyCare America, 2012).

Acute Care Services

Acute care services address health issues that have recently developed, quickly worsened, or resulted from a recent accident. The primary goal of acute care services is to provide recovery through a short-term stay. The services primarily supplied through acute care include those of physicians, physician assistants, nurse practitioners, nurses, or other skilled professionals offering short-term medical assistance (Administration on Aging, 2012; FamilyCare America, 2012).

Custodial Care

Custodial care is yet another option available within nursing home settings. Individuals receiving custodial care need supervision with personal care and other ADLs but do not require the help of a practical nurse. Individuals suffering from dementia, including AD, are often given this type of care (Administration on Aging, 2012; FamilyCare America, 2012).

Hospice Care

Hospice care is an infusion of home care and facility care provided to benefit terminally ill patients and support their families through their tough times. This option can be offered within a long-term care facility and is covered through Medicare. Hospice care can also be provided directly in one's home as well. Medicare will provide funding for this option if a physician indicates that a person probably has 6 months of less to live.

The hospice care program also offers medical and social support/ services to people who have been diagnosed with a terminal disease. The approach to hospice care is that *comfort care* is stressed through the control of pain control management of symptoms. Social support is offered to individuals and their families during the process leading up to the persons' passing, and grief counseling is often offered to family members for several months postmortem. At the current time, grief counseling and supportive services are not extended to the nursing home staff who provided care to the individuals who have passed (Jurkowski, 2013).

Adult Day Care
Adult day care programs work just like any other day care programs where people may send their children. Adult day care programs provide services during the day, while a caregiver may be at work or in need of respite. The services can be offered in a nursing facility or a separate facility. The program provides meals, structured activities, and care services to older adults in a community facility or within a nursing facility during the day for a specific time period. Generally, people who attend adult day care are in need of social interactions and have some level of cognitive and functional impairments (Administration on Aging, 2012; FamilyCare America, 2012).

Respite Care
This aid is offered only on a temporary basis. Respite care allows the primary caregiver or family member relief for a few days or even just a few hours. Respite care can be delivered through a nursing facility or assisted-living facility and, when it takes this form, generally provides relief for caregivers who need a short break from their caregiving roles. (Jurkowski, 2013).

POVERTY

The review of housing options and discussion about the startling cost of living lead to the question of how people can afford to remain in the best housing option possible and age in place. These also beg the question, To what extent is poverty a real factor within rural communities?

According to data collected from the U.S. Department of Agriculture (USDA; 2013), rural and nonmetro communities find themselves with a median income of at least $10,000 less than their urban counterparts. As illustrated in Table 4.1, household income is at least 25% less, consistently, across a decade of comparisons. This showcases the impact poverty may have on rural residents because their limitations in income

TABLE 4.1   Household Money Income By Residence, 2000–2009*

	Nonmetro		Metro		
Year	Median household income ($)	Change from previous year (%)	Median household income ($)	Change from previous year (%)	Nonmetro as % of metro
2009	40,135	–1.2	51,522	–0.3	77.9
2008	40,630	–3.3**	51,656	–3.7**	78.7
2007	42,024	3.1**	53,630	–0.4	78.4
2006	40,750	–1.2	53,864	1.2**	75.7
2005	41,264	NA (not available)	53,249	NA	77.5
2004	NA	NA	NA	NA	NA
2003	40,939	–1.0	53,704	–0.6	76.2
2002	41,350	1.6	54,001	–1.4**	76.6
2001	40,704	–0.7	54,778	–1.6**	74.3
2000	40,999	–3.8**	55,674	1.7**	73.6

*In 2009 dollars.
**Indicates a statistically significant change in median income, at the 90% confidence level.
Note: Estimates for 2004 are not available because the definition of metropolitan areas changed during the course of that year. The post-2004 estimates reflect the new metro/non-metro definitions.
Calculated by the U.S. Department of Agriculture, Economic Research Service using data from the Annual Social and Economic Supplement (ASEC) of the Current Population Survey (P-60), U.S. Bureau of the Census. Adjusted for inflation using CPI-U.

would also lead to less in resource availability, and rural-dwelling consumers would be less likely to afford many resources available in urban centers.

Earnings: Rural Versus Urban Status

Although we traditionally think of people living in rural communities as farmers, the reality is that the majority of older adults living in rural communities probably held nonfarm-oriented jobs. Their wages in comparison to wages for urban counterparts were considerably lower. The real nonfarm earnings per job were essentially unchanged in 2009. Nonfarm earnings make up 96% of total farm and nonfarm earnings (from wages, salaries, and self-employment) in nonmetro counties and fully 99.6% of earnings in metro counties.

The trend in average nonfarm earnings per job in metro/urban versus nonmetro/rural areas is one measure of the changing urban-rural wage gap. In 2009, the average metro job paid $53,373, whereas the average job in a nonmetro/rural county paid $36,920. Over the last 30 years, average metro earnings per job have grown faster than nonmetro/rural earnings per job. As a result, average nonmetro/rural earnings per job equaled 69% of the metro average in 2009, compared with 81% in the late 1970s. This gap, however, appears to have narrowed in the wake of the 2001 recession, and also during the 2007–2009 recession (USDA, 2013).

Since 1978, nonmetro/rural per capita transfer payments have risen faster than payments in metro/urban areas. Most of this increase comes from the rising cost of government programs such as Medicare and Medicaid that provide medical benefits. Because nonmetro/rural areas have an older population and a higher proportion of persons with disabilities than do metro/urban areas, nonmetro/rural areas receive more transfer payments for retirement and medical costs (USDA, 2013).

Medical benefits are the single largest transfer payment category in both nonmetro/rural and metro/urban areas. The USDA (2013) found that by comparison, in 1978, medical benefits accounted for 18.9% of all nonmetro transfer payments (the second-largest category), and by 2011 these had risen to 41.7% (the largest category) of all nonmetro/rural transfer payments. Similarly, in metro/urban areas, medical benefits increased from 22.7% of all transfer payments in 1978 to 42.1% of payments in 2011. Overall, between 1978 and 2011, nonmetro transfer payments for medical benefits increased 581.5%, compared with 498.9% in metro areas. The rising cost of health care, which has far outpaced the overall rate of inflation, is a major source of this increase (USDA, 2013).

Transfer payments for retirement and disability insurance are also increasing but, in contrast to medical benefits, have been declining as a proportion of total transfer payments. In 1978, nonmetro/rural retirement and disability payments accounted for 51.7% of total transfers; by 2011, this percentage had fallen to 34.8%. Nonmetro/rural retirement and disability transfer payments increased by 107.9% over this period. Metro retirement and disability payments fell from 46.1% of total transfers in 1978 to 31.8% in 2011, but increased by 122% over this period (USDA, 2013). Barring changes in program eligibility and support, per capita transfer payments in rural America are likely to increase as a result of the aging of the baby boom population, many of whom are expected to move to rural areas as they retire.

Despite the War on Poverty, which was a major initiative that began at least 50 years ago, there are still many people, especially older adults, living in poverty within the robust United States. Poverty impacts housing, housing options, neighborhoods, and, ultimately, one's health. Whereas health was the focus of Chapter 3, it is clear that the impacts of lower incomes and poverty will affect older adults in a myriad of ways—as is described elsewhere in this book.

> Glenn and Ruby explored housing options and began to try to identify some choices for themselves for 5 years to 10 years into the future. As the couple examined their finances and reviewed their spending patterns over the last 5 years, they were amazed to learn how much their expenses had increased—now putting them below the poverty line. They joked that they qualify for a number of government subsidies; however, silently the two lamented that they had not worked hard during their lifetimes to be categorized as below the poverty line in terms of their earnings.

TRANSPORTATION

As has been seen earlier in this chapter and book, many rural communities where older adults live may be limited in terms of housing. Glenn in this chapter's case study makes use of a golf cart for traveling around the community. Although this may make the reader smile, the sad reality is that there may not be transportation services available to the degree that many older adults require. This section of the chapter reviews what is currently known about transportation services and sheds some light in terms of options available.

The issue of access to transportation is a critical issue that older adults face in rural communities. Although transportation strategies can be viewed within a range of options (Coughlin & Ambrosio, 2012), the reality is that few options, outside of emergency medical services (EMS) exist for rural older adults (Marx et al., 2010; Mnres & Halseth, 2012). Because of the limited transportation resources for rural communities, EMS systems become strained when people inappropriately seek emergency medical services. People might misuse EMS in rural areas because of a lack of education on what EMS is for, lack of transportation (Marx et al., 2010), or a misunderstanding of the severity of their medical condition. Although these are just some of the many reasons why people may inappropriately seek EMS, they contribute to a wealth of issues. When ambulances are deployed helping nonemergency patients, there are fewer ambulances available to help patients with true medical emergencies. Conversely, what issues related to transportation needs face older adults? This chapter explores the nature of transportation and its role with older adults in rural communities.

The EMS system is an important component of the health care community, providing emergent medical care and transportation for all individuals. However, it is often misused by the public for a myriad of complex social and economic reasons. EMS personnel understand that this current system design fails to meet the needs of patients who should be using the EMS system and are not, and patients who are transported by an ambulance when they do not have a medical emergency (Schmidt et al., 2000). The following review identifies the definitions for appropriate and inappropriate uses of EMS, some of the reasons for inappropriate use of the EMS system, perceptions of the EMS system by both EMS providers and patients, and describes alternative programs to EMS in order to alleviate some of the financial and social costs on the system.

The EMS system is considered to be misused when patients with nonemergent medical issues call 911 in order to be transported to a medical care facility (Richards & Ferrall, 1999). When these services are misused, fewer ambulances are able to respond to true emergencies. Richards and Ferrall (1999) define a true medical emergency as "a medical condition or injury requiring medical care as soon as possible at the emergency department" (p. 15). Although emergency dispatchers and EMS responders might realize that a patient is calling with a nonemergent issue, they are required to transport the patient because of liability issues and the risk of malpractice (Richards & Ferrall, 1999). However, 7% of EMS agencies in the United States have implemented programs that allow EMS personnel to refuse transportation to patients who do not meet the criteria for having a medical emergency (Millin, Brown, & Schwartz, 2011). Whereas these programs do exist, little research has been done to support their effectiveness (Millin et al., 2011). Because many U.S. states do not allow EMS-initiated refusal of transport, it is important to explore options that should help lessen the misuse of EMS systems. Some of these options include, but are not limited to, treating the patient in the field without urgent transport to a medical care facility; transporting patients by other modes than an ambulance; developing programs that educate patients on when to call 911; and offering alternative resources for patients who need to be seen by a medical professional but do not have an emergent need for care (Krohmer, 1999).

The general lack of public transportation options within rural communities gives rise to individuals utilizing the EMS system for their transportation needs. Averill (2012) in her qualitative study identified themes from older adults about access to transportation in rural areas. Noted were expensive services and lack of access due to isolated rural locations between home and destinations. Patients often call 911 because they believe that they or someone they are calling for has a true medical emergency. Conversely, patients seek emergency services knowing that they don't have a medical emergency but do not have other forms of transportation or money to pay for transportation (Krohmer, 1999). Patients sometimes do not understand when to call 911 and this can result in a misuse of services (Richards & Ferrall, 1998). Snooks and colleagues (1998) argued that there is a public perception that an ambulance might be faster than utilizing other forms of transportation. Parents of young children often believe that their children need an ambulance for reasons that are not considered a true emergency (Millin et al., 2011). In addition, variables such as patients' age, race, gender, type of insurance, and their reasons for calling 911 can contribute to why patients misuse EMS (Richards & Ferrall, 1999). Unfortunately, there are a higher proportion of people age 60 and older who utilize the EMS system to meet their transportation needs in rural communities.

Richards and Ferrall (1999) conducted a study to determine the extent of inappropriate EMS use from the perspectives of both EMS providers and patients. Their study sought to better understand any correlations or differences between provider and patient perceptions of what EMS is meant for and what constitutes a true emergency. The researchers conducted a consecutive, prospective study of EMS providers and patients transported by an ambulance during the month of February 1997 to an urban university hospital. All the 1,264 ($N = 1,264$) patients who were transported to the hospital during February were eligible for the study. The investigators used to a consecutive cross-sectional survey of both EMS providers and eligible patients. Of the eligible participants, 887 patients and 887 EMS providers were included in the study. EMS providers were specifically asked, "Do you think that the patient's medical problem represented a true emergency requiring

EMS transport?" (The researchers defined true emergency as "a medical condition or injury requiring medical care as soon as possible at the emergency department" [Richards & Ferrall, 1999, p. 15].) Patients were asked, "Do you think your medical problem is a true emergency requiring an ambulance?" as well as questions regarding demographic information (see the independent variable descriptions that follow). Patients were also asked about their ability to transport themselves to the hospital. Odds ratios (ORs) and 95% confidence intervals (CIs) were used to describe the relationship between emergency and nonemergency transports by ambulance. The kappa statistic was used to assess the agreement between groups. Statistical significance was assumed at a level of $p < .05$. The independent variables used in the study were gender, age, race, level of education, and type of insurance. Gender was defined as male or female; age ranges were 0 years to 17 years, 18 years to 30 years, 31 years to 40 years, 41 years to 50 years, 51 years to 60 years, and 61 years and older; race/ethnicity was defined as White, Black, Hispanic, or Asian; education was defined as high school or equivalent, grade school, unknown, college, or postgraduate; and insurance was defined as none, MediCal (California's version of Medicaid), Medicare, HMO/MCO, private, or self-pay. Descriptive statistics were used for each independent variable and a univariate analysis was performed with chi-square comparing each of the variables.

Richard and Ferrall (1999) found that the age range of patients was between 2 months and 95 years. The highest percentage of people using EMS were ages 41 years to 50 years (n = 214, 24%). The EMS providers believed that patients 31 years to 40 years of age were significantly less likely to have true emergencies compared with other age groups (OR 0.6, 95% CI [0.4–0.9], p = .004). Patients who identified their race as White were found to use EMS transport the most (n = 406, 46%) commonly. Both EMS providers and patients believed that this was the race of patients who most likely did not have true medical emergencies. Patients who identified their race as Black were more likely to consider their medical problems as true emergencies. Patients with a high school education or equivalent used EMS transport the most (n = 454, 51%). From the perspectives of both patients and EMS providers, patients with a high school education or equivalent had conditions that were not likely to be true emergencies. EMS provider perspectives indicated that patients with no insurance or MediCal were least likely to have conditions that were true emergencies. From the patients' perspectives, patients with MediCal were least likely to have conditions that were true emergencies. Finally, a large number of patients (n = 415, 47%) had their own transportation and the ability to utilize it but chose to use ambulance services instead.

Richards and Ferrall (1999) identified the limitations of their study as well as recommendations for future researchers. Because this study used a survey and responses were voluntary, the results were subjective. There were also a considerable number of EMS providers who chose not to participate in the study (n = 71). The investigators also noted that their study was conducted in an urban environment and therefore their work might not be relevant for smaller or more rural communities. Finally, the researchers recommended that future studies should explore the development of alternative transportation to the emergency department for nonemergent patients, while creating a system for EMS providers to triage patients at the scene. They also argued that in order for patients to misuse ambulance services less often, there need to be consequences or disincentives for inappropriate use of the EMS system.

Richards and Ferrall (1999) found that specific populations misuse the EMS system more than others. Understanding why different populations misuse the EMS system more than others is important, when trying to develop interventions that can positively benefit both the system and the patients who seek services. One of the populations found to misuse the EMS system more than others are people age 65 and older (Platts-Mills, Leacock, Cabañas, Shofer, & McLean, 2010). Because the number of people age 65 and older is rapidly increasing, it is crucial to develop services that are relevant to their specific needs. According to previous studies, patients age 65 and older and, more specifically, patients age 85 and older use EMS services for transportation to the emergency department more than any other age group (Platts-Mills et al., 2010). Based on this understanding, Platts-Mills and colleagues conducted a study using a comprehensive statewide emergency department database known as the North Carolina Disease Event Tracking and Epidemiologic Collection Tool (NC DETECT). The researchers queried the database for all emergency department visits between January 1, 2007 and December 31, 2007. Platts-Mills and coworkers used information on the patients within that database that included demographic information, EMS use, and disposition. EMS use included ground, helicopter, and fixed-wing air ambulances and also included basic life support (BLS) and advanced life support (ALS). Disposition was defined as admission or discharge from hospital and death. Patients who left against medical advice were classified as being discharged from the hospital. The total numbers of emergency room department visits were classified by age groups. During the period that the study was conducted, 3,853,866 patients visited the emergency departments at a total of 105 hospitals in North Carolina. Of those patients, 2,743,221 (71.2%) had data on both mode of transport and disposition. There were no significant results when comparing these patients with patients who were missing data on either mode of transport or disposition in regard to mean age (55.4% vs. 56.1%), percentage without insurance (24.1% vs. 23.8%), and use of EMS (16.9% vs. 16.8%). Patients who had complete data consisted of people age 65 and older (403,248 or 14.7%), patients younger than 18 years of age (624,798 or 22.3%), and patients who were considered nonolder adults (n = 1,715,175 or 62.5%). According to the investigators, "the proportion of patients using EMS for emergency department transport increased steadily with age" (Platts-Mills et al., 2010, p. 330). These researchers also found that 6.7% of pediatric patients, 14.5% of nonolder adults, and 43.2% of patients age 65 and older were transported to the emergency department via EMS. These systems were the most common form of transportation to the emergency department for patients age 85 and older. Admission rates for patients who arrived via EMS versus non-EMS were 29.2% versus 9.0% for nonolder adult patients and 52.7% versus 30.3% for older patients.

Based on the U.S. Bureau of the Census and current EMS utilization in North Carolina, Platts-Mills et al. (2010) predicted that patients using EMS to get to the emergency department will increase from 38.3% to 49% by 2030. In addition, the population of people age 65 and older will increase nationally from 1.16 million to 2.17 million, an increase of 87.2%. Platts-Mills and colleagues (2010) used these predictions to demonstrate the need for patients who are age 65 and older using EMS currently and in the near future. "The very high rates of admission (for this population) . . . transported by EMS suggest a high level of severe illness and injury . . . and provide additional evidence to question the appropriateness of alternative transport protocols" (Platts-Mills et al., 2010, p. 331). The researchers noted that there are social factors such as institutionalization and access to transportation that influence inappropriate EMS utilization among patients age 65 and older. Finally, Platts-Mills and coworkers recommended that EMS community prevention models should be considered for patients with chronic illnesses who use EMS frequently. If patients are educated about their problems and learn how to manage them, they might need to use EMS systems only when they have a true emergency.

The patients' age can be a significant variable in whether or not they seek to use EMS systems. Whereas age can be an important component in determining who seeks EMS transportation, socioeconomic factors can also impact the patients' perceived need for EMS. Kawakami, Ohshige, Kubota, and Tochikubo (2007) conducted a self-administered, questionnaire-based study that targeted residents living in Yokohama, Japan. The researchers recognized that unnecessary ambulance use has become an issue in industrialized nations such as Japan, the United States, and the United Kingdom. Although these nations don't necessarily have the same health care systems, their EMS systems are similar in that they all provide emergency transportation to patients who call EMS and believe they have a medical emergency.

Kawakami and colleagues' (1997) anonymous, self-administered, questionnaire-based survey targeted 3,600 people. These residents were randomly selected from the city resident registration list. Three groups of 1,200 residents were selected based on age-range groups from 20 years to 39 years, 40 years to 64 years, and age 65 and older. The questionnaire consisted of three parts. Part 1 covered demographic questions and socioeconomic characteristics such as participants' age, gender, and pretax annual household income. Part 2 discussed three hypothetical situations pertaining to ambulance use. Part 3 included questions about the participants' perceptions of the city's emergency medical system. Kawakami and coworkers defined gender as male or female and age groups as 20 years to 29 years, 30 years to 39 years, 40 years to 49 years, 50 years to 59 years, 60 years to 69 years, 70 years to 79 years, and age 80 and older. Participants' pretax annual household income was defined in groups of less than $19,000, $19,000 to $37,999, $38,000 to $56,999, $57,000 to $75,999, $76,000 to $94,999, and $95,000 and more. Participants were also asked if they had a car, if they felt hesitant or not to call an ambulance, and if they were aware of a private patient transport service.

Kawakami et al. (1997) mailed out the questionnaires to a total of 3,600 residents. Of the 3,363 deliverable questionnaires, 2,029 were completed, returned, and used in the study (a response rate of 60.3%). A total of 1,279 participants reported that they owned a car (63.0%). A total of 240 participants (11.8%) reported that they would call an ambulance for Scenario 1, 255 (12.6%) reported that they would call for Scenario 2, and 124 (6.1%) reported that they would call for Scenario 3. In Scenario 1, men were more likely to call an ambulance ($p = .046$), as well as people who were living alone ($p = .015$). In Scenario 2, men were more likely to call an ambulance for a child or young relative facing a nonemergent medical situation ($p = .001$). In Scenario 3, men were more likely to call an ambulance when an older relative faced a nonemergent medical situation (p = .001). In addition, Kawakami and colleagues (2007) also found that older participants tended to call an ambulance more easily than did younger adults. Medicaid recipients accounted for 59% of unnecessary ambulance reports, and participants' household incomes negatively influenced the decision to call an ambulance when a family member was experiencing a nonemergent situation. If participants owned a car and had hesitation to use an ambulance, then it negatively influenced their decision to call an ambulance based on the hypothetical scenarios in the questionnaire ($p < .05$).

Kawakami and colleagues (2007) recognized that their study faced some limitations because of the hypothetical scenarios used in their questionnaire rather than actual calls. The response rate for the questionnaire was also limited (60%), and 41.4% of the total respondents were considered to be older based on the demographic information they provided. Based on the response rate and demographics, the responses might not have represented a true sample of the total population. In addition, Kawakami and colleagues noted that people who call an ambulance might have chosen not to participate in their survey. Finally, the investigators made some recommendations based on their findings. These recommendations included "education for appropriate ambulance use, promotion of less resource-intensive transportation systems than an ambulance system, and provision of information on the city's primary emergency medical services deserve consideration as policy interventions" (Kawakami et al., 2007, p. 123). Although these recommendations could positively impact this population, they need to be researched further to see if they are feasible and effective.

In a study conducted by Knaus (2012) examining EMS agencies in Illinois, it was found that there were 30 ambulances owned and operated within the total sample. Of the participants, 60% (n = 18) reported that they were municipal (public) EMS agencies, whereas 40% (n = 12) reported that they were private EMS agencies. When agencies was asked if they were compliant with the National Emergency Medical Services Information System (NEMSIS), 53.3% (n = 16) responded yes; 23.3% (n = 7) responded no (sheriff dispatch handles all of their data collection), no contact was made and therefore no data were collected from 13.3% (n = 4) of the agencies, and 3.3% (n = 1) responded no (an outside billing company handles all of their data collection; Table 4.2).

When agencies were asked if they recorded data on callers' race, age, gender, and form of payment for services, 60% (n = 18) responded

TABLE 4.2   Emergency Medical Services Agencies Experience Inappropriate Use of Systems

Response	n	%
Yes	20	66.7
Seldom	4	13.3
No—sheriff dispatch	2	6.7
Unable to contact	4	13.3
Total	30	100

TABLE 4.3   Emergency Medical Services Agencies that Log Instances of Inappropriate Use

Response	n	%
Yes	4	13.3
No—but aware	10	33.3
No	8	26.7
No—sheriff dispatch	3	10.1
No—outside billing company	1	3.3
Unable to contact	4	13.3
Total	30	100

yes, 23.3% ($n = 7$) responded no (sheriff dispatch handles all of their data collection), no contact was made and therefore no data were collected from 13.3% ($n = 4$) of the agencies, and 3.3% ($n = 1$) responded no (an outside billing company handles all of their data collection; Table 4.3).

When agencies were asked if they experienced callers seeking EMS services for inappropriate reasons (nonemergent medical issues), 66.7% ($n = 20$) responded yes, 13.3% ($n = 4$) responded that they *seldom* do, no contact was made and therefore no data were collected from 13.3% ($n = 4$) of the agencies, and 6.7% ($n = 2$) responded no (sheriff dispatch handles all of their data collection). If agencies reported that they had experienced inappropriate use of their services, they were then asked if they formally logged these instances. When asked this question, 33.3% ($n = 10$) responded *no but aware* (these agencies keep these instances in mind but do not record or log them formally), 26.7% ($n = 8$) responded no, 13.3% ($n = 4$) responded yes, no contact was made and therefore no data were collected from 13.3% ($n = 4$) of the agencies, 10.0% ($n = 3$) responded no (sheriff dispatch handles all of their data collection), and 3.3% ($n = 1$) responded no (an outside billing company handles all of their data collection). Agencies were also asked if they chose to intervene when inappropriate use occurred by informing the caller during or after transport or by reporting it to local authorities. When asked this question, 36.6% ($n = 11$) reported yes, or after transport or by reporting it to local authorities.

Overall, there is a dearth of transportation services available within rural communities to meet the needs of an older adult population. Transportation companies often do not find service delivery within rural communities profitable (Averill, 2012), and often informal support systems are not available to provide rides or transport to medical appointments. Conversely, as we have seen in this chapter, many older adults living in rural communities become reliant upon the EMS system as a substitute for transportation. Innovative solutions such as a Patient Navigator program offer some promise for solutions.

The Patient Navigator program has proved to be an effective strategy to impact transportation and EMS misuse. Frequent callers receive an intervention from a case manager or social worker, who helps identify the legitimacy of class. Through education, inappropriate callers learn appropriate mechanisms to help them cope with their crises. This strategy has been effective in reappropriating resources.

CONCLUSION

Housing, Poverty, and Transportation Service Within Rural Communities

A series of conclusions have been conceptualized in efforts to plant seeds in fresh minds with the hopes of building a new team of advocates to support the development of policies and practices within the areas of housing, poverty, and transportation that will equalize the landscape for older adults living in rural communities. These include the following:

1. Work with state legislatures, Medicare, and Medicaid funding agencies to begin to define what types of housing options could be funded through waiver programs.
2. Continue to support financial subsidy options to supplement incomes for older adults living slightly above the poverty line.

3. Educate the public on options for transportation through various forms of media advertisement.
4. Help create more alternative medical transportation services through cooperative entities in rural communities.
5. Identify, within one's scope of practices, strategies to reach advocacy for solutions at the micro, mezzo (middle), and macro levels of practice. Social workers can help to solve problems surrounding inappropriate use of the EMS system by (a) educating their clients, (b) conducting research, and (c) drafting legislation for policy changes.

USEFUL WEBSITES

eHow Grants for Rural Housing

http://www.ehow.com/list_6749634_grants-rural-housing.html

Smart Growth America: An advocacy group for rural transportation

http://www.smartgrowthamerica.org/complete-streets/implementation/factsheets/rural areas-and-small-towns/

USDA Economic Research Service

http://www.ers.usda.gov/topics/rural-economy-population/rural-poverty-well-being/geography-of-poverty.aspx

United States Department of Transportation: Rural Issues

https://www.fhwa.dot.gov/planning/publications/rural_areas_planning/page03.cfm

United States Housing Development and Rural Development Communities

http://www.rurdev.usda.gov/LP_Subject_HousingAndCommunityAssistance.html

REFERENCES

Administration on Aging. (2012). *Services and providers.* National Clearinghouse on Long Term Care Information. Retrieved from http://www.longtermcare.gov/LTC/Main_Site/Understanding/Services

Averill, J. B. (2012). Priorities for action in a rural older adults study. *Family Community Health, 35*(4), 358–372. doi:10.1097/FCH.0b013e318266686e

Auh, S., & Cook, C. (2009). Quality of community life among rural residents: An integrated model. *Social Indicators Research, 94*(3), 377–389. doi:10.1007/s11205-008-9427-0

Behr, R., Sciegaj, M., Walters, R., Bertoty, J., & Dungan, R. (2011). Addressing the housing challenges of an aging population: Initiatives by Blueroof Technologies in McKeesport, Pennsylvania. *Journal of Architectural Engineering, 17*(4), 162–169. doi:10.1061/(ASCE)AE.1943-5568.0000033

Coughlin, J., & Ambrosio, L. D. (2012). *Aging America and transportation: Personal choices.* New York, NY: Springer Publishing Company.

Community development/affordable housing update. (2010). *Journal of Housing & Community Development, 67*(3), 30–31.

FamilyCare America. (2012). An overview of resources for long-term care settings. Retrieved from http://www.caregiverslibrary.org

Heuberger, R. (2011). Impact of housing type on nutritional status and oral health of rural older adults residing in the midwestern United States. *Seniors Housing & Care Journal, 19*(1), 49–63.

Jurkowski, E. T. (2013). *Culture change: Benchmarks and strategies for management in long term care.* New York, NY: Springer Publishing Company.

Kawakami, C., Ohshige, K., Kubota, K., & Tochikubo, O. (2007). Influence of socioeconomic factors on medically unnecessary ambulance calls. *BMC Health Services Research, 7,* 120–128.

Knaus, L. (2012). *Emergency medical services in rural communities.* Unpublished manuscript.

Krohmer, J. (1999). Appropriate emergency medical services transport. *Academic Emergency Medicine: Official Journal of the Society for Academic Emergency Medicine, 6*(1), 5–7.

Latimer, M., & Woldoff, R. A. (2010). Good country living? Exploring four housing outcomes among poor Appalachians. *Sociological Forum, 25*(2), 315–333. doi:10.1111/j.1573-7861.2010.01178.x

Marx, J., Davis., C., Miftari, C., Salamone, A., & Weise, W. (2010). Developing brockered community transportation for seniors and people with disabilities. *Journal of Gerontological Social Work, 53*(5), 449–466. doi:10.1080/016344372.2010.487886

McKee, K. (2012). Understanding Community. *Housing Studies, 27*(5), 720–721. doi:10.1080/02673037.2012.617917

Millin, M., Brown, L., & Schwartz, B. (2011). EMS provider determinations of necessity for transport and reimbursement for EMS response, medical care, and transport: Combined resource document for the National Association of EMS Physicians Position Statements. *Prehospital Emergency Care, 15*(4), 562–569. doi:10.3109/10903127.2011.598625

Mnres, L. D., & Halseth, G. (2012). Resolving mobility constraints impeding rural seniors access to regionalized services. *Journal of Aging and Social Policy, 24,* 328–344.

Platts-Mills, T., Leacock, B., Cabañas, J., Shofer, F., & McLean, S. (2010). Emergency medical services use by the elderly: Analysis of a statewide database. *Prehospital Emergency Care, 14*(3), 329–333. doi:10.3109/10903127.2010.481759

Richards, J., & Ferrall, S. (1999). Inappropriate use of emergency medical services transport: Comparison of provider and patient perspectives. *Academic*

Emergency Medicine: Official Journal of the Society for Academic Emergency Medicine, 6(1), 14–20.

Schmidt, T., Atcheson, R., Federiuk, C., Mann, N., Pinney, T., Fuller, D., & Colbry, K. (2000). Evaluation of protocols allowing emergency medical technicians to determine need for treatment and transport. *Academic Emergency Medicine: Official Journal of the Society for Academic Emergency Medicine*, 7(6), 663–669.

Snooks, H., Wrigley, H., George, S., Thomas, E., Smith, H., & Glasper, A. (1998). Appropriateness of use of emergency ambulances. *Journal of Accident & Emergency Medicine*, 15(4), 212–215.

U.S. Department of Agriculture. (2013). *Rural America at a glance, 2013 edition*. Retrieved September 12, 2013, from http://www.ers.usda.gov/publications/eb-economic brief/eb24.aspx#.UsRnvLTHmFA

5

Work, Retirement, and Leisure in Rural Places

M. HELEN HOGUE

ELAINE T JURKOWSKI

MAOR RUBINSTEIN

After 35 years of intensive work, Sara, a high school teacher, couldn't wait to retire. She even applied for early retirement at age 55. She loved her workplace and her students and enjoyed being a teacher. Sara was very pleased her objectives for a successful career and fulfillment of job expectations had been achieved, and yet she also felt physically and mentally exhausted. Sara wanted to attempt some other life goals while she still could, and while she still had strength, vivacity, and vitality. She imagined all the things she could do in her leisure time. She made plans but decided that she wanted to be relaxed: nothing to rush to, no pressure, no commitment, no responsibilities, no worrying about others, no need to be on time for anything. Thus, she decided to wait until the right time to begin to plunge into new activities. Sara looked forward to being able to fulfill and accomplish many of the things that she had pushed aside for years, and looked forward to being able to do things for herself for a change. Her fantasy was to indulge in all the things she had postponed for the years. So Sara retired and had an exciting farewell party filled with greetings and praises.

The first week of Sara's retirement passed, and she sat in her bathrobe at home. She didn't wake up early as she used to. She began each day with a late breakfast, the newspaper, and coffee amid the quiet around. The phone did not ring. She read a book. "What will I do today? I don't feel like doing anything." She went back to sleep. She woke up troubled. She checked to see if anyone had called. No one had called. She picked up the phone and thought about calling someone. "Whom should I call? Everyone is at work. I have no one to call. And what would I say? That I did nothing today?!" She went back to sleep but felt uneasy.

Sara felt out of place and emptiness. It was too quiet for her. There was no reason to get out of bed. She wondered, "How come they don't call me from the school? Don't they have any questions for me? Don't they need my advice? Are they really getting along without me? They forgot about me. I am not needed anymore. They are getting along without me. Is this the retirement I have been waiting for? Did I make a mistake? What do I do with all of this free time now?"

Time passed and things got better.

Looking back, Sara admitted that going from an intensive work schedule to complete freedom generated days of grief for what she had lost, and from this grief something new needed to grow. She learned that clinging to the past only hurt her. She soon realized that she had to cut off/break away from the past and start over in a new chapter of the journey known as retirement. Consequently, Sara signed up for extracurricular activities, began to travel with fellow older adults, spent time with her grandchildren, volunteered, arranged meetings with her friends in local cafes, and attended social events and movies. Sara also took on a part-time job working at the local day care center, where she helped serve meals and work with the students in their after-school reading programs. Sara's diary became filled with events, and her life began again in the retirement phase of living.

The well-being of U.S. rural people and places depends upon many things: the availability of good-paying jobs; access to critical services such as education, health care, and communication; vibrant communities; and a healthy natural environment—to name a few. Although the urban United States is equally dependent upon these things, the challenges to well-being look very different in rural areas. Small-scale, low-density settlement patterns make it more costly for communities and businesses to provide critical services. Declining jobs and incomes in the natural resource-based industries that many rural areas depend upon are forcing workers in those industries to find new ways to make a living. Often those new ways are found only in the city. Low-skill, low-wage rural manufacturing industries must find new ways to challenge the increasing number of foreign competitors. Distance and remoteness impede many rural areas from being connected to the urban centers of economic activity. Finally, changes in the availability and use of natural resources located in rural areas affect the people who earn a living from those resources, as well as those who derive recreational and other benefits from them.

Some rural areas have met these challenges successfully, achieved some level of prosperity, and are ready for the challenges of the future. Other rural areas have met these challenges but have little capacity to adapt further. Still other rural areas have neither met the current challenges nor positioned themselves for the future. Thus, concern for the rural United States, its conditions, and its future is real. And, although the rural United States is a producer of critical goods and services, the concerns go beyond economics. Rural regions are also home to one fifth of the nation's people, keeper of natural amenities and national treasures, and safeguard of a unique part of U.S. culture, tradition, and history.

Translating concern into effective policy for the betterment of the rural United States is, however, no easy task. The challenge lies, at least partly, in the complex nature of the subject. The rural United States, like the rest of the country, is changing. Similarly, rural areas, like other areas of the country, are diverse. These are simple, if not obvious, facts. Yet, in the course of policy debate and formulation, those simple, obvious facts often get lost. In matters of policy, it is tempting to think of rural America as unchanging and homogeneous, to think of it as it once was or as it is now in only some places.

This chapter explores employment opportunities, employment for older adults living in rural communities, retirement, and leisure and recreation opportunities. It explores change and diversity from several angles: its people and places, its economies and industries, its concerns and future. The chapter concludes with some considerations for practitioners working with older adults in rural communities and next steps for the future.

RURAL AMERICA

Rural America has been and continues to be a vital part of the nation. Today, rural America comprises 2,288 counties. It contains 83% of the nation's land and is home to 21% (51 million) of its people. In 1992, non-metro/rural counties supplied 18% of the country's jobs and generated 14% of its earnings. Rural people and communities today are engaged in and depend upon a wide range of economic activities—from manufacturing to mining, from recreational services to agriculture, and everything in between. Yet, older adults who are rural residents are likely to have many of their needs—shopping, medical care, banking—at least partially met by providers in urban areas.

At the beginning of the 20th century, rural America was the center of American life. It was home to most of the population and was the source of food and fiber for the nation's sustenance and commerce. And most of its people were involved in producing that food and fiber. The typical rural community in 1900 consisted of a small town or village with numerous small farms within a few miles. Most people lived their lives and fulfilled most of their needs, economic and otherwise, within this community. They had little contact with areas beyond the community.

The rural United States has changed in many ways over the century. The rural economy in particular has changed—shifting from a dependence on farming, forestry, and mining to a striking diversity of economic activity. Another significant change has been in the connection between rural areas and cities. Improvements in communication and transportation between the two have reduced rural isolation and removed many of the cultural differences between them. Television, phone service, and transportation systems have helped bring rural and urban dwellers much closer together in terms of culture, information, and lifestyles.

RURAL EMPLOYMENT

Shifting From Farming to Manufacturing and Services

In the not too distant past, farming was nearly synonymous with rural. However, that is no longer the case. Although farming remains important as a source of jobs and income in many rural areas and is the largest single user of rural land, it is no longer the dominant rural industry it once was—nor will it likely be again. However, it has been the major source of income and livelihood for many older adults currently living in rural communities.

In the last 40 years, farming employment dropped from just under 8 million to slightly more than 3 million. The number of farms has gone from 5.8 million to 2.1 million. In the last 20 years, the percentage of the rural workforce employed in farming has gone from 14.4% to 7.6%. Even by including agricultural services, forestry, and fishing, the share has gone from only 15.3% to 8.5% (AOA, 2013; DHHS, 2012; U.S. Department of Agriculture [USDA], 2013). Today, only about 5 million people, less than 10% of the rural population, live on farms. In addition, in 1990, 58% of U.S. farm-operator households received wages and salary (averaging nearly $30,000 per reporting household) from off-farm employment. For example, one or more household members might work at a manufacturing plant, telemarketing office, or in retail trade. Therefore, even for the remaining farm households, the nonfarm rural economy is a critical source of employment and income. The decline of farming employment is, in many ways, a consequence of success. Improvements in technology, crop science, and farm management have all boosted output while reducing the need for labor. Productivity growth has, in turn, led to farm consolidation, declining farm numbers, decreases in farm employment, and consequently a surplus of farm labor. Thus, the ability to produce more with less, although benefiting many, has caused economic hardship for others.

Today, the largest share of rural jobs and employment growth comes from the services sector, which employs more than one half of all rural workers. This dominance of the services sector mirrors the urban employment picture. Rural services related to recreation, retirement, and such natural amenities as mountains, lakes, shorelines, and so forth have emerged as important new sources of rural employment and growth. Other services (e.g., financial, insurance, real estate, retail stores, dry cleaners, restaurants, etc.) are also important. There is evidence that advances in telecommunications are enabling still other types of services (e.g., telemarketing and data processing) to move to rural areas (Riding-Malon & Werth, 2014; U.S. Federal Communications Commission, 2013).

Manufacturing also is a major provider of both rural jobs and income, providing jobs for nearly 17% of the rural workforce and employing more people than farming, agricultural services, forestry, fishing, and mining combined (AOA, 2013; DHHS, 2012; USDA, 2013).

Manufacturing also provides roughly one fourth of all rural earnings. However, like farming, the share of manufacturing jobs in rural areas has declined. From 1969 to 1992, that share dropped from 20.4% to 16.9% of rural employment.

Given these changes in the rural economy, and its current structure, the economic future and well-being of most rural people now depend on the availability and quality of jobs in the rural services and manufacturing sectors and the entrepreneurial opportunities in those sectors.

The decline in the number of farming-dependent counties is, in part, a consequence of agricultural success. Increases in farm productivity through advances in production technology, crop science, and management have led to decreases in farm employment. Simply put, fewer people are needed to produce an increasing amount of farm goods.

In addition to changes in farming, the remoteness of these counties (the most rural of the county types discussed here) creates a barrier to development. With very few urban centers or nearby major metropolitan areas, these counties have limited access to the information, innovation, trade, services, and finance that drive today's economy.

Distances between communities and low average population densities (11.8 persons per square mile compared with 36.3 per square mile for all nonmetro/rural counties; USDA, 2013) also increase per capita costs of infrastructure and other investments, making it hard for people in these communities to maintain transportation systems, utilities, public institutions, and other services that urban areas take for granted.

As farming employment has declined, other types of industry have not replaced all the jobs that were lost. Thus, many young people have left to seek jobs elsewhere, often moving to a different part of the country. This end result finds people working longer in rural communities, and retiring at a much older age, with limited younger people available to take over.

As farm employment declines, other types of employment need to be found to replace those jobs. However, the out-migration of working-age and well-educated people may act as a barrier to creating and maintaining those other economic activities. Growth in the services sector has been the dominant force in nonmetro/rural (as well as national) industrial trends over the last 20 years, giving rise to the popular term "service economy." The services sector includes transportation and public utilities, wholesale and retail trade, finance, insurance, real estate, agricultural services, and so forth. During a 10-year period, more than 3 million nonmetro (rural) jobs were lost.

The previous discourse about employment opportunities in rural communities begs the question as to what this means for older adults living in rural communities.

Employment opportunities are more important today than ever before for older adults living in rural communities. Older adults are working longer, and maintaining some form of part-time employment, despite being retired, due to the rising costs of living and inadequate pension income. Changes in pension benefits have also led to the desire of older adults to continue to work. Despite this desire, the opportunities may not exist in many rural communities.

Older adults find meaning in their lives through employment, in addition to income (Fragar et al., 2010). Mor-Barak (1995) proposed four factors that contribute to the meaning of work for older adults: financial, personal, social, and generativity. Whereas the first three are obvious, generativity relates to the manner of teaching, training, and sharing skills with younger generations. Although older adults living in rural communities may want to share their skills in a manner that promotes their self-esteem, the changing nature of the workforce may pose new challenges (e.g., training, cognitive skills, and retirement anxiety) for this target population (Johnson, Mermin, & Resseger, 2012; Lee & Lassey, 1980; Liu & Besser, 2003). Employers in a rural setting may be reluctant to hire older adults, simply because they may feel that older individuals may not be as quick to learn through training or may require cognitive skills that are beyond their abilities (Chou & Choi, 2011; Johnson et al., 2012). Conversely, some strategies that may be helpful to create a niche for older adults in rural communities may include the development of markets that capitalize on skills in which older adults may excel— tapestries, high-end carpentry, and culinary skills.

Older adults (age 55 and older), who are living below the poverty line, can qualify for help with seeking employment and developing some new job skills. Created as part of the Older Americans Act (OAA) in 1965, the Senior Community Service Employment Program (SCSEP) is the nation's oldest program to help low-income, unemployed people ages 55 and older find work. This program helps older adults by matching them with part-time jobs for community service organizations. One of the strengths of this program is that older adult participants build skills and self-confidence, while earning a modest income. The SCSEP experience has had a track record of leading participants to permanent employment. Employment opportunities include child care providers, teachers' aides, customer service representatives, computer technicians, health care workers, and maintenance workers, to name a few (National Council on Aging [NCOA], 2013). This program has held promise for older adults living in rural areas, although the opportunities and available options may be more limited in rural communities than in urban centers.

> Sara learned about the SCSEP through a friend with whom she attended a yoga class. Although Sara did not qualify to use the service because her pension rendered her income well above the poverty level, she was inspired to take a job as a teacher's aide in a local after-school program. The opportunity gave Sara a sense of well-being because it offered her financial resources, a way to utilize her teaching skills, a social outlet, and the chance to teach and share her skills with younger generations.

RETIREMENT

Retirement, a term sometimes characterized as the "golden parachute," may or may not be perceived as golden for older adults living in rural communities. Within many rural communities, where children have left their areas of origin, couples may be left with empty nests and only each other to rely upon in retirement. This can pose stress and push strained relationships (Dorfman, 2003). Traditional married couples may have had a patriarchal or matriarchal relationship during the course of their lives together; once in retirement, they find there is a need for a more egalitarian relationship in order to have balance within the household (Dorfman & Heckert, 1988). Husbands may perceive retirement in a more satisfactory manner than their wives do, as a result of trying to chart new territory within the home and community networks. Establishing new boundaries within the home and community, as a result of retirement, can be a source of excitement for one family member but a source of stress for another marital partner (Dorfman, Lieckeri, Hili, & Kohous, 1988).

Retirement satisfaction may not be static and consistent across the country, community, or rural settings because much depends upon the community, the resources available within the community, the profession or occupation prior to retirement, education level, and socioeconomic status (Dorfman, Kohout, & Heckert, 1985). Leisure and recreational outlets are also critical factors in one's level of satisfaction with retirement.

> Sara found her adjustment to retirement much easier than the women she discussed retirement with in her quilting group.

As she thought about it, she realized that she did not face the adjustment issues with space and territory that her married counterparts experienced. Sara had adjusted to living alone, following her husband's passing 5 years earlier. She found that her concerns differed from those of her friends with husbands who had recently retired.

LEISURE AND RECREATION

All too often we refer to the health care sector as facing the most challenges when considering older adult issues; however, rural areas probably face greater needs in the areas of leisure and recreation when trying to meet the needs of older adults (Adams, Leibbrandt, & Moon, 2011; Filkins, Allen, & Cordes, 2000; Glasgow & Brown, 2012; Kirk & Alessi, 2002; Li, 2006; Leitner & Leitner, 2012; Turner, 2004). It has been established in the literature that communities are not always well equipped to help older adults remain connected to their social support systems (Cromartie & Nelson, 2010), or to remain active (Adams, Leibbrandt, & Moon, 2011; Hanson & Hildenbrand, 2011; Kochera & Bright, 2006). Kang and Russ (2009) suggested that recreational and leisure activities should integrate six dimensions of wellness (physical, social, intellectual, emotional, occupational, and spiritual) to help maintain a healthier older adult segment. Thus, leisure and recreation programs in rural communities need to be designed to be attractive and culturally relevant for older adults, specific to their rural community. For example, outdoor hiking programs may be very attractive to older adults in the Colorado area, where hiking was an integral component of younger persons' leisure activities. But this activity may not be attractive to older adults living in rural New Orleans.

An increasingly rich knowledge-base provides evidence that positive relationships, recreation, and leisure activities are often tied to sources of social support. Older adults with strong support systems are likely to report being more satisfied with their lives and less socially isolated (Infeld & Whitelaw, 2002; Kochera & Bright, 2006; Stalker, 2011; Torgerson & Edwards, 2013; Walker et al., 2013). Studies have shown that older adults see their quality of life (QOL) more positively and experience less social isolation when they have sustained support networks and ongoing affectionate relationships (USDHHS, 2012). The oldest older people (age 85 and older) are probably at the greatest risk of isolation and most in need of leisure/recreational activities because they may suffer from physical and medical conditions that prevent them from full participation in social and leisure activities (Li, 2006).

The impact of social connectedness and health in the older population is well documented (Cromartie & Nelson, 2013; Infeld & Whitelaw, 2002; Kochera & Bright, 2006; Walker et al., 2013). Older adults who lack social ties are at risk for health-related problems (Kirk & Alessi, 2002; Turner, 2004). Social connectedness can prove to be more difficult in rural areas, especially in areas where weather causes much seasonal variation and forces people to remain in their homes. Snow and blizzard conditions may make it difficult for people to travel outside their homes and visit with their friends.

Older adults in rural communities engage in a range of activities to maintain their levels of engagement. According to the Pew Research Center (2013), the most frequent leisure activities of older adults, age 65 and older, in rural communities include talking with family and friends (90%); followed by the use of cell phones (85%); and reading books, magazines, or the newspaper (83%). Watching more than 1 hour of television per day was noted by 77% of participants, followed by prayer (76%). Respondents felt that spending time on hobbies or interests was only engaged in by 43% of participants, and exercise was only engaged in less than 22% of the time (Pew Research Center, 2013). The study also found that women over the age of 65 used social media as a form of leisure in 74% of the sample, as compared to men in 62% of the sample (Pew Research Center, 2013).

A unique feature of rural living is the outdoors and opportunities for utilizing parks and walking trails. The use of parks is a unique feature that contributes to the QOL of older adults in rural communities. The development of community parks and recreational areas is a critical need for rural communities. Physical activity has been identified as an underutilized intervention for recreation and leisure activity among older adults (Fei, Norman, & White, 2013). However, a number of strategies to help people become more active in rural communities have proved to be quite successful (Son, Shinew, & Harvey, 2011; Torgerson & Edwards, 2013). Hughes and colleagues have made strides within rural communities to help motivate increased physical activity through their evidence-based physical activity program Fit and Strong (Hughes et al., 2004, 2006; Seymour, Hughes, Campbell, Huber, & Desai, 2009).

Civic engagement is an active form of leisure activity for people living in rural communities. People may choose to retire but remain active within their communities through community participation, including civic engagement. Experts within the field of civic engagement include board membership, volunteerism, mentorship, and community leadership activities all as viable forms of civic engagement (Hinterlong, 2010; Hong, Morrow-Howell, Tang, & Hinterlong, 2009).

Leisure and recreational activities are strongly tied to health and well-being in older adults living in rural communities. Older adults in rural communities, however, can run the risk of being in poorer health, overweight, and in poorer physical condition. Strategies to promote healthy leisure activities are important in the process of building leisure options for older adults living in rural communities.

> Sara struggled with the initial process of retirement; however, as she settled into a host of leisure activities, she found herself confident, self-assured, and her overall health improved. Her new friends rooted in her various social activities gave her a new social network and a sense of social support.

CONCLUSION

Older adults living in rural communities may think of rural settings as a panacea of bliss. However, if one chooses to retire into a rural community, the nature of being in a rural setting may pose challenges in terms of employment opportunities during one's golden years. Retirement may not be the hub of activity that people envisioned as they planned for their golden-parachute experience. Older adults who wanted to retire into rural communities may be forced to locate alternative employment to help with paying their bills and making ends meet. Social engagement through leisure activities, the telephone, and social media are all major strategies for older adults in rural settings to employ in their leisure time and to stay connected to others.

USEFUL WEBSITES

AARP Employment in Retirement
www.aarp.org/work
Active for Life Newsletter
www.activeforlife.info/resources
Fit and Strong Physical Activity Evidence-Based Intervention
www.fitandstrong.org/about/staff.html

National Council on Aging: Senior Community Service Program
www.ncoa.org/enhance-economic-security/mature-workers/
senior-community-service-employment-program-scsep
Social Security Retirement Planner
www.ssa.gov/retirement
The Urban Institute on Retirement Policy
www.urban.org/retirement_policy/older-age-employment.
cfm#data
WHO: Physical Activity and Older Adults
www.who.int/dietphysicalactivity/factsheet_olderadults/en

REFERENCES

Adams, K., Leibbrandt, S., & Moon, H. (2011). A critical review of the literature on social and leisure activity and well-being in later life. *Ageing & Society, 31*(4), 683. doi:10.1017/S0144686X10001091

Administration on Aging. (2013). A profile of older Americans. Retrieved from http://www.aoa.gov/AoARoot/Aging_Statistics/Profile/2013/docs/2013_Profile.pdf

Chou, R., & Choi, N. G. (2011). Prevalence and correlates of perceived workplace discrimination among older workers in the United States of America. *Aging and Society, 31*(6), 1051–1070. doi:10/1017/S0144686X10001297

Cromartie, J. M., & Nelson, P. (2010). Baby boom migration tilts toward rural America. *Montana Business Quarterly, 48*(2), 2.

Donnelly, E. A., & Hinterlong, J. (2010). Continuity of social participation and changes in volunteer activity among recently widowed older adults. *The Gerontologist, 50*(2), 158–169.

Dorfman, L. T. (2003). Older rural workers and retirement preparation. *Journal of Gerontological Social Work, 41*(3/4), 213–228. doi:10.1300/j083v4 1n03_2

Dorfman, L. T., & Heckert, D. (1988). Egalitarianism in retired rural couples: Household tasks, decision making, and leisure activities. *Family Relations, 37*(1), 73.

Dorfman, L. T., Kohout, F., & Heckert, D. (1985). Retirement satisfaction in the rural elderly. *Research on Aging, 7*(4), 577–599.

Dorfman, L. T., Lieckeri, D., Hili, E. A., & Kohout, F. I. (1988). Retirement satisfaction in rural husbands and wives. *Rural Sociology, 53*(1), 25–39.

Fei, S., Norman, I. J., & While, A. E. (2013). Physical activity in older people: A systemic review. *BMS Public Health, 13*(1), 1–17. doi:10, 1186/1471-2458-13-449

Filkins, R., Allen, J., & Cordes, S. (2000). Predicting community satisfaction among rural residents: An integrative model. *Rural Sociology, 65*, 72–86.

Fragar, L., Strain, H. J., Perkins, D., Kelly, B., Fuller, J., Coleman, C., . . ., Wilson, J. M. (2010). Distress among rural residents: Does employment and occupation make a difference? *Australian Journal of Rural Health, 18,* 25–31.

Glasgow, N., & Brown, D. (2012). Rural ageing in the United States and contexts. *The Journal of Rural Studies, 38*(4), 422–431.

Hanson, T., & Hildebrand, E. (2011). Can rural older drivers meet their needs without a car? Stated adaptation responses from a GPS travel diary survey. *Transportation, 38*(6), 975–992.

Hong, S., Morrow-Howell, N., Tang, F., & Hinterlong, J. (2009). Engaging older adults in volunteering: Conceptualizing and measuring institutional capacity. *Nonprofit and Voluntary Sector Quarterly, 38,* 200–219.

Hughes, S., Seymour, R., Campbell, R. T., Huber, G., Pollak, N., Sharma, L., & Desai, P. (2006). Long-term impact of Fit and Strong! on older adults with osteoarthritis. *The Gerontologist, 46*(6), 801–814.

Hughes, S., Seymour, R., Campbell, R., Pollack, N., Huber, G., & Sharma, L. (2004). The impact of the Fit and Strong! intervention on older adults with osteoarthritis. *The Gerontologist, 44*(2), 217–228.

Infeld, D., & Whitelaw, N. (2002). Policy initiatives to promote healthy aging. *Clinics in Geriatric Medicine, 18,* 627–642.

Johnson, R. W., Mermin, B. T., & Resseger, M. (2012). *Will older adults be able to keep working as the employment picture changes?* (AARP Issue Paper #2007–20). Washington, DC: Public Policy Institute.

Kang, M., & Russ, R. (2009). Activities that promote wellness for older adults in rural communities. *Journal of Extension, 47,* 1–5.

Kirk, A., & Alessi, H. (2002). Rural senior service centers: A study of the impact on quality of life issues. *Activities, Adaptation and Aging, 26,* 51–64.

Kochera, A., & Bright, K. (2006). Livable communities for older people. *American Society on Aging, 29,* 32–36.

Lee, G. R., & Lassey, M. L. (1980). Rural-urban differences among the elderly: Economic, social, and subjective factors. *Journal of Social Issues, 36*(2), 62–74.

Leitner, M. J., & Leitner, S. F. (2012). *Leisure in later life* (4th ed.). Urbana, IL: Sagamore Publishing.

Li, H. (2006). Rural older adults' access barriers to in-home and community-based services. *Social Work Research, 30,* 109–118.

Liu, A., & Besser, T. (2003). Social capital and participation in community improvement activities by elderly residents in small towns and rural communities. *Rural Sociology, 68*(3), 343.

Mor-Barak, M. E. (1995). The meaning of work for older adults seeking employment: The generativity factor. *The International Journal of Aging and Human Development, 41*(4), 325–344.

National Council on Aging (NCOA). (2013). SCSEP for older adults. Retrieved October 4, 2013, from http://www.ncoa.org/enhance-economic-security/mature-workers/senior-community-service-employment-program-scsep/for-older-adults.html#sthash.nApHRkYT.dpuf

Pew Research Center. (2013). *Growing old in America: Expectation vs. reality.* Retrieved from http://www.pewsocialtrends.org/2009/06/29/growing-old-in-america-expectations-vs-reality

Riding-Malon, R., & Werth, J. L. (2014). Psychological practice in rural settings: At the cutting edge. *Professional Psychology: Research & Practice, 45 I*(2), 85–91. doi:10.1037/a0036172

Sevilla, A., Gimenez-Nadal, J., & Gershuny, J. (2012). Leisure inequality in the United States: 1965–2003. *Demography, 49*(3), 939–964. doi:10.1007/s13524-012-0100-5

Seymour, R., Hughes, S., Campbell, R. T., Huber, G., & Desai, P. (2009). Comparison of two methods of conducting the Fit and Strong! program. *Arthritis Care and Research, 61*(7), 876–884.

Stalker, G. (2011). Leisure diversity as an indicator of cultural capital. *Leisure Sciences, 33*(2), 81–102. doi:10.1080/01490400.2011.550219

Son, J. S., Shinew, K. J., & Harvey, I. (2011). Community readiness for leisure-based health promotion: Findings from an underserved and racially diverse rural community. *Journal of Parks & Recreation Administration, 29*(2), 90–106.

Torgerson, M., & Edwards, M. (2013). Demographic determinants of perceived barriers to community involvement: Examining rural/urban differences. *Nonprofit & Voluntary Sector Quarterly, 42*(2), 371. doi:10.1177/0899764012440181

Turner, K. W. (2004). Senior citizens centers: What they offer, who participates and what they gain. *Journal of Gerontological Social Work, 43,* 36–47.

U.S. Department of Agriculture. (2013). *Rural America at a glance, 2013 edition.* Retrieved September 12, 2013, from http://www.ers.usda.gov/publications/eb-economic brief/eb24.aspx#.UsRnvLTHmFA

U.S. Department of Health and Human Services. (2012). Aging trends and rural issues: 2012 key indicators of well-being. Federal Interagency Forum on Age-related Statistics. Retrieved from http://www.agingstats.gov/aging-statsdotnet/Main_Site/Data/Data_2012.aspx

U.S. Federal Communications Commission. (2013). Access to telecommunications technology: Bridging the digital divide in the United States. *Congressional Digest, 92*(4), 2–5.

Walker, J., Orpin, P., Baynes, H., Stratford, E., Boyer, K., Mahjouris, N., Patterson, C., Robinson, A., & Carty, J. (2013). Insights and principles for supporting social engagement in rural older people. *Ageing & Society, 33,* 938–963. doi:10.1017/S0144686X12000402

III

Providing Health and Human Services to Rural Older Adults

6

Providing Services to Rural
Older Adults

JOHN A. KROUT

Charles Anderson is 82 years old and lives alone in an old farm-house in the countryside in upstate New York, where he was born. The youngest of seven children, he grew up on a farm and attended school through the 10th grade before working full-time on the family farm and serving honorably in the army for 6 years. He returned to his hometown at the age of 25 and worked in farming and the timber industry until he was age 50, then in a small manufacturing business until he was age 65. He was married for 50 years until his wife died in 2006. They had four children and one (a son) lives close by, as does his one sur-viving sibling, a younger sister who also lives alone. Charles was always socially gregarious but goes out much less often now, partly because his eyesight is failing. He only drives to church, the local grocery, and the Dollar General; his doctor has men-tioned that perhaps he should not drive anymore.

Many years of hard labor outdoors have left Charles with arthritis and foot problems that inhibit his walking. The closest medical specialists are 25 miles away; thus, he has not received any medical attention for his problems. He is able to carry out his activities of daily living (ADLs) but lately has had difficulty going up stairs. Charles is getting forgetful about paying bills and having small repairs done around the house. He has a poor diet and is especially fond of pastries. He was recently diagnosed with high blood pressure and has been somewhat depressed lately. His son tries to visit once a week and helps take care of the house; however, he may have to move because his new job requires a 2-hour round-trip commute. Charles has about $5,000 in savings and lives mostly on Social Security (SS) and a small veteran's pension. He refuses to apply for Supplemental Security Income (SSI) or to check if he is eligible for Medicaid, and he is unaware of the local senior center and the programs it offers such as Meals on Wheels and a van service to medical appointments and shopping.

Charles's case illustrates a situation that sadly is all too often faced by rural older adults and their families—a lack of available, accessible, and affordable social and health services. Indeed, one of the most consistent findings in the gerontological literature is that significant gaps can be found in the continuum of rural aging services, and that rural older adults are disadvantaged, in this regard, compared to urban older adults (Coward & Krout, 1998; Goins & Krout, 2006a). Concerns also exist regarding the appropriateness and effectiveness of services that are available and the low levels of awareness and knowledge of such services (Krout, 1994a). Some have argued that older adults who have spent a lifetime in rural places face a cumulative service disadvantage that begins at a young age and has significant and negative impacts on their health and well-being. Further, the combination of a lack of formal services and demographic changes affecting rural communities and families may put rural older adults at greater risk of social isolation. This is often seen as an important factor in a poorer quality of life (QOL) for older adults.

The causes of this variation and the rural–urban service gap are many and complex, including factors such as lower population size and density, smaller proximate population centers, greater distances between people and existing services, rural population and economic decline, diminished rural political clout, geographic isolation, increased centralization of health care providers, and flat federal funding for human services (Coward & Krout, 1998; Glasgow & Berry, 2013a; Krout, 1994a). Although federal programs such as SS, Medicare and Medicaid, and the Older Americans Act (OAA) are intended to ensure that all older Americans have their basic service needs met, a lack of focus on rural issues and a variety of factors have diminished the capability of these programs to adequately address the service needs of rural older adults. Additionally, data to assist policy makers and practitioners develop effective responses to rural service needs (e.g., best practices) are lacking.

This chapter focuses on the nature and degree of the deficits in rural health and social services, the barriers rural older adults and their families face in accessing those services, and the challenges practitioners face in providing them. The elements of effective service provision and information on effective evidence-based practices are also presented.

SERVICE NEEDS OF RURAL OLDER ADULTS

Previous chapters discuss the characteristics and needs of rural older adults. By and large, we have seen that rural compared to urban older adults have poorer health and nutrition, lower incomes, fewer employment opportunities, fewer transportation options, and less adequate housing. These realities suggest that rural older adults have a greater need for a wide range of services (Bull, 1993; Coward & Krout, 1998; Glasgow & Berry, 2013; Goins & Krout, 2006; Krout, 1994a). Several of these needs are examined in more detail in the following paragraphs.

Home ownership is significantly higher for rural compared to urban older adults (85% vs. 67%). Of those rural older adults, 10% live in mobile homes, twice the number found in urban areas (Housing Assistance Council, 2003). However, housing for older rural residents is more likely to be older and substandard than in urban places (Folts, Muir, Peacock, Nash, & Jones, 2006). This translates into a need for repairs and maintenance that, when coupled with lower rural incomes, often results in housing problems that remain unfixed. This is the reality for Charles Anderson in this chapter's case study. He lives in an old farmhouse, and it can be surmised that it has an antiquated heating system, is poorly insulated, and lacks air-conditioning. The bedrooms are upstairs, where there is one bathroom, with a possible washroom on the first floor. For older adults with arthritis and walking difficulties like Charles, this means a lack of fit between his living environment and abilities that may lead to costly home modifications or even a premature relocation to other housing. For many lower income rural older adults, unattended small repairs on steps and roofs can turn into major safety and QOL issues. Lower rural housing values mean less income when older adults choose to or have to leave their homes due to health declines or other reasons.

Home-owning, independent-living older adults usually come to mind when housing is discussed; however, another important issue is the availability of in-home services and housing options for those whose needs lead to a move to other housing arrangements (e.g., assisted living or skilled care). These options are notoriously lacking for rural older adults (Folts et al., 2006; Glasgow & Berry, 2013b). For those needing assistance to stay in their homes (be it a house or an apartment), in-home services such as home health care can be critical. Unfortunately, such services are less likely to be available in rural areas and are less affordable for older adults not covered by government-subsidized programs (Goins & Krout, 2006).

Transportation issues have long been recognized as one of the, if not the, most pressing rural service access problem (Bull & Bane, 2001; Glasgow & Berry, 2013; Goins & Krout, 2006). Low population densities and centralization of services, coupled with the lack of public transit systems, create significant problems of service access for older rural residents. For example, Firestine (2011) reported that 3.5 million rural residents lost access to intercity bus transportation between 2005 and 2010. Rural dwellers of all ages are particularly dependent on the private vehicle because this is often their only transit option. Older adults who do not or cannot drive or own a vehicle largely rely on friends and neighbors. These facts lead to concerns about the ability of rural older adults to meet their daily needs through shopping, going to the bank, making medical appointments, maintaining social relationships, and staying involved in the fabric of community life (e.g., religious services and social activities). Overreliance on private vehicles as a source of transport can jeopardize rural older adults' mobility if other options are ignored (Shergold, Parkhurst, & Musselwhite, 2012). Charles Anderson in this chapter's case study is facing these issues. His driving is beginning to be limited by his health problems, and he faces the prospect of losing the ability to drive. His son may soon move farther away; however, Charles clearly does not yet seem accepting of programs that could help him access services.

Older rural residents, especially the very old, face acute and chronic health problems that require formal services (Morton & Weng, 2013; Sharkey & Bolin, 2006). Research has shown that rural older adults experience a greater number of years with physical impairments than urban older adults (Laditka, Laditka, Olatosi, & Elder, 2007) and have a higher prevalence of mental health problems (Scheidt, 1998). However, as is shown in this chapter, rural areas are underserved by a wide variety of health care professionals. Charles Anderson has health issues, but appropriate professional help is quite a distance away.

Exacerbating the impact of these needs is the fact that rural older adults have fewer economic resources than their urban counterparts, including lower incomes, less savings, and fewer opportunities to earn income in retirement (Dorfman, 1998; Goins & Krout, 2006). Rural communities, likewise, have fewer economic resources to attract and support health care services (Morton & Weng, 2013). Charles Anderson evidences this economic vulnerability; his savings are insufficient to meet unexpected medical or housing expenses or simply keep pace with inflation. He has a strong sense of self-reliance and is reluctant to accept services to which he is entitled, traits not uncommon among rural older adults.

One way to view the need for services among rural areas is through Lawton and Nahemow's (1973) concept of "environmental press." Lawton and Nahemow used this term to refer to the demands that natural and built environments place on individuals. Various features of rural environments seem particularly relevant to the press notion, including lack of basic shopping as well as social and health care options, greater distances to specialty services, lower quality housing, and lower incomes. The impact of such press is seen in relation to the resources and competencies of individuals and, as it can be argued, communities. Since both rural older individuals and communities often lack the resources necessary to meet needs, one can argue that the press is higher. Formal services as well as informal supports then become even more important for rural older adults.

SERVICE AND SERVICE UTILIZATION

A large number of community-based health and social services have developed over the years to address the needs of the older population. One useful way to identify these services is presented in the Older Adult Service Matrix shown in Table 6.1. The Older Adult Service Matrix was developed by the Social Work Leadership Institute of the New York Academy of Medicine (n.d.). The matrix identifies life stages including well-elderly, functionally impaired, and end of life and matches them with corresponding health and social services. These services

TABLE 6.1 Practicum Partnership Program (PPP), Older Adult Service Matrix

	Wellness/ prevention	Social, community, and spiritual engagement	Housing	Mental health care	Health care	Legal system	Planning/ advocacy
Well-elderly	Exercise programs Congregate meals Nutritional services Health clubs Wellness programs Health fairs Health education programs	Recreation programs Congregate meal programs Information/referral services Volunteer opportunities – RSVP – Older companions – Foster grandparents – Tutoring Educational programs Employment opportunities Spiritual opportunities Pastoral care opportunities	Home repair services Independent older adult housing Retirement communities Retirement homes Home-sharing devices Transportation services	*See social and health* Support groups Psychoeducational groups Retirement adjustment programs Later life transition programs	Home emergency response programs Primary medical services Emergency Room services Home health care Acute in-hospital medical services	Elder law services – Estate planning – Designated POA – Representative payee – Health proxy – Living will – Crime prevention awareness	Needs assessment Public hearings Lobbying Program planning Legislative advocacy AARP
Functionally impaired	*See above* Caregiver support services	*See above* Homemaker and chore services Caregiver psychoeducational support groups Case management Money management Adult protective services Respite care Adult day care Nursing home ombudsman services	*See above* In-home support services Board and care homes Shelters for abuse, homeless Assisted living– Continuous care communities	*See above* Outpatient treatment services Outpatient mental health rehabilitation services Support groups Peer counseling Psychiatric day hospital Inpatient treatment Residential dementia care Substance abuse services	*See above* In-home nutritional services Acute hospital care Outpatient rehabilitation Outpatient dialysis Medical day care Nursing homes	*See above* Guardianship/ conservator	*See above*
End of life	*See above*	*See above* Caregiver support services, including hospice	*See mental health and health care*	*See above* Hospice/home Bereavement services Support groups	*See above* Hospice/home Palliative care Hospice: inpatient or residential	*See above*	*See above*

AARP, American Association of Retired Persons; POA, power of attorney; RSVP, Retired and Senior Volunteer Program.
Reprinted with permission from Social Work Leadership Institute (SWLI), n.d., *Practicum Partnership Program (PPP)*, Older Adult Service Matrix.

include wellness/prevention; social, community, and spiritual engagement; housing; mental health care; health care; legal; and planning/advocacy.

Research on rural older adults indicates that their needs would be well served by a number of these services, including housing repair, long-term care options, food and nutrition, physical and mental health, income support and employment, transportation, recreation and leisure, disease prevention and health promotion, and caregiver education and support (Bull, 1993; Coward, Bull, Kukulka, & Galliher, 1994; Coward & Krout, 1998; Goins & Krout, 2006; Krout, 1994a, 1998). As noted earlier, however, rural older adults generally have a smaller number and variety of such services available and accessible to them (Johnson, Brems, Warner, & Roberts, 2006; Nemet & Bailey, 2000).

Existing data support the argument that many rural communities are disadvantaged compared to urban and suburban ones in regard to the availability of services and practitioners (Coward & Krout, 1998; Goins & Krout, 2006; Krout, 1991, 1994a). For example, rural older adults compared to their urban counterparts receive fewer days of home care (McAuley, Spector, & Van Nostrand, 2009) and have lower rates of hospice use (Vining, Moscovice, Durham, & Casey, 2004). Very small and remote rural places are often at the greatest disadvantage (Vining et al., 2004). It is not uncommon to find no adult day care, mental health, specialized medical, respite care, assisted living, public transportation, or geriatric assessment available in very rural communities (Krout & Bull, 2006). However, it should be recognized that some rural communities are much more service rich (or poor) than others and the rural disadvantage has diminished for some services over the years.

Many rural service needs are long-standing and seem unlikely to be fully ameliorated. The system of services and service providers that has developed through the OAA of 1965 provides a good example of the rural/urban service gap. The OAA created and funds a network of some 630 local Area Agencies on Aging (AAAs) operating under the direction of 56 State and Territorial Units on Aging (SUAs) and ultimately the titles of the federal OAA (Administration on Aging, 2011). OAA services are available to any American age 60 and older and are provided by AAAs as well as some 20,000 local service providers (Administration on Aging, 2011). The OAA was allocated $1.9 billion for the 2012 fiscal year with State and Community Programs (Title III) receiving 71%, and Community Service Employment (Title V) receiving 23% of those funds. Title III funding is weighted heavily toward nutrition programs (congregate and in-home) and supportive services. Health promotion and activities for health, independence, and longevity received only 1.5% of total OAA funding (Napili & Colello, 2013). Although the OAA allocation of almost $2 billion sounds impressive, one must remember that this amount is dwarfed by Medicare and Medicaid expenditures and amounts to approximately $40 for every person age 60 and older in the nation. In addition, OAA funding has rarely kept pace with inflation over the years.

Services funded via the OAA are provided by AAAs either directly or by contracts with local providers. A detailed discussion of AAAs is given here because services are more likely to be provided directly by them in rural compared to urban areas due to the lack of other provider organizations. As established under the OAA, AAAs are required by federal and state laws to provide certain services to all persons age 60 and older, regardless of income; nonetheless, their activities and resources vary considerably and rural–urban differences are particularly notable (Krout, 1991; Peters, 1981). AAAs play a broad variety of roles that include identifying service needs through mandated needs assessments, funding contractors to provide services, developing services and service providers, coordinating services, identifying and mobilizing community resources, implementing state and federal program mandates, establishing and supporting new and innovative service delivery approaches, evaluating service provider outcomes, providing information to consumers, and offering technical assistance to service providers (Krout, 1991; Peters, 1981).

Every AAA is responsible for these and other roles in a planning and service area (PSA), typically encompassing one or more counties. Due to lower population densities and sizes of rural communities, rural AAAs cover more counties and larger geographic areas than do urban ones. Research conducted in the early 1990s found that the median number of counties and square miles for rural PSAs were six counties and 3,600 square miles versus one county and 460 square miles for more urban PSAs (Krout, 1991, 1994b). Whereas population figures may have changed for some rural AAAs, these parameters have not.

OAA funding for SUAs is based on a state's number population of those age 60 years and older relative to the nationwide total; however, funding for AAAs is based on complicated intrastate funding formulas (IFFs) that include a variety of factors such as population size, income, and race. Most states provide rural AAAs a base allocation that is intended to help the smallest AAAs provide minimum services.

Some SUAs even provide a rural "factor" in the IFFs; nonetheless, smaller population sizes still translate into smaller budgets and fewer services (Coward, Vogel, Duncan, & Uttaro, 1995). In addition, AAAs receive funding from state and local government agencies as well as foundations and not-for-profit organizations. Rural AAAs are often at a disadvantage here as well (Krout, 1994b). It is clear that rural AAAs have smaller budgets and staff than urban ones and many studies have shown that rural AAAs support a smaller number and variety of services (Krout, 1994b; Nelson, 1980). Furthermore, often services that are available through rural AAAs are very limited and inadequate to meet the needs of rural older adults.

There is some evidence that the rural-AAA disadvantage had diminished somewhat by the end of the 20th century (Krout, 1994b). Based on anecdotal evidence, it would appear that progress is being made by AAAs in meeting the service needs of older rural residents. To get a better handle on current trends, the question of rural AAA service gaps was explored in the summer of 2010 via a survey of all the rural AAAs in New York State—one of the more service robust states in the nation. In New York, a county is considered rural by the state if it has fewer than 200,000 in total population. Of New York's 62 counties, 43 meet this criterion, and 25 of them responded to an open-ended survey about service needs and challenges. In many ways, the results mirrored those reported nationally 20 years ago. Transportation topped the list of the greatest unmet need and lack of funding the biggest barrier (each selected by 75% of respondents). Transportation, in-home, and nutrition services were noted as those most in need of expansion. Lack of home care and home care aides were also noted as major service needs, and distance, cost, and transportation were seen as the biggest rural disadvantages (Krout, 2010).

BARRIERS TO SERVICES FOR RURAL OLDER ADULTS

Many factors underlie the rural service disadvantages noted in the previous section. Goins and Krout (2006) and Krout (1994a) identified four main underlying factors. First, a lack of adequate service funding exists for people of all ages. Programs that can have significant impacts on community-based services for older adults, such as the OAA, job training, transportation, housing, and so forth are generally underfunded and do not have enough of a rural focus. Older rural residents and communities have fewer resources to pay for services. Concomitantly, there is a need for economic development in many rural parts of the country to generate revenues that support public and private services, retain and grow young adult populations, and maintain more robust health care networks. Fortunately, for some rural parts of the country, the last 5 years have seen economic growth due largely to expansion in the energy, agriculture, and retirement industries (see Chapter 1). This growth has not only provided more revenues for public services but also put pressure on existing service infrastructures.

Second, the ecological realities of rural areas are often problematic. These include smaller populations and lower (sometimes stagnant) population growth, low population density, and long distances to population centers. These ecological factors combine with others to create transportation and service delivery challenges to providers. Dispersed rural populations often combine with terrain and weather challenges to reduce the feasibility of centralizing services and bringing assistance to people. An urban meal provider can serve a large number of congregate or home meals in an urban high-rise apartment building. A rural provider may have to support multiple satellite sites and lengthy routes to do the same. Simply put, rural providers do not have the same economies of scale available to them. Unfortunately, small rural places have also lost retail options that have concentrated in regional centers.

Third, deficits in human as well as economic capital create challenges to service sustainability and delivery to rural older adults. A lack of dollars for services means a smaller and less diverse pool of professionals for all types of health and social services. Smaller rural provider organizations cannot afford the same number and diversity of trained personnel, especially in specialty areas. Increasingly, rural areas are not able to attract doctors. Rural organizations often have fewer resources to provide training to staff, especially on specialty care issues. This also means fewer professional incentives to both attract and retain well-trained professionals.

Fourth, too little attention has been given to designing rural solutions to rural problems. Many federal policies and programs do not focus on residence as a significant factor and often assume that a scaled-down version of an urban program will work for rural places.

Effective practices developed at the local rural community level are not widely disseminated. A lack of research on rural aging results in a lack of understanding of the unique challenges faced by rural professionals and providers or of the skills needed. Very few universities and colleges provide courses on rural aging or instruction within various professional disciplines on serving older rural residents.

Research suggests that these underlying factors lead to a deficit in services for rural older adults by negatively impacting six aspects of service development and delivery. These factors are availability, accessibility, affordability, awareness, appropriateness and adequacy (Goins & Krout, 2006, p. 28). Each of these presents challenges and need to be addressed, if the service needs of rural older adults are to be met. Service planners and providers should take these into account to identify areas of weaknesses and strengths.

Availability

- Number and diversity of formal services and providers
- Qualified human and social service professionals
- Basic and high-tech equipment
- General lack of human services and infrastructure

Accessibility

- Adequate, appropriate, and affordable transportation systems
- Population density and geographic isolation
- Cultural and social isolation, especially of the vulnerable
- Terrain and weather
- Political isolation and lack of policy input

Affordability

- Economic resources to support service (economic development)
- Economies of scale
- Poverty and lack of income to access services, cost share
- Challenges to rural economies in a multinational economy

Awareness

- Levels of service awareness and knowledge
- Information dissemination and referral
- Levels of literacy and education opportunities

Appropriateness

- Fit of service approaches with values and expectations of rural people and communities; levels of service awareness and knowledge
- Services that address underlying needs
- Recognition of rural reliance on self-care

Adequacy

- Skill of rural professionals
- Evidence that services are effective and address needs successfully
- Data that support evidence-based practice
- Lack of training and technical assistance

Some of these issues are illustrated very well by Charles Anderson in this chapter's case study. His health is declining, and his health care needs are becoming more complex; however, he lives near a small community where specialty care is not available. Health problems indicate that he may soon be unable to drive, severely limiting his ability to meet basic needs and access to health care. His son may have to move to be closer to his new job, depriving Charles of a key link to services. Charles lives on a limited income and will be unable to afford services that are not subsidized by public funding. It is also apparent that he lacks knowledge of available services that could help him meet his needs and remain in his home.

Unfortunately, few if any inventories of effective service practices provide information on how to address these challenges and best meet the needs of rural older adults. More than 20 years ago, the author conducted a national survey of rural AAAs to learn about program issues and innovations, and many of the approaches that were identified would seem relevant today (Krout, 1991, 1994b). Many of these approaches creatively used volunteers and existing community resources; established partnerships to make the most out of available physical and human resources; and transcended traditional geographic and political boundaries to tap into government funding sources. One program involved paying volunteers mileage to drive neighbors to services under an umbrella insurance policy that limited their individual liability. Another involved a collaboration between local clergy and public health nurses to identify parishioners in need of caregiver education and support. A third program took advantage of the meal-preparing and nutrition expertise in schools and hospitals to reduce costs of congregate and in-home meal programs (Krout, 1990). Other chapters in this section provide more examples of innovative and effective services for rural older adults.

CONCLUSION

Rural older adults have a variety of needs that are generally less likely to be met than is the case for their urban counterparts. These include affordable and adequate housing, housing options for those unable to live independently, economic resources and opportunities, transportation options to access a wide range of services, and accessible and appropriate health care. Service deficits found in most rural areas stem from a combination of problems including a lack of community economic and organizational resources, inadequate attention to the needs of older rural residents in public policy and programs, demographic and geographic realities of rural areas, and a lack of interest in rural issues among educators. Further, rural providers must confront challenges related to service availability, accessibility, affordability, awareness, appropriateness, and adequacy.

In addition to considering the previously mentioned challenges, it is useful to consider what is distinctive about rural places and people. These include distinctive features of rural population characteristics and needs; rural social and physical environments; and the provision of services to rural older adults (Coward, DeWeaver, Schmid, & Jackson, 1983). Although emphasis should be placed on developing service delivery "models" that can be duplicated in a variety of rural places, the reality is that successful programs need to be tailored to the unique distinctive features noted. Sociodemographic characteristics, geography, community economic and social resources, and so forth all factor into designing and maintaining an effective program. Existing community resources and potential partners as well as values and social patterns must be identified and utilized. The impact of demographic shifts and local, state, and federal policies and expenditures need to be anticipated (Krout & Bull, 2006).

Despite decades of progress, challenges remain and the needs of too many rural older adults continue to be unmet. Solutions require the collaboration, dedication, and imagination of all those involved in planning and providing services to older adults. The research reviewed in this chapter suggests a number of priorities for the future, including more research on existing and projected service needs; awareness and utilization patterns; identifying and disseminating evidence-based and effective rural practices; raising the visibility and priority of rural older adults' service needs; examining the impacts of social, economic, and demographic change on service needs; and identifying and measuring the consequences of state and federal policy changes on service availability and effectiveness. Elevating the visibility of the needs of older rural residents in discussions of major entitlements such as SS, Medicare and Medicaid, and the OAA as well as rural transportation, housing, and economic development is essential. Studies have repeatedly shown that rural service gaps stem from a lack of funding and provider organizations and personnel, as well as a lack of access due to limited transportation services and options. Addressing these problems for rural people of all ages should be a priority at the local, state, and national levels.

USEFUL WEBSITES

Administration on Aging (AOA)

www.aoa.gov

Eldercare Locator

www.eldercare.gov/Eldercare.NET/Public/Index.aspx

National Association of Area Agencies on Aging (AAAs)

www.n4a.org

Older Americans Act and the Aging Network

www.aoa.gov/AOA_programs/OAA/index.aspx

USA.gov-Senior Citizens' Resources

www.usa.gov/Topics/Seniors.shtml

REFERENCES

Administration on Aging. (2011). *A profile of older Americans.* Washington, DC: U.S. Department of Health and Human Services.

Bull, C. N. (Ed.). (1993). *Aging in rural America.* Thousand Oaks, CA: Sage.

Bull, C. N., & Bane, S. D. (2001). Program development and innovation. *Journal of Applied Gerontology, 20*(2), 184–194.

Coward, R. T., Bull, C. N., Kukulka, G., & Galliher, G. M. (1994). *Health services for rural elders.* New York, NY: Springer Publishing Company.

Coward, R. T., DeWeaver, K. L., Schmidt, F. E., & Jackson, R. W. (1983). Distinctive features of rural environments: A frame of reference for mental health practice. *International Journal of Mental Health, 12,* 3–24.

Coward, R. T., & Krout, J. A. (Eds.). (1998). *Aging in rural settings: Life circumstances and distinctive features.* New York, NY: Springer Publishing Company.

Coward, R. T., Vogel, W. B., Duncan, R. P., & Uttaro, R. (1995). Should intrastate funding formulae for the Older Americans Act include a rural factor? *The Gerontologist, 35,* 24–34.

Dorfman, L. T. (1998). Economic status, work, and retirement among the rural elderly. In R. T. Coward & J. A. Krout (Eds.), *Aging in rural settings* (pp. 47–66). New York, NY: Springer Publishing Company.

Firestine, T. (2011). *The U.S. rural population and scheduled intercity transportation in 2010: A five-year decline in transportation access.* Washington, DC: U.S. Department of Transportation.

Folts, W. E., Muir, K. B., Peacock, J. R., Nash, B., & Jones, K. L. (2006). Housing for rural elders. In R. T. Goins & J. A. Krout (Eds.), *Service delivery to rural older adults* (pp. 163–182). New York, NY: Springer Publishing Company.

Glasgow, N., & Berry, E. H. (Eds.). (2013a). *Rural aging in twenty first century America.* Dordrecht, Netherlands: Springer Science+Business Media.

Glasgow, N., & Berry, E. H. (2013b). Introduction to rural aging in twenty-first century America. In N. Glasgow & E. H. Berry (Eds.), *Rural aging in twenty first century America* (pp. 1–13). Dordrecht, Netherlands: Springer Science+Business Media.

Goins, R. T., & Krout, J. A. (Eds.). (2006a). *Service delivery to rural older adults: Research, policy and practice.* New York, NY: Springer Publishing Company.

Goins, R. T., & Krout, J. A. (2006b). Aging in rural America. In R. T. Goins & J. A. Krout (Eds.), *Service delivery to rural older adults: Research, policy and practice* (pp.3–20). New York, NY: Springer Publishing Company.

Housing Assistance Council. (2003). *Rural seniors and their homes.* Washington, DC: Author.

Johnson, M. E., Brems, C., Warner, T. D., & Roberts, L. W. (2006). Rural-urban health care provider disparities in Alaska and New Mexico. *Administration and Policy in Mental Health Services Research, 33*(4), 504–507.

Krout, J. A. (1991). Rural area agencies on aging: An overview of activities and policy issues. *Journal of Aging Studies, 5*(4), 409–424.

Krout, J. A. (1994a). *Providing community-based services to the rural elderly.* Thousand Oaks, CA: Sage.

Krout, J. A. (1994b). *Area agencies on aging: A national longitudinal rural-urban comparison* (Final report submitted to the AARP Andrus Foundation). Fredonia, NY: Fredonia State College.

Krout, J. A. (1998). Services and service delivery in rural environments. In R. T. Coward & J. A. Krout (Eds.), *Aging in rural environments: Life circumstances & distinctive features* (pp. 247–266). New York, NY: Springer Publishing Company.

Krout, J. A. (2010). Ithaca College Gerontology Institute, Ithaca, NY.

Krout, J. A., & Bull, C. N. (2006). Service delivery to rural elders: Barriers and challenges. In R. T. Goins & J. A. Krout (Eds.), *Service delivery to rural older adults: Research, policy and practice* (pp. 21–36). New York, NY: Springer Publishing Company.

Laditka, J. N., Laditka, S. B., Olatosi, B., & Elder, K. T., (2007). The health trade-off of rural residence for older adults: Long life, more impairment. *National Rural Health Association, 23*, 124–132.

Lawton, M. P., & Nahemow, L. (1973). Ecology and the aging process. In C. Eisdorfer & M. P. Lawton (Eds.), *Psychology of adult development and aging* (pp. 619–674). Washington, DC: American Psychological Association.

McAuley, W. J., Spector, W., & Van Nostrand, J. (2009). Formal home care utilization patterns by rural-urban community residence. *Journal of Gerontology: Psychological and Social Sciences, 64B*(2), 258–268.

Morton, L. W., & Weng, C. (2013). Health and health care among the rural aged. In N. Glasgow & E. H. Berry (Eds.), *Rural aging in twenty first century America* (pp. 179–194). Dordrecht, Netherlands: Springer Science+Business Media.

Napili, A., & Colello, K. J. (2013). *Funding for the Older Americans Act and other aging services programs.* Washington, DC: Congressional Research Service.

Nelson, G. T. (1980). Social services to the urban and rural aged: The experience of area agencies on aging. *The Gerontologist, 20*, 200–207.

Nemet, G. F., & Bailey, A. J. (2000). Distance and health care utilization among the rural elderly. *Social Science and Medicine, 50*(9), 1197–1208.

Peters, G. F. (1981). Area agencies on aging and the service delivery network. In F. D. Berghorn (Ed.), *The dynamics of aging* (pp. 243–253). New York, NY: McGraw-Hill.

Scheidt, R. T. (1998). The mental health of the elderly in rural environments. In R. T. Coward & J. A. Krout (Eds.), *Aging in rural settings: Life circumstances & distinctive features* (pp. 85–103). New York, NY: Springer Publishing Company.

Sharkey, J. R., & Bolin, J. N. (2006). Health and nutrition in rural areas. In R. T. Goins & J. A. Krout (Eds.), *Service delivery to rural older adults* (pp. 79–101). New York, NY: Springer Publishing Company.

Shergold, I., Parkhurst, G., & Musselwhite, C. (2012). Rural car dependence: An emerging barrier to community activity for older people. *Transportation Planning and Technology, 35*(1), 69–85.

Social Welfare Leadership Institute of the New York Academy of Medicine. (n.d.). Older Adult Service Matrix.

Vining, B. A., Moscovice, I. S., Durham, S. B., & Casey, M. M. (2004). Do rural elders have limited access to Medicare hospice services? *Journal of the American Geriatrics Society, 52*(5), 731–735.

Providing Services to Well Older Adults in Rural Areas

LENARD W. KAYE

SARAH A. HARVEY

Evelyn Netting is a widowed 85-year-old woman with the energy and spunk of someone decades younger. She still lives alone, drives a car, manages her own finances, and is very independent. She is in excellent health and, in fact, once a year she takes her roller skates out of the closet, brushes the dust off, and goes for a spin around the dining room for old times' sake. She has provided child care in her home in Downeast Maine for more than 50 years and continues to the present day, although with fewer children in her care now. As one of the few child care providers in a small, rural town, Evelyn has cared for multiple generations of families and has a strong network of client-families and friends in the area; however, because she is working with children in her home all day, she has less time for other activities. The town she lives in offers few formal recreational, social, and educational opportunities, and has very few amenities. There is a small market, a post office, a coffee shop, a church, and a senior center that offers occasional transportation for meals and events, which Evelyn attends when her schedule allows. The

nearest large community to access shopping and medical facilities is 30 miles away. If her car were to break down or if she were
no longer able to drive, Evelyn would have difficulty meeting
her basic needs. The sidewalks in town are in disrepair; and in
order to access any programs or services on foot, Evelyn would
have to cross a rural but busy highway. Evelyn's son had been
living nearby and providing any assistance she might need, such
as home repairs, snow shoveling, and grocery shopping, but
he recently passed away. Her only other living family member
is her younger son, who lives several states away and cannot
travel long distances due to a chronic health condition.

Living in the same small Maine town are Ted and Sheila
Johnson, a well-educated couple in their late 60s who are pho-
tographers in semiretirement. They raised their children in the
town, and they love the area for its natural, unspoiled beauty
and its proximity to several lakes and mountains. However, due
to Sheila being diagnosed in her 40s with Raynaud's syndrome,
which causes the blood vessels in her fingers and toes to overreact
to the cold, they travel frequently and spend a greater part of the
year in a warmer climate. When in town, they are quite engaged
in the community. They have planned musical, educational, and
cultural events for everyone in town to enjoy. Ted serves on a
nonprofit advisory board; Sheila volunteers in a program at a
local nature preserve teaching people how to grow and cultivate
herbs. Both participate in the many informal recreational opportunities in the area such as swimming and hiking. Although they
are active and well known in the community, they feel the town
is lacking in enough social and educational opportunities, especially in terms of intergenerational activities. They could attend
events at the senior center, but they do not feel that they have
much in common with the people who regularly go there.

In thinking about the lives and experiences of Evelyn and the Johnsons,
the question arises as to how this and other rural communities can meet
the various needs and desires of these well older adults with limited
resources and a lack of infrastructure. Notwithstanding the very real
and challenging gaps in health and social services for older adults in
rural areas identified in Chapter 6, this chapter highlights specific programs and services that currently exist for well older adults in rural
locales. These include recreational opportunities, socialization, volunteering and civic engagement, work, and educational initiatives.

This chapter focuses on the programs that fall under the wellness/ prevention and social, community, and spiritual engagement domains of the Older Adult Service Matrix (Social Work Leadership Institute, n.d.) described in Chapter 6. Both formal and informal programs and opportunities are discussed in this chapter, although acknowledging the challenges to availability that rurality presents. In addition, new models are explored for conceptualizing the program and service needs of older adults who wish to remain active, mobile, and engaged.

Defining Wellness, Engagement, and Successful Aging

First, it is important to briefly explain what is meant by the term "well older adults." Being well can be conceived of in many different ways. Generally speaking, it refers to those who live independently and are mobile. Belza and Wooding Baker (2000) defined well older adults as "those with physical, mental, social, and spiritual function or resources to meet the needs of everyday living" (p. 12). In the framework of this chapter, wellness is not composed of a narrowly defined set of criteria; rather, wellness can be thought of as a state of health that allows individuals to use their minds and/or bodies for productive purposes. However, as Kaye (2005) pointed out, what is considered to be "productive" is likely best defined by individuals themselves. The term *well* should not be limited to only those in peak physical or mental health. For example, in the case study of the Johnsons, Sheila's Reynaud's syndrome influenced her decision to live in a warmer climate for part of the year; however, most people would not characterize her as "unwell," and her diagnosis does not prevent her from continuing to engage in the relatively broad range of activities that she enjoys.

For Sheila Johnson, remaining engaged, as defined in her own terms, enables her to live her life actively and productively. A useful way to conceive of remaining engaged as we age is to recognize at least four ways in which older adults can choose to stay connected to the world around them: educational activities, volunteering, caregiving, and paid employment. In turn, engagement can also be conceptualized as one of the three critical components in realizing a successful aging experience, along with avoidance of disease and disability, and high cognitive and physical function (James, Besen, Matz-Costa, & Pitt-Catsouphes, 2010). The concepts of engagement and successful aging serve to add nuance to understanding who the well older adults are and remind us that individuals need to be able to determine for themselves how they define wellness.

Today's Older Adults

Despite common stereotypes, the large majority of older adults (76%) describe their health to be good, very good, or excellent. These individuals are able to live independently without support from a caregiver (Federal Interagency Forum on Aging-Related Statistics, 2012). Older adults today are mobile, active, and engaged. The numbers of well older adults are increasing as the baby boomer generation ages. In general, the baby boomers tend to be in better health (Cutler, Ghosh, & Landrum, 2013) and are more educated than the preceding generation (Administration on Aging, 2013). It stands to reason that they are likely to desire a wide range of well older adult programs. There are some well older adults, like the Johnsons, who will create and shape their own opportunities without asking for the assistance of others. Others, like Evelyn, may benefit from a service infrastructure that reflects a range of programs and services to choose from. It is important that a continuum of options and alternatives be available, given the diversity reflected among older adults in terms of life experiences, backgrounds, and personal interests. Yet, meeting this need in small towns and rural communities can be extremely challenging.

In the past, some programs for older adults may have reflected stereotypical societal notions of what older people should do or be interested in. These may not have wholly represented the scope and breadth of interests exhibited by older adults. Fortunately, these notions are gradually being replaced with more open, positive, and constructive models of aging. As such, ideas about programming for older adults are also changing. With that in mind, this chapter inventories a variety of productive aging-oriented programs and opportunities for older rural adults, as well as informal programs and activities available in rural areas that should appeal to various interests.

RECREATION

Physical Activity

Physical activity is a critically important component of healthy, successful aging. Regular exercise has been shown to increase energy and improve mood, reduce pain levels, decrease many of the risk factors for chronic disease, and enable older adults to maintain their independence later in life (Adams-Fryatt, 2010). Rural communities vary in the extent to which formal opportunities for physical activity are available (U.S. Environmental Protection Agency, U.S. Department of Housing and Urban Development, and U.S. Department of Transportation, 2011). Unfortunately, many rural settings may lack a system of well-maintained roadways and do not have an abundance of sidewalks and walking paths that promote an active lifestyle. Despite their immediate proximity to the pristine outdoors, many rural communities are not particularly walkable because they lack public space for people to assemble, have not incorporated universal design principles that are sensitive to people of differing physical abilities, and have few streets and trails that are controlled and well linked. Visit the website (www.walkable.org/about.html) of the Walkable and Livable Communities Institute to learn more. However, for all that some rural areas may lack in the way of formal recreational programs or physical infrastructure, there is often an abundance of informal recreational opportunities. Many rural communities, for example, have easy access to forests for walking and hiking, mountains for skiing, natural areas for snowshoeing, and many lakes and coastlines for activities like swimming, canoeing, and kayaking.

Increasingly, older adults are taking advantage of formal recreational venues previously considered as places only for younger people—including fitness clubs and indoor recreation centers that may be available in or near small towns and rural communities. Activities such as yoga, Zumba, and tai chi have been gaining in popularity and availability. These activities can be learned and practiced in a group setting or in-home at one's own pace according to fitness level. Evidence-based exercise programs designed for older adults such as Silver Sneakers and Active Living Every Day can be found or organized by social workers, exercise instructors, and Area Agencies on Aging (AAAs) and at fitness centers, community centers, and senior centers nationwide. Bone Builders is a community-based osteoporosis prevention program conducted nationally through lay leaders who are trained to implement the program in their own communities. There are also programs offered remotely, such as Active Choices that is facilitated through a telephone-based activity coach. Walk With Ease is a self-directed program with a guidebook and online tools to improve arthritis symptoms and increase strength and balance (National Council on Aging, 2014); U-ExCEL (*Exercise and Conditioning for Easier Living*) Balancing Act (a falls prevention program) is currently being tested for effectiveness as an in-home, self-implemented program. For exceptionally active and physically robust older adults looking for the excitement of a physical challenge, the State and National Senior Games (for age 50 and older) offer a venue to compete in a variety of sports with others in their own age category.

Gardening

Creating and maintaining a garden is another excellent way to get exercise that is inexpensive. This can be done in one's own yard or in a community setting, and has been shown to have a variety of health benefits. Wang and MacMillan (2013) reviewed 22 empirical studies of older adults in indoor and outdoor gardening, limiting their synthesis to those studies that reported on physical or mental health outcomes. The benefits of gardening found in these studies included improved overall health and well-being, higher levels of physical activity, decreased physical pain, increased strength in the hands and body, greater flexibility, higher likelihood of vegetable consumption, increased social interaction, cognitive improvements, and higher sense of life satisfaction, among others (Wang & MacMillan, 2013). Gardening is an activity that can be tailored to various fitness and skill levels and can therefore be enjoyed by diverse groups of older adults, as well as multigenerational groups.

Community gardens can offer a place for older rural adults to engage in community life and socialize with people of all ages while also providing a place to be active. Sheila Johnson enjoys volunteering at the nature preserve because it gives her the opportunity to meet new people and share her extensive knowledge of herbs with others. Gardening can also bring the community together for a shared purpose, such as growing produce for community members in need. Maine Harvest for Hunger and Friends of Aroostook are two successful community gardening endeavors in Maine working to reduce food insecurity in local communities through the use of volunteers. Similar such programs can be found in other rural states and communities.

For gardening enthusiasts looking for a more formal opportunity, the Cooperative Extension of every public university system in the United States offers a Master Gardener training program. For example, the University of Maine Cooperative Extension's Master Gardener program offers 40 hours of training in horticulture in return for 40 hours of volunteer work in the community, including activities such as teaching workshops, coordinating community projects, helping older adults tend a garden, and mentoring children in home gardening. Arrangements may vary from state to state but the mission of each program is the same: to educate people about home horticultural practices and enable them to give back to their local community and to share the knowledge they have acquired. Farm-to-school programs strive to bring fresh produce from farms to school lunchrooms and provide agriculture, health, and nutrition education to children in Grades K–12 while supporting local farms and communities. Active in all 50 states, these programs are another excellent venue for combining a recreational activity with an intergenerational volunteer project that benefits the community.

Group Activities and Travel Programming

Shores, West, Theriault, and Davidson (2009) found that for rural older adults, having social support, a safe environment, and the ability to walk to a local park are correlated with getting enough physical activity. Group activities that can be enjoyed in a socially supportive environment with a trained facilitator or guide can provide a sense of structure and safety that may encourage some older adults to pursue a wider range of progressively more challenging activities.

Organizations such as the Appalachian Mountain Club (AMC) offer guided tours and outdoor trips, volunteer opportunities, leadership, and outdoor skill-building programs to promote both enjoyment and stewardship of the environment. These may have a cost associated with them such as an annual membership fee or trip fee; however, these opportunities are available in many rural areas in the United States and worldwide. Older adults living in rural areas have the option to engage in these outdoor recreational pursuits close to home (or farther away, if they choose). Road Scholar offers travel experiences designed to promote and enhance lifelong learning that are not limited to outdoor activities in the natural environment.

Road Scholar trips can be found for almost any type of interest— arts and music, food and wine, photography, science and nature, sports-themed tours, city tours, and much more. Both the AMC and Road Scholar organize intergenerational trips. However, whereas the AMC offers general family programs, Road Scholar has programs specifically tailored for an older adult to enjoy with a child or teenager (such as for a grandparent and grandchild). For those who are mobile and have the financial means, facilitated day trips and longer sojourns can promote an active, healthy lifestyle.

SOCIALIZATION

Opportunities for socialization are encompassed in all of the programmatic areas discussed in this chapter, whether arising from recreational pursuits, civic engagement, educational programs, or employment. Informal socialization with friends, relatives, and neighbors promotes the health and well-being of older adults (Gardner, 2011). Informal socialization has been found to increase a subjective sense of well-being in rural older adults, in particular (Mair & Thivierge-Rikard, 2010) Formal opportunities for socialization, such as the programs held at senior centers, have shown to have a positive effect on physical and mental health of participants as well (Aday, Kehoe, & Farney, 2006).

Senior Centers

Senior centers are partially funded by the Older Americans Act (OAA) and have traditionally offered a wide array of programs and services including those for individuals age 50 and older. Senior centers have provided opportunities for socialization, community education, recreation and exercise, health screenings, health promotion, and nutrition. They have streamlined access to a network of social services including transportation (Administration on Aging, n.d.). There are 11,000 senior centers situated nationwide (National Council on Aging, 2012), and this is a venue that has an important role to fill, especially in a rural community where there may be few other resources that are specifically geared to older adults.

Some senior centers report to be experiencing a "graying" of their participants over time, as the current participants grow older or "age out" and those in the younger old age group may not be joining in at the same rate (Pardasani, 2010), Krout (1994, as cited in Pardasani & Thompson, 2012). People like the Johnsons and others like them in the younger old cohort may hesitate to get involved at their local senior centers for a variety of reasons including perceptions that they cater to particular age, racial, or gender-specific participants. Studies show that, demographically, Caucasian women older than age 75 with lower income are the most likely to utilize senior centers (Pardasani, 2010). Other older adults may feel that they do not need the services provided at senior centers or that the available programs are not aligned with their interests (Pardasani, 2010; Pardasani & Thompson, 2012). The offerings of senior centers are, however, evolving in response to the changing needs and interests of the extremely large baby boomer cohort (born between 1946 and 1964) that began turning age 65 at the rate of 10,000 a day beginning in January 2011 (Lassiter, 2007).

Older adults should not discount the idea of becoming involved in senior centers on the basis of what has been offered in the way of past programming. AAAs, many of which administer senior center funding in their catchment areas, are afforded the flexibility to implement the programs and services needed and desired by older adults in their area (Administration on Aging, n.d.). Older adults, then, should inquire about what programs are available at their local senior centers and even advocate for programs they would like to see offered. Some senior centers now include features such as fitness centers, cafes, computer labs, organized group trips overseas, support for employment and volunteer placements, and broadcasts of professional concerts and performances for those unable to travel to see them in person (National Council on Aging, 2012).

Programming at Religious Institutions

Religion can play a prominent role in the social lives of many rural older adults (Gesler, Arcury, & Koenig, 2000). No matter how small the community, there is likely to be a church, synagogue, or other spiritual gathering place that often serves as a primary location for opportunities for both socialization and volunteerism. Religious and spiritual practices, and the social supports received in these settings, have been shown to have a positive effect on the psychological health and ratings of life satisfaction of rural older adults (Yoon & Lee, 2007). Religious venues also allow for a variety of multigenerational experiences. These have been shown to promote learning and improve the health and emotional well-being of older adults, improve academic performance and social skill development in younger generations, and enhance and strengthen the entire community (Generations United, 2007). Churches or synagogues may also support the community by serving as a gathering place, or a place to hold meetings for nonreligious community activities.

The Role of Technology

Technology is playing an increasingly significant role in how we socialize with one another today, and that is increasingly true for older adults as well. Social networking website use by older adults is rapidly rising, with rates of use in those over age 74 quadrupling between 2008 and 2010 (to 16%); rates increased 30% and 34% for younger and older baby boomers, respectively (Zickuhr, 2010). Older adults primarily use social networking for e-mail, researching health information, getting the news, buying products, and making travel reservations (Zickuhr, 2010). For older adults in rural areas especially, technology allows them to transcend their locations to remain engaged and connected with others (Feist, Parker, Howard, & Hugo, 2010). Although only 9% of Americans have used online dating, it is becoming a more common and socially acceptable way to meet a like-minded potential partner, regardless of one's geographic home (Smith & Duggan, 2013). In addition to broad-based and interest-specific online dating websites, there are also specialized sites exclusive to older adults, such as AARP Dating, OurTime, SeniorMatch, and a senior platform of the eHarmony dating site.

CIVIC ENGAGEMENT AND VOLUNTEERING

Volunteering is an excellent way for older adults to stay active, use their minds, and share their expertise to benefit the community in a variety of ways—whether on a local, state, or national level. Kaskie, Imhof, Cavanaugh, and Culp (2008) found that as many as one in four older adults may be involved in civic engagement as a formal retirement role. Profiles of those who volunteer indicate that they are in better health, have higher education levels, and are more physically active than older adults who do not volunteer (Kaskie et al., 2008, p. 374). Rozanova, Keating, and Eales (2012) pointed out that there can be structural inequalities that impact the degree to which a person is able to engage in the community. It is important to consider the wide range of factors that influence a person's interest in and inclination to volunteer, and tap into the skills of people of all ages, backgrounds, and abilities (Kaskie et al., 2008; Morrow-Howell, Carden, & Sherraden, 2005).

Joseph and Skinner (2012) highlighted the important role volunteers play in the community for meeting the needs of people in rural areas aging in place; they provide a "community response to the changing roles and responsibilities of the state and civil society whereby NPOs (nonprofit organizations), community groups, family members and individual volunteers take on a more central role in meeting the needs of people aging in place" (p. 381). As local, state, and federal funding sources are dwindling, older adult volunteers have much to offer in the way of knowledge and life experience to help address pressing issues in their communities (Joseph & Skinner, 2012). Older adults are an untapped resource to serve on advisory groups, planning councils, and school boards and can help serve the needs of all types of organizations. Placing older adults in volunteer leadership roles can contribute to long-term organizational stability and counteract the scarce resources with which many rural-based community programs are forced to operate. However, the challenge for institutions is conducting a thorough needs assessment and adequately recruiting and training volunteers to maximize their benefit to the organization (Luckie, 1999). Organizations must also remember that volunteers require that a range of ongoing supports be provided, such as responsible supervision and adequate incentives including performance recognition, to ensure the effectiveness of their efforts. Those organizations that create a sound infrastructure to work with the growing numbers of potential volunteers will realize the most gain from the talents and energy of older adults (Morrow-Howell, 2010).

Leadership and Environmental Stewardship

Drawing upon community, organizational, and leadership development theory, Sandmann and Vandenberg (1995) developed a conceptual model around the leadership needs of the future. Their community action leadership framework incorporates an overarching philosophy of community, vision, learning, and action and is operationalized by seven action values: visioning together, leading together, learning together, building community, developing energy, acting together, and communicating. It envisions a process of people coming together with their individual strengths to develop a collective vision and collaborate toward action or change in the community (Sandmann & Vandenberg, 1995).

Sandmann and Vandenberg's (1995) classic empowerment principles have contributed to the development of various leadership development initiatives for older adults that are on the rise in some communities including those in rural regions of the country. For example, Encore Leadership Corps (ENCorps) is a program in Maine for people age 50 and older to give back to their communities in the areas of environmental stewardship and community development. Volunteers have worked on projects such as grooming snowmobile and hiking trails; starting food co-ops, food pantries, and farmers' markets; grant writing; and serving on town planning boards. Training and networking opportunities, as well as a 2-day annual leadership summit, are a part of this program, and stipends may be available for certain volunteer projects. Comparable programs exist in New York and Florida, organized through Cornell University, called RISE (Retirees in Service to the Environment), and similar programs are sure to develop in other areas of the country to tap into the environmental inclinations and concerns of the baby boomer generation. The U.S. Environmental Protection Agency, recognizing the potential of older adults to contribute their time and talents to environmental stewardship, created the Aging and Environment Initiative to promote programming for older adults as well as intergenerational programming opportunities.

Pillemer, Fuller-Rowell, Reid, and Wells (2010) conducted a comparison study of adults in the Alameda County Study from the 1974 and 1994 cohorts who volunteered in general areas with those who specifically did environmental volunteering. They found that the group that did environmental volunteering had better ratings of self-reported health, fewer depressive symptoms, and greater levels of physical activity at the 20-year mark, after controlling for other variables. Engagement in environmental sustainability initiatives may be of particular interest to older adults living in small towns and rural communities because of their affinity to the land and outdoor living.

Programs in Civic Engagement

There are access points to volunteering for people with a variety of experience and interests in all counties in all states. Senior Corps is a program that was developed through the Corporation for National Community Service (CNCS) in the 1960s. It connects adults age 55 and older to volunteer opportunities with organizations that match with their interests. Senior Corps is operated in every state and is comprised of three distinct programs: Senior Companions, RSVP (Retired and Senior Volunteer Program), and Foster Grandparents.

Senior Companions is a program for older adult volunteers to pro-vide in-home support for older people struggling to maintain inde-pendent living. Senior companions provide friendship and may run errands or help with other daily living tasks. These volunteers may serve a particularly vital role in reducing the isolation and loneliness experienced by older and disabled individuals who reside in sparsely populated rural and frontier communities. RSVP is the largest national volunteer organization, with 300,000 volunteers annually. RSVP has six core focus areas: disaster services, economic opportunity, educa-tion, environmental stewardship, healthy futures, and veterans and military families. This program offers a great deal of flexibility so vol-unteers can choose to serve in different capacities because their inter-ests or availability may change. Volunteers have engaged in activities such as renovating homes, teaching English as a second language, and mentoring youth. The Foster Grandparents program is an inter-generational program connecting older adults with opportunities to mentor children in school and child care settings, hospitals, and cor-rectional facilities. Volunteers in each of these programs receive train-ing and orientation from the organization they are linked with and, depending on the program and sponsoring organization, they may also receive supplemental insurance during volunteer hours, meals while volunteering, or mileage reimbursement. Stipends may be available depending on the organizational placement. In the Foster Grandparents program, receipt of a stipend is based on income eligi-bility criteria.

The Service Corps of Retired Executives, or SCORE program, is also a part of the CNCS, and boasts 11,000 volunteers across 62 industries to help small businesses grow and succeed. SCORE mentors are former business leaders who offer counseling and guidance at low or no cost within the local area of the small business owner needing assistance. SCORE sponsors local or online workshops, and the SCORE website provides business tools, templates, and guidance for general business advice, also for starting a business, handling finances, marketing, man-agement, and technology. In addition, SCORE provides resources for specific categories of entrepreneurs, including those who are age 50 and older, and for those starting or operating a rural business endeavor. Volunteers with the SCORE program can transmit critical knowledge and business acumen to help one's own community and local economy thrive.

EDUCATION AND LIFELONG LEARNING

The educational needs of rural older adults are as diverse as older adults themselves: Age, gender, and level of education all play a role in shaping their educational interests (Mott, 2008). Being rural does not preclude older adults from engaging in formal educational opportunities. In fact, Maine, the most rural state in the nation in 2010 (61.3% of its population live in rural areas; Wickenheiser, 2012), leads the country in lifelong learning programming for older adults, with 17 senior colleges that are part of a statewide consortium called the Maine Senior College Network. Courses in foreign languages, genealogy, woodworking, financial planning and investing, historical and literary topics, and more, are taught by volunteers for a modest fee to support program operation. There are no tests, papers, or graded assignments.

Computer Technology and Internet Connectivity

Computer technology can facilitate self-directed online learning through Internet-based distance learning programs or free open access courses offered by numerous colleges and universities. Also, less formal means, using online instructions, can be found for learning a craft or conducting a project. It is increasingly common to find do-it- or learn-it-yourself video tutorials on websites such as YouTube, or simply by using a search engine to look for videos or instructions. Self-directed learning is one way that older adults in rural communities can meet their own educational needs, informally (Roberson & Merriam, 2005). Roberson and Merriam (2005) found that learning among adults ages 75 to 87 was associated with the need to adapt or adjust to developmental life changes, such as retirement or having more time in one's day, taking an interest in the activities of a family member, or loss (e.g., loss of a spouse, change in health status). Older adults in this study also conveyed that they felt that rural living promoted the process of self-directed learning because the "communal aspects of rural life" afforded them the support and accessibility of friends, family, and neighbors in the learning process (Roberson & Merriam, 2005, p. 284).

Increasingly widespread Internet connectivity and computer use will enable a growing number of older adults in rural areas to remain engaged in various activities and endeavors, even when issues like geographic isolation or a lack of transportation create initial barriers to their participation. Those who are comfortable with technology and open to using it in new and innovative ways will be able to benefit in myriad ways—for socialization, volunteer work, continuing employment, and even to enhance their medical care using technology for remote monitoring and telehealth conferencing (Cimperman, Brencic, Trkman, & de Leonni Stanonik, 2013). Lack of familiarity with computers is an issue that is expected to decrease as the youngest baby boomers—many of whom are computer literate—grow older (Githens, 2007). Until such time, there are good learning and instructional resources for older adults to gain basic computer skills. SeniorNet, a program nearly 30 years old with 4,000 volunteers and 20,000 students, offers computer instruction as well as courses on hundreds of other topics taught by older adult volunteers to learners age 50 and older, both online and in community settings. The website (everyoneon.org) launched by a public and private partnership working to bring computers and Internet access to low-income families provides a venue where novice Internet users can learn how to navigate the Internet, use e-mail, investigate the various types of social media sites that exist, find out more about Internet safety, locate computer classes in their local communities, and more. Though not specifically designed for older adults, this site makes it easy for anyone to become more familiar with computer technology and can promote digital literacy.

Increasingly, technology is enabling rural citizens to transcend physical distance to the library and is facilitating access to reading for educational pursuits and/or pleasure. The state of Maine has a particularly robust network of library resources, including MARVEL, Maine's Virtual Library, which provides streamlined database searching to locate and access journals, magazines, newspapers, and reference books. Through the Maine InfoNet Download Library patrons can search for and download audio and e-books in formats for 13 different types of electronic devices. Most e-reader devices include features for enlarging text and changing the screen contrast and brightness, which can benefit older adults with varying visual abilities. Text-to-speech capability is another excellent feature of some e-readers, but it is not yet available across all types of devices. In addition, online book clubs encourage reading and lifelong learning, and can be found for a wide variety of interests. Some specifically market themselves to the older adult reader, such as the one operated through SeniorNet.

MaineCat, run through Maine InfoNet, is an electronic interlibrary loan service that enables patrons to request library materials throughout the state. Books by Mail is a grant-funded program run by the Maine State Library that delivers library books and materials by mail to people who are homebound or live in communities that do not have a full-service library, such as those in rural areas. However, this program can also be accessed by requesting books by telephone, and a computer is not required. As the most rural (U.S. Bureau of the Census, 2012a) and one of the oldest states in the nation (U.S. Bureau of the Census, 2012b), Maine offers a fine example for other states with aging rural populations in regard to making library materials widely available to just about anyone who wants them. Similar programs can be found in other rural states throughout the United States. Despite these opportunities, there is still concern about the "digital divide" and the availability of high-speed Internet services in rural areas ("Access to Telecommunications Technology," 2013).

Educational Program Planning and Design

There are important considerations for designing formal educational programs for older adults in rural communities. Collaborating with older adults, as well as providers and stakeholders in the community, is vital to ensuring a program is successful (Mott, 2008). By including older adults in the planning process, their voices will help to inform the interests and needs of those in the community. Additionally, "It is important to consider factors such as transportation, cost, age, health, and technological capability, while not assuming these influences to be barriers to participation and success" (Mott, 2008, p. 56). Luckie (1999) outlined four working hypotheses of the features of successful older adult education programs: professional staff leadership to ensure program stability when changes and transitions occur; using older adult volunteers as program leaders in all phases and program functions; situating the placement of programs appropriately to assist in stability and funding; and utilizing institutional partnerships to create long-term, multilevel strategies for funding and support at the policy level. In rural settings, thoughtful decisions around program planning and design will be especially important to ensure the programs that are developed can be accessed with the least amount of difficulty and effort on the part of older adult consumers.

WORK AND EMPLOYMENT

The Trend Toward Later Employment

Older adults are working later in life than ever before regardless of whether they reside in rural or urban communities. The labor force participation rates of people older than age 50 that were in decline for much of the 20th century have been steadily increasing since the 1990s (Harootyan & Sarmiento, 2011). In 2012, 18.5% of the population older than age 65, or 7.7 million people, were either working or looking for work (Administration on Aging, 2013). The better health and higher education levels of the baby boomer generation have increased the likelihood that they will work beyond traditional retirement ages (Rix, 2011). However, those with more physically or cognitively demanding jobs will tend to retire sooner (Johnson, Mermin, & Resseger, 2011).

Some continue to work for personal fulfillment or because they want to contribute to society; others need to do so for financial reasons (Curl & Hokenstad, 2006). Older adults have much to gain from remaining in or returning to the workforce. Additional earnings will increase their eventual Social Security (SS) benefits, enable additional money to be put into investments and savings, and decrease the number of years living on a fixed amount of retirement funds (Johnson et al., 2011). The relatively lower levels of assets available to older adults in rural settings place additional pressures on these individuals to remain in the workforce.

Older adults are particularly well suited for alternative types of employment, such as telecommuting or working from a virtual office; doing contract, part-time, or temporary work; and working nontraditional hours. They report that flexibility, part-time work, "snowbird" programs, or phased-retirement arrangements are especially appealing incentives that could enable them to work longer (Eyster, Johnson, & Toder, 2008; Rix, 2011).

There are also benefits to the economy when older adults work longer. Working older adults can help offset the anticipated workforce shortages as many in the baby boomer generation retire, and help reduce the current stressors on the SS program (Eyster et al., 2008). The traditional out-migration of younger people from rural communities to urban centers in search of greater employment opportunities and related attractions creates additional advantages for employers to seek the services of older workers in rural communities. An additional work incentive was created when the "retirement earnings test" was removed in 2000, allowing people to work and receive their full retirement benefits as long as they are over full retirement age (Curl & Hokenstad, 2006). Organizations can benefit from the knowledge and experience of older workers who delay their retirement and utilize the wide range of skills they have acquired over the course of their lives.

Retooling for Continued Employment

There are barriers for older adults remaining in or reentering the workforce. For some, a mismatch of job skills and employer needs will necessitate additional training. The Senior Community Service Employment Program (SCSEP) is a program authorized through Title V of the Older Americans Act (OAA) to provide work-based job training opportunities for older adults in community service positions. Nearly 77,000 adults participated in SCSEP in program year 2011; 65.3% were women and 46.9% were minorities. Participants work approximately 20 hours per week earning the highest local, state, or federal minimum wage. More than one half (55.9%) of the job opportunities are subsidized; the remainder are unsubsidized. SCSEP works with participants to create an Individualized Employment Plan (IEP); links them to employment assistance through American Job Centers (formerly Career Centers); and provides access to additional retraining through seminars, formal training programs, and college courses. In order to participate, older adults must be age 55 or older with family income less than 125% of the poverty level and be unemployed and facing challenging job prospects. Preference is given to veterans and their qualified spouses, adults older than age 65, minorities, those with limited English skills, Native Americans, and those with particular economic or special needs (U.S. Department of Labor, Employment and Training Administration, n.d.).

The Workforce Investment Act (WIA) is an age-integrated program that provides assistance searching for a job, assessments of skills and abilities, and help preparing for a job through 800 American Job Centers across the country. Although not specifically geared for older adults in most states, their programs are targeted for lower income adults and displaced workers. Ohio is one state where the SCSEP and WIA funding has been used to create four employment centers through the Mature Services program specifically geared for the needs of older adults (Eyster et al., 2008). The Senior Services division of the National Able Network provides special assistance to job seekers older than age 55, in addition to the vocational and job readiness training they provide for all ages.

Challenges for Older Workers

Age discrimination is another barrier to work for older adults that has seen an increase with the aging of the population as evidenced by the rise in age-related claims of discrimination with the Equal Employment Opportunity Commission (EEOC; Rothenberg & Gardner, 2011). The Age Discrimination in Employment Act of 1967, or ADEA, was implemented to prevent age discrimination for workers age 40 and older; however, only 2.4% of the 21,396 cases received in 2013 were found to have reasonable claims (U.S. Equal Employment Opportunity Commission, n.d.). It is often hard for a claimant to prove, for example, that retirement incentive programs or downsizing has occurred as a result of age, even if older workers are predominantly impacted (Rothenberg & Gardner, 2011). Older adults statistically have a harder time finding work than younger workers (younger than age 45) after a period of unemployment (Harootyan & Sarmiento, 2011) or after a return to work following retirement (Rothenberg & Gardner, 2011). Higher unemployment rates and lower paying jobs may make it even more difficult for older adults in rural areas to gain and maintain employment that earns a decent wage (U.S. Department of Agriculture [USDA], 2012). AAAs, job placement agencies, and other programs that work with older adults interested in seeking employment are increasingly providing job counseling services. Such services can help ensure that older adults who want to work will be competitive during the job search and successful once hired. Their assistance includes training in job interviewing, skills assessment, conducting a job search, and résumé writing.

Encore Careers

Current and future predicted trends in the number of well older adults who will choose to remain in the workforce for extended periods of time point to the greater likelihood that they will also want to pursue "encore careers." These are work and volunteer experiences in which they have the opportunity to search for a new calling in the second half of life that can result in a variety of rewards. These rewards include serving as a source of continued income, but also prove to be personally fulfilling and have a positive social impact on the world in which we live (Freedman, 2011). Local community and 4-year colleges in both rural and urban communities are beginning to offer job training programs for midlife and older adults who are in search of new career paths and perhaps discovering their own encore careers.

CONCLUSION

The cohort of well older adults is as heterogeneous as any age group and deserves alternatives to select from in determining how they will spend their active years later in life. Even so, the availability of recreational, educational, volunteer, and work opportunities will certainly vary from one community to another in rural areas. The relative economic health of a given community will be an influential factor in predicting the extent to which there will be both job opportunities for older adults and active older adult programming. It is best to resist the urge to oversimplify the solutions that will be offered to them. The older adult population of the future will be increasingly diverse, both racially and ethnically. At the same time, they will be more educated, mobile, and well informed than their predecessors. Their expectations will also be heightened and their voices will be heard more loudly and clearly than those of their parents and grandparents. Increasingly, they will want to be genuinely engaged in the planning and design of the opportunities made available to them. Their engagement needs to be both anticipated and encouraged.

USEFUL WEBSITES

American Job Centers
jobcenter.usa.gov
Appalachian Mountain Club
www.outdoors.org

Encore.org
www.encore.org
Encore Leadership Corps
www.encoreleaders.org
EPA Intergenerational Activities
www.epa.gov/aging/inter-gen-resources.html
EveryoneOn
www.everyoneon.org
Generations United
www.gu.org
Maine Senior College Network
www.maineseniorcollege.org
Master Gardener Program
www.ahs.org/gardening-resources/master-gardeners
National Able Network
www.nationalable.org
National Council on Aging
www.ncoa.org
National Senior Games Association
www.nsga.com
Osher Lifelong Learning Institute (OLLI)
www.usm.maine.edu/olli/national/index.html
Road Scholar
www.roadscholar.org
Senior Community Service Employment (SCSEP)
www.doleta.gov/seniors
Senior Corps Programs
www.nationalservice.gov/programs/senior-corps
Senior Corps of Retired Executives (SCORE)
www.score.org
Senior Environmental Employment (SEE)
www.epa.gov/ohr/see/brochure/backgr.html
Silver Sneakers
www.silversneakers.com

REFERENCES

Access to telecommunications technology: Bridging the digital divide in the United States. (2013). *Congressional Digest, 92*(4), 2–5.

Adams-Fryatt, A. (2010). Facilitating successful aging: Encouraging older adults to be physically active. *The Journal for Nurse Practitioners, 6*(3), 187–192.

Aday, R. H., Kehoe, G. C., & Farney, L. A. (2006). Impact of senior center friendships on aging women who live alone. *Journal of Women & Aging, 18*(1), 57–73. doi:http://dx.doi.org/10.1300/J074v18n01_05

Administration on Aging, Administration for Community Living, U.S. Department of Health and Human Services. (2013) *A profile of older Americans: 2012.* Retrieved December 1, 2013, from http://aoa.gov/AoARoot/Aging_Statistics/Profile/2012/docs/2012profile.pdf

Administration on Aging. (n.d.). Supportive services and senior centers program. Retrieved December 1, 2013, from http://www.aoa.gov/AoA_programs/HCLTC/supportive_services/index.aspx#data

Belza, B., & Wooding Baker, M. (2000). Maintaining health in well older adults: Initiatives for schools of nursing and the John A. Hartford Foundation for the 21st century. *Journal of Gerontological Nursing, 26*(7), 8–17.

Cimperman, M., Brencic, M. M., Trkman, P., & de Leonni Stanonik, M. (2013). Older adults' perceptions of home telehealth services. *Telemedicine and e-Health, 19*(10), 786–790. doi:10.1089/tmj.2012.0272

Curl, A. L., & Hokenstad, M. C. (2006). Reshaping retirement policies in postindustrial nations: The need for flexibility. *Journal of Sociology and Social Welfare, 33*(2), 85–106.

Cutler, D. M., Ghosh, K., & Landrum, M. (2013). *Evidence for significant compression of morbidity in the elderly U.S. population* (National Bureau of Economic Research [NBER] Working Paper No. 19268). Cambridge, MA: NBER. Retrieved December 1, 2013, from http://www.nber.org/papers/w19268

Eyster, L., Johnson, R. W., & Toder, E. (2008). *Current strategies to employ and retain older workers.* Washington, DC: The Urban Institute. Retrieved January 30, 2014, from http://www.urban.org/UploadedPDF/411626_older workers.pdf

Federal Interagency Forum on Aging-Related Statistics. (2012). *Older Americans 2012: Key indicators of well-being.* Washington, DC: U.S. Government Printing Office.

Feist, H., Parker, K., Howard, N., & Hugo, G. (2010). New technologies: Their potential role in linking rural older people to community. *International Journal of Emerging Technologies and Society, 8*(2), 68–84.

Freedman, M. (2011). *The big shift: Navigating the new stage beyond midlife.* New York, NY: Perseus Books.

Gardner, P. J. (2011). Natural neighborhood networks: Important social networks in the lives of older adults aging in place. *Journal of Aging Studies, 25*(3), 263–271.

Generations United. (2007). *The benefits of intergenerational programs.* Retrieved December 1, 2013, from http://www.gu.org/LinkClick.aspx?fileticket= 71wHEwUd0KA%3D&tabid=157&mid=606

Gesler, W., Arcury, T. A., & Koenig, H. G. (2000). An introduction to three studies of rural elderly people: Effects of religion and culture on health. *Journal of Cross-Cultural Gerontology, 15*(1), 1–12.

Githens, R. (2007). Older adults and e-learning: Opportunities and barriers. *The Quarterly Review of Distance Education, 8*(4), 329–338.

Harootyan, B., & Sarmiento, T. (2011). The future for older workers: Good news or bad? In *Older workers: Problems and prospects in an aging workforce* (Public Policy & Aging Report, Vol. 21, No. 1, pp. 3–9). Washington, DC: National Academy on an Aging Society.

James, J. B., Besen, E., Matz-Costa, C., & Pitt-Catsouphes, M. (2010). *Engaged as we age: The end of retirement as we know it* (Issue Brief No. 24). Boston, MA: Sloan Center on Aging and Work at Boston College.

Johnson, R. W., Mermin, G. B. T., & Resseger, M. (2011). Job demands and work ability at older ages. *Journal of Aging and Social Policy, 23*(2), 101–118.

Joseph, A. E., & Skinner, M. W. (2012). Voluntarism as a mediator of the experience of growing old in evolving rural spaces and changing rural places. *Journal of Rural Studies, 28*(4), 380–388.

Kaskie, B., Imhof, S., Cavanaugh, J., & Culp, K. (2008). Civic engagement as a retirement role for aging Americans. *The Gerontologist, 48*(3), 368–377.

Kaye, L. W. (2005). A social work practice perspective on productive aging. In L. W. Kaye (Ed.), *Perspectives on productive aging: Social work with the new aged* (pp. 3–17). Washington, DC: National Association of Social Workers Press.

Lassiter, M. (2007). Nation's first baby boomer files for Social Security retirement benefits—online! [Press release]. Retrieved from http://www.ssa.gov/ pressoffice/pr/babyboomerfiles-pr.htm

Luckie, J. C. (1999). Case studies on success variables in older adult learner programs. *Educational Gerontology, 25*(3), 253–268.

Mair, C. A., & Thivierge-Rikard, R. V. (2010). The strength of strong ties for older rural adults: Regional distinctions in the relationship between social interaction and subjective well-being. *International Journal of Aging and Human Development, 70*(2), 119–143.

Morrow-Howell, N. (2010). Volunteering in later life: Research frontiers. *The Journals of Gerontology: Series B, 65B*(4), 461–469. doi:10.1093/geronb/gbq024

Morrow-Howell, N., Carden, M., & Sherraden, M. (2005). Productive engagement of older adults: Volunteerism and service. In L. W. Kaye (Ed.), *Perspectives on productive aging: Social work with the new aged* (pp. 83–105). Washington, DC: National Association of Social Workers Press.

Mott, V. W. (2008). Rural education for older adults. *New Directions for Adult and Continuing Education, 117,* 47–57.

National Council on Aging. (2012, September 4). *What you don't know about your local senior center.* Retrieved from http://www.ncoa.org/national-institute- of-senior-centers/nisc-news/what-you-dont-know-about.html

National Council on Aging. (2014). *Title III-D highest tier evidence-based health promotion/disease prevention programs.* Retrieved December 1, 2013, from http://www.ncoa.org/improve-health/center-for-healthy-aging/content-library/Title-IIID-Highest-Tier-Evidence-FINAL.pdf

Pardasani, M. (2010). Senior centers: Characteristics of participants and nonparticipants. *Activities, Adaptation & Aging, 34*(1), 48–70.

Pardasani, M., & Thompson, P. (2012). Senior centers: Innovative and emerging models. *Journal of Applied Gerontology, 31*(1), 52–77.

Pillemer, K., Fuller-Rowell, T. E., Reid, M. C., & Wells, N. M. (2010). Environmental volunteering and health outcomes over a 20-year period. *The Gerontologist, 50*(5), 594–602.

Rix, S. E. (2011). Boomers sail into retirement—or do they? (In *Public policy & aging report.* Older workers: Problems and prospects in an aging workforce.) *National Academy on an Aging Society, 21*(1), 34–39.

Roberson, D. N., & Merriam, S. B. (2005). The self-directed learning process of older, rural adults. *Adult Education Quarterly, 55*(4), 269–287.

Rothenberg, J. Z., & Gardner, D. S. (2011). Protecting older workers: The failure of the Age Discrimination in Employment Act of 1967. *Journal of Sociology and Social Welfare, 38*(1), 9–30.

Rozanova, J., Keating, N., & Eales, J. (2012). Unequal social engagement for older adults: Constraints on choice. *Canadian Journal on Aging, 31*(1), 25–36. doi:10.1017/S0714980811000675

Sandmann, L. R., & Vandenberg, L. (1995). A framework for 21st century leadership. *Journal of Extension* [Online version], *33*(6), Article 6FEA1. Retrieved December 15, 2013, from http://www.joe.org/joe/1995december/a1.php

Shores, K. A., West, S. T., Theriault, D. S., & Davidson, E. A. (2009). Extraindividual correlates of physical activity attainment in rural older adults. *Journal of Rural Health, 25*(2), 211–218.

Smith, A., & Duggan, M. (2013). *Pew Research Center: Online dating & relationships.* Retrieved from http://pewinternet.org/~/media//Files/Reports/2013/PIP_Online%20Dating%202013.pdf

Social Security Press Release October 15, 2007. *News Release Nation's First Baby Boomer Files for Social Security Retirement Benefits—Online!* Mark Lassiter, Press Officer. Retrieved from: http://www.ssa.gov/pressoffice/pr/baby-boomerfiles-pr.htm

Social Work Leadership Institute (SWLI), Older Adult Service Matrix. (n.d.). *Practicum partnership program (PPP).* Retrieved September 24, 2013, from http://www.hartfordpartnership.org/index.php?/downloads/document/get/D2_Older_Adult_Service_Matrix.pdf

U.S. Bureau of the Census. (2012a). *Growth in urban population outpaces rest of nation, Census Bureau reports.* Retrieved December 15, 2013, from http://www.census.gov/newsroom/releases/archives/2010_census/cb12-50.html

U.S. Bureau of the Census. (2012b). *The 2012 statistical abstract: Resident population by age and state.* Retrieved December 15, 2013, from http://www.census.gov/compendia/statab/cats/population.html

U.S. Department of Agriculture. (2012, December). *Rural America at a glance, 2012 edition* (Economic Brief No. 21). Washington, DC: U.S. Department of Agriculture, Economic Research Service. Retrieved August 27, 2013, from http://www.ers.usda.gov/media/965908/eb-21_single_pages.pdf

U.S. Department of Labor, Employment and Training Administration. (n.d.). *About SCSEP*. Retrieved from http://www.doleta.gov/seniors/html_docs/aboutscsep.cfm

U.S. Environmental Protection Agency, U.S. Department of Housing and Urban Development, and U.S. Department of Transportation. (2011). *Supporting sustainable rural communities*. Retrieved from http://www.epa.gov/dced/pdf/2011_11_supporting-sustainable-rural-communities.pdf

U.S. Equal Employment Opportunity Commission. (n.d.). *Age discrimination in Employment Act: FY 1997–FY 2013*. Retrieved from http://www.eeoc.gov/eeoc/statistics/enforcement/adea.cfm

Wang, D., & Macmillan, T. (2013). The benefits of gardening for older adults: A systematic review of the literature. *Activities, Adaptation & Aging, 37*(2), 153–181.

Wickenheiser, M. (2012, March 26). Census: Maine most rural state in 2010 as urban centers grow nationwide. *Bangor Daily News*. Retrieved from http://bangordailynews.com/2012/03/26/business/census-maine-most-rural-state-in-2010-as-urban-centers-grow-nationwide

Yoon, D. P., & Lee, E. O. (2007). The impact of religiousness, spirituality, and social support on psychological well-being among older adults in rural areas. *Journal of Gerontological Social Work, 48*(3/4), 281–298.

Zickuhr, K. (2010). *Pew Research Center: Internet & American life project: Generations 2010*. Retrieved December 1, 2013, from http://www.pewinternet.org/~/media//Files/Reports/2010/PIP_Generations_and_Tech10.pdf

8

Providing Services to Frail Older Adults in Rural Areas

DENISE GAMMONLEY

KRISTINA M. HASH

LORIANN SONNTAG

Frank and Ida Rogers live in a small home that Frank built in a quiet hollow in Kentucky. Frank is 85 years old and was a "lifer" in the U.S. Army. He worked in the coal mines for 10 years after leaving the army to support his loving wife Ida. Ida is 84 years old and served her country as a member of the Women's Army Corps (WACs) during World War II. She met Frank in 1944 and they married 2 years later. Frank continued his army career, and Ida stood by his side as he completed tours of duty in both Korea and Vietnam. Ida never worked outside the home but has always been actively involved in her faith community and charitable activities. Even now, at her advanced age, she knits blankets for newborns at the nearby critical access hospital (CAH) and remains a leader in her church. Although their marriage has lasted for more than 67 years, Frank and Ida were never able to have children.

Like many veterans coping with combat, Frank used alcohol to dull the nightmares and the images of war in his head. Frank's alcoholism led to many physical complications including cirrhosis of the liver and pulmonary fibrosis, as well as problems in his marriage and work life. A recent diagnosis of diabetes explains his recent significant weight loss and complications with his eyesight. Pain and numbness (neuropathy) in his feet have resulted in an unsteady gait, limiting his ability to walk comfortably for any distance outside the home. Ida has been his primary caregiver up to this point, but there has been a recent change in her as well. She experiences chronic arthritis in her knees and hands, has recently developed hypertension, and has been complaining of frequent fatigue, requiring long naps each afternoon. Neighbors and friends have also reported short-term memory loss, forgetting church meetings, and mistakes in her job as treasurer at the church.

Frank and Ida both require trips to a physician—the closest doctor is more than 60 miles away. Frank and Ida still drive, but neither one is comfortable enough to make the long trip alone. Frank and Ida live mainly on Social Security (SS) and a small pension from his years in the mines. Frank refused to apply for Medicare when he was eligible because he believes that the Veterans Administration (VA) owes him his medical care. This means that all of his care must come through the VA, or it is not covered at all. He is too proud to apply for Medicaid or food stamps, refuses to use the food pantry at the church, and will not allow Ida to accept "charity" from anyone.

In rural communities, couples like Frank and Ida confront numerous challenges surrounding access to the extensive range of services needed to cope with the physical, psychological, and community living consequences of frail health. "Frailty" represents a composite of factors that has been described as a clinical syndrome significantly increasing vulnerability to stress. Fried, Ferrucci, Darer, Williamson, and Anderson (2004), in a widely cited review of this condition, characterized frailty as consisting of the following elements: weight loss and/or fatigue, weakness, balance or gait difficulties, and slow motor performance. Numerous medical conditions as well as cognitive impairment can contribute to frailty. However, cognitive impairment alone is not synonymous with frailty. Long-term care services are often needed for frail older adults like Frank and Ida Rogers, and include services that help individuals meet activities of daily living (ADLs) such as eating, bathing, and toileting, as well as instrumental activities of daily living (IADLs) including bill paying, meal preparation, and medication administration in either a home- or institutional-based setting. Medicaid and Medicare are the primary funders of these services when they are medically necessary (U.S. Department of Health and Human Services [HHS], n.d.-a).

Institutional-based, long-term care options in rural areas include assisted-living residences, small adult family board and care homes, and nursing homes. Assisted-living facilities in rural areas are undersupplied, have fewer professional staff, offer limited privacy, and are more likely to be private pay—reducing their accessibility for low-income rural older adults (Hawes, Phillips, Holan, Sherman, & Hutchinson, 2005). Slightly more than 30% of U.S. nursing homes are located in rural areas; however, concerns about lesser quality, relative to homes in urban centers, are an important limitation of these care settings (Lutifyya, Gessert, & Lipsky, 2013). Community-based, long-term care systems are often fragmented and lack access to specialty care providers within reasonable transportation distances. In many cases, small community health care and other services are disappearing or being acquired by larger organizations that are distant from the local community (Lynch, 2013; Nelson & Gingerich, 2010). This chapter focuses on services for frail older adults within the Older Adult Service Matrix (Social Work Leadership Institute, n.d.), categories of functionally impaired, and end of life. Services available to Frank and Ida for health and behavioral/mental health care—within the realms of acute (short-term) care, long-term care, and end of life—are highlighted.

ACUTE CARE

Hospital Care

An episode of fainting at a church luncheon landed Ida in the closest CAH for a 48-hour period of observation. Frank was unable to travel to the hospital to be with her and remained at home alone. After 1 day, a fellow church member checked in on Frank and provided him with a hot meal. Ida was discharged home with a prescription to treat her newly discovered angina and also received care for a wide gash on her leg resulting from the fainting fall. After talking with Ida and completing a cognitive impairment screening assessment, the hospital discharge planner recognized that Ida was at a high risk for readmission to the hospital. Although her cognitive screening indicated she had mild impairment, adjusting to her new medication, cleaning the wound, and changing the bandages would require Ida to adhere to a new and complex treatment regime.

The discharge planner recommended that she receive some home health and homemaker services for the next couple of weeks so that Ida could keep off her feet to allow the leg to heal. Because Ida was adamant that Frank would not allow any outsider into the home, the discharge planner explored a bit more with Ida about her home life with Frank. She learned that Ida had a couple of close friends from church who would look in on her and that Frank's diabetes and shortness of breath required daily attention by Ida. The discharge planner recognized that Frank's health concerns were also significant and recommended that Ida and Frank discuss the possibility of home visits by the VA during Frank's next scheduled appointment at the VA clinic in 1 month.

Critical Access Hospitals (CAHs) were formed under the Balanced Budget Act of 1997 in response to a trend in the closures of small, rural hospitals. Among other requirements, to be certified as a CAH, hospitals must have no more than 25 beds and be at least 35 miles from the next nearest hospital (Joynt, Orav, & Jha, 2013; HHS, n.d.-b). Joynt and colleagues (2013) found that compared to non-CAHs, the mortality rates in critical access hospitals for several conditions had grown since 2002. The authors suspected that this might be the result of CAHs not being required to participate in federal quality improvement programs. Dellasega and Fisher (2001) followed 70 patients, posthospital discharge, from an urban hospital to a rural home setting and examined their patterns of service usage. Not surprisingly, informal caregivers were relied upon heavily as opposed to formal services. An arrangement bridging both informal and formal support from home health and homemaker services would promote a good transition back to home for Ida (Magilvy & Congdon, 2000).

Ambulance services and emergency care are related to hospital care and access to these for older adults is an important component of the safety net for frail older adults in rural communities. Unfortunately, ambulance services are more limited in rural areas due to travel distances (Shah et al., 2010). Paramedics have been used successfully to help screen and identify at-risk older adults using assessments for fall risk, depression, and infectious diseases (Shah et al., 2006). Among rural older adults, the presence of respiratory or cardiac disease, eligibility for

Medicaid, fair or poor self-rated health, and residing in the U.S. western or southern region have been associated with use of hospital emergency departments (Fan, Shah, Veazie, & Friedman, 2011). Wolinsky and coworkers (2008) noted that, compared to urban older adults, rural older adults were more likely to use emergency departments for reasons that were non–life-threatening. This finding is consistent with the lack of access to adequate preventative or primary care services characteristic of rural communities.

Home Health Care

Rural hospitals often also offer their own home health care services. Home health care can be acute or long term in nature, and is provided in the home of an individual either following a hospital or nursing home/ rehabilitation discharge. The service is also used to help individuals avoid admissions to acute settings by providing skilled nursing care, occupational and physical therapy, medical supplies and equipment, and medical social services. Magilvy and Congdon (2000) noted these arrangements are helpful for rural older adults confronting the crisis of a hospital admission and discharge. However, rural home health agencies are often smaller than their urban counterparts, more likely to be hospital-owned, nonprofit, and offer fewer services. Hartman, Jarosek, Virnig, and Durham (2007) found in their study of Medicare-certified home health care that rural residents are more likely to live in areas of lower utilization. It is unclear whether this can be attributed to not having access to the services. McAuley, Spector, and Van Nostrand (2009) found that rural home care patients received fewer provider days than do their urban counterparts. These features of rural home health services underscore the need for geriatric professionals to engage an array of home-based health care and informal supports to address needs adequately.

LONG-TERM CARE

In-Home and Community-Based Services

After being encouraged by her primary care doctor, Ida agreed to invite a home health care nurse to visit her during the 3 weeks following her hospital admission to help her clean and dress the wound on her shin. The LPN (licensed practical nurse) assigned to care for Ida was an acquaintance of one of Ida's church friends, allowing Ida and Frank to accept this stranger into their home more easily. By the end of the second week of visiting twice per week the LPN had built an easy rapport with Ida; Frank remained distant and uninvolved in their interactions. The LPN knew that Ida only had 1 additional week of her Medicare home health benefit available for this episode of care and was concerned about the home situation once home health services concluded. She convinced Ida to allow her to invite the medical social worker (MSW) to come with her to talk about support services during her next wound-care visit. Because the home health agency program was a part of the CAH where Ida was discharged, the MSW had access to her hospital discharge records and was prepared with some ideas for home- and community-based service referrals when she first met Ida and Frank. When the MSW arrived, introductions were eased by the LPN, who was careful to first introduce Frank and ask him to explain what was most important to their comfort. Unfortunately, Frank's respiratory symptoms were flaring up that day, and he mentioned that he was running low on his medication and not feeling up to the long drive to the VA to take the spirometry test for his refill. This allowed the MSW to mention a new home-based primary care program she knew about through the VA that might be especially helpful for him.

In-home and community-based supportive services help individuals meet ADLs and IADLS. Services are most often provided by unpaid caregivers (often family and friends) but can be offered by paid professionals. In Ida and Frank's case several services may be particularly useful to help maintain independence in their own home for as long as possible, while addressing their fragile health status. Home-delivered meals, telephone reassurance, and friendly visiting programs are familiar services used across urban and rural settings. Community-based information and referral services exist to provide assistance in finding these services and supports for well and frail older adults. These services operate under a variety of auspices, including Area Agencies on Aging (AAAs), and offer information and connection to community- and institutional-based services and programs. A federal program operated at the state and local levels, Aging and Disability Resource Centers (ADRCs) provide information and referral related to aging and disability services for individuals, caregivers, and providers. ADRCs also serve as the "entry point" for services funded by the Older Americans Act (OAA), VA, Medicaid, and other programs and are designed to improve awareness of and access to long-term care services. ADRCs are instrumental in helping individuals and families complete Medicaid applications. In the majority of states, ADRCs provide assistance in transitions from nursing homes to the community. Geographically, the program is available to almost 70% of the United States (HHS, n.d.-c).

A few service models would be of particular benefit to Frank and Ida Rogers, including the Program for All Inclusive Care of the Elderly (PACE). This program offers an interdisciplinary health care approach to providing long-term care services to individuals with Medicare and Medicaid who would qualify for nursing home care and who reside in a PACE service area. The services provided are focused on keeping individuals age 55 and older in the community, as opposed to being institutionalized. Services include primary medical care, dental services, social services, physical and occupational therapy, counseling, adult day care meals, and so forth. PACE also offers model practices for care of persons with various chronic conditions such as diabetes, heart failure, and kidney disease. In addition, the federal PACE has a Rural PACE Assistance Program and has funded rural-specific PACEs.

Home-based primary care (HBPC) services offered by the VA may also assist Frank and Ida and may provide the full continuum of services inclusive of home visits by medical professionals along with home-delivered communication, occupational and physical therapies, mental health services, nutrition counseling, pharmacy services, and personal care. A recent case study adaptation of HBPC in a rural setting linked services with a telehealth intervention, achieving positive patient outcomes in social functioning, patient strength, and reported easing of caregiver burden (Sorocco, Bratkovich, Wingo, Qureshi, & Mason, 2013). In addition, to help Ida succeed in coping with her new medication regime, additional support from a community lay health advisor might also prove beneficial. One randomized trial used community health volunteer educators to teach rural older adults with chronic illnesses about medication safety. Results indicated improved knowledge and safety behaviors among rural older adults receiving this education (Wang, Fetzer, Yang, & Wang, 2013).

Several new innovations in home- and community-based services using technology and alternative delivery strategies have been targeted toward rural communities. Telehealth monitoring devices, for example, can provide more frequent observation of vital signs and perceived health status for fragile rural patients such as Frank. Luptak and colleagues (2010) successfully used an individualized training and support approach to implement a telehealth device project with rural older veterans. This intervention used a simple LCD (liquid crystal display) screen device on which patients answer simple questions about their health along with instruments that measure blood pressure and weight and transmit readings directly to the VA. A care coordinator monitors readings daily using a website, and is alerted to contact the veteran should findings indicate important health concerns. Telehealth also has an important role to play for rural caregivers. Caregiver education using telephone support, videophones, and web-based information and referral systems has been in use for many years. New and more easily accessible interactive technologies will promote increased use (Buckwalter, Davis, Wakefield, Kienzle, & Murray, 2002). However, geriatric practitioners must be careful to assess the technology resources and capabilities of rural older adults to promote effective use. Ida and Frank, as members of the oldest older cohort, might be expected to make more use of technologies that have been available in their homes for many years than of newer technologies (Calvert, Kaye, Leahy, Hexem, & Carlson, 2009).

As another area of innovation, advances in technologies to monitor the home environment have been proposed as one strategy to provide support for frail older adults in rural communities but may be cost prohibitive in poor communities. Behr, Sciegaj, Walters, Bertoty, and Dungan (2011) cluster home technologies into three categories: (a) environmental safety, (b) health and wellness of the individual, and (c) technologies to promote community social connectedness. Homes can be retrofitted with contact and motion sensors to track movement, falls, and use of appliances and medical devices, and wireless communication products to allow visual and telephone communication with family members, informal, and formal care providers. However, the reliability and complexity of these systems have been problematic in some studies introducing these products to older adults (Charness, 2014). Not all devices are suitable for older adults with cognitive impairments and may have other limitations as well. Some versions of panic buttons, often worn as a pendant around the neck, for example, are of limited use when an older adult is unconscious after a fall or otherwise unable to push a button. Newer innovations, such as the pressure-contact sensors described by Behr et al. (2011), avoid this problem by inserting sensors into furniture or flooring. Technological advances will continue and the future of home care for frail and cognitively impaired older adults may include assistive robots and systems guided by artificial intelligence (Bakola et al., 2014; Wu et al., 2014). These innovations will require geriatric health care professionals to establish assessment tools to match older adults' technology preferences and abilities with the appropriate devices, and translational research to determine the most appropriate methods to deploy them.

> Ida's leg healed nicely and, although she still had some mobility problems making it difficult for her to walk long distances, she gradually returned to her usual routine of twice-weekly outings to church activities. Ida had always enjoyed her role as a homemaker and resumed her caregiving role for Frank once her leg wound healed. At times she was too tired to make the homemade meals she once had and relied on frozen foods to feed them. She was adjusting to her new medication well, but others continued to notice her forgetfulness. Frank had not been very social throughout his life and preferred to remain at home most of the time except for occasional trips to the closest convenience store to purchase beer.
>
> Over the next 6 months Frank's pulmonary fibrosis symptoms worsened, and he was diagnosed with advanced COPD (chronic obstructive pulmonary disease). This further restricted his ability to move about the home. The VA home-based primary care team developed a care plan that included providing a respiratory therapist to visit Frank at home to provide pulmonary rehabilitation once per week. In between, Frank relied upon oxygen at times, making him mostly homebound by the end of that year. One day, upon returning home from church, Ida discovered Frank sprawled out on the floor turning blue. She quickly called for the EMS (emergency medical service) to come to the house. The paramedics attempted to resuscitate Frank while he was being transported to the CAH, where he was pronounced deceased.

Behavioral Health and Dementia Care

Now approaching her 86th year, Ida's health had taken a turn for the worse recently with the development of serious knee and ankle pain from chronic rheumatoid arthritis and the development of hypertension. Ida was no longer driving after dark and would only venture to the nearest grocery store (a 20-mile drive) or to church. Even her church attendance had declined, especially since she had given up her role as coordinator of the infant blanket project, feeling too fatigued to pursue it after Frank's death.

Accepting Frank's death was quite difficult for Ida emotionally. Receiving grief counseling from her pastor helped Ida through some of the difficulties. Nearly 1 year after Frank died, the pastor became concerned with Ida's persistent depression and asked a member of his congregation who was serving as the faith community nurse to check on Ida and see if she needed more attention to mental health care. The faith community nurse was the daughter of an old friend of Ida's who had passed away. Ida was very happy to invite her into her home. The nurse noticed immediately that Ida's home had many hazards and was in need of many repairs—gutters in disrepair, frayed throw rugs in many rooms, inadequate lighting, and furniture items in need of fixing. Ida enjoyed reminiscing with the nurse and admitted that since Frank's death she was feeling isolated and sometimes afraid to be alone at night, unable to sleep, and restless. Ida described these feelings as her "nerves." The nurse noticed too that Ida seemed to respond slowly to some of her questions and provided vague answers to questions about what she had eaten recently, whom she had talked with on the phone, and what medicines she had taken that morning. Ida reluctantly agreed to answer a few screening questions about her depression symptoms and memory, after the nurse reassured Ida she was not "crazy" for sharing her concerns.

Numerous barriers to accessing behavioral health services exist for rural older adults. Sanders, Fitzgerald, and Bratteli (2008) found that some of the barriers included factors related to the older adults themselves. Barriers include the older adults' attitudes toward and stigma about receiving services, cognitive challenges to detecting a mental health problem, physical limitations preventing access to providers, and older adults' lack of knowledge about available services. Professionals' lack of knowledge about older adults and aging or mental health issues is another significant barrier. The lack of family involvement or acknowledgment of a mental health problem, as well as the scarcity of services nearby and transportation to services were also mentioned as significant barriers.

Rural residents of all ages may be more likely to receive psychopharmacology and less likely to receive psychotherapy for depression. Disparity in using psychotherapy is associated with availability of mental health specialists (Fortney, Harman, Xu, & Dong, 2009). Probst, Laditka, Moore, Herun, and Powell (2005) also found higher prevalence of depression among adult rural residents. Hayslip, Maiden, Thomison, and Temple (2010) found in their comparison between rural and urban older adults that rural older adults held less favorable attitudes toward and were less likely to seek mental health services. In addition, they had a lesser understanding of psychological symptoms and problems. In his review of the literature on rural suicide, Hirsch (2006) found that rural areas often have higher suicide rates. Specific risk factors in these areas include "cultural ideals, geographic and interpersonal isolation, and economic and sociopolitical distress" (p. 191).

Despite these challenges, several promising models of behavioral health care have been created or tailored to serve rural communities. Outreach programs to heighten community awareness of behavioral health and addiction issues include the Mental Healthiness Aging Initiative, which formed a partnership with rural home extension agents in Kentucky to educate the community about geriatric mental health using personal engagement and social marketing (Zanjani, Kruger, & Murray, 2012). Establishing consortia in rural communities is an important strategy to meet the diverse mental health and substance abuse needs of rural older adults who are also physically frail. Four County Mental Health Center in Kansas achieved increased service use among older adults through this effort along with reductions in serious symptoms of depression and anxiety (Geriatric Mental Health Foundation, 2011).

Gatekeeper programs that utilize first responders, bankers, postal employees, hairdressers and other laypersons to recognize and refer older adults in need of behavioral health assessment have been utilized for many years (Bartsch, Rodgers, & Strong, 2013; Buckwalter, Smith, Zevenbergen, & Russell, 1991). Rural older adults have endorsed gatekeepers as a valid source to help facilitate their access to behavioral health services but express a preference for seeking behavioral health care services through their primary care provider (Andren Kitchen et al., 2013).

Telemental health services using videoconferencing, web-based, and mobile services have emerged as a promising practice to address lack of access to specialty psychiatric care in rural communities. In a review of published studies, Hilty and colleagues (2013) suggested research evidence supports the benefits of telemental health for accurate assessment and diagnosis and applicability across a range of home and provider office settings. Martin-Khan and coworkers (2012) found diagnoses of dementia obtained through videoconferencing equally reliable as those obtained through face-to-face procedures in a memory disorder clinic. Holden and Dew (2008) found patients and family members satisfied with telemental health services provided through a geropsychiatry inpatient unit in a rural community.

One service model that might be particularly helpful for a frail older adult such as Ida could be Alabama's Project to Enhance Aged Rural Living (PEARL), which delivers home-based cognitive behavioral treatment in 16 sessions to 20 sessions using social worker providers (Kaufman, Scogin, Burgio, Morthland, & Ford, 2007). A randomized trial of this approach achieved reductions in depressive symptoms (Scogin, Moss, Harris, & Presnell, 2013) and improved quality of life (QOL) for participants receiving the cognitive behavioral therapy compared to rural older adults in the minimal support control condition (Scogin et al., 2007).

Ida's nurse friend from the church helped to arrange medical transportation for Ida to make more regular visits to her internist, and provided a personal emergency response system she could attach to her wristwatch. Internist Dr. Small, who had known Ida for many years, was pleased concerning her cardiac status but had some concerns about her cognitive status, which seemed to be at the mild to moderate level of cognitive impairment. During her visit with Dr. Small, Ida insisted that her memory was fine but admitted that she was very nervous and anxious most days. Dr. Small prescribed a benzodiazepine, lorazepam, for Ida to use only occasionally when her nerves were acting up. He encouraged Ida to continue checking in with her nurse friend from church as well.

Thanks to a new countywide initiative, a multipurpose community center in the next small town over from Ida's small crossroads area was establishing some new older adult programming. This was part of a new effort to create shared community spaces (Grandparents United, www.gu.org/OURWORK/SharedSpaces.aspx), where generations could come together for some joint activities while also providing space for older adult-specific social activities and health supports. Thanks to a grant from a local foundation, a new bus was purchased allowing older adults from outlying areas to access the center. With encouragement from her nurse friend, Ida began visiting the center on a weekly basis. She often did not feel up to attending the exercise class but did enjoy having coffee, visiting with the other participants, and especially enjoyed interacting with the young children who came in to work in the community garden.

Having this time together each week was helpful for Ida, as was having easier transportation access. Unfortunately, Ida still experienced periods of anxiety and depression made worse by the chronic pain from her arthritis. The lorazepam provided by her internist helped Ida to sleep sometimes; however, now she began to forget to take it and her cardiac medications. One cold winter day, 8 months after she began attending the new center, the bus driver noticed that Ida was not sitting out on her front stoop as she usually was waiting to be picked up. The bus driver discovered Ida fallen on the bathroom floor, having taken off her personal alert system earlier that morning to prepare to bathe. Ida was alert but experiencing considerable pain in her right leg. After being evaluated in the hospital, it was determined that Ida had broken her hip. This would require hip replacement surgery, high risk for someone so frail. A long period of rehabilitation would follow and Ida would first require skilled care in a nursing home. The outcome of her rehabilitation would determine if she could ever return home to live independently.

Skilled and Long-Term Residential Care in Assisted-Living and Nursing Homes

Medicare, Medicaid, and other federal programs are the primary payers for long-term care nursing home services, whereas assisted-living residences are funded privately (HHS, n.d.-a). Assisted-living settings in rural communities are not abundant and rural residents, compared to urban residents, have less access to this residential option (Averill, 2012; Hawes et al., 2005; Stevenson & Grabowski, 2010). A particular challenge in identifying the best array of services that promote good outcomes for frail older adults in assisted living is related to the variety of residents served in terms of their physical, psychosocial, and functional abilities and limitations (Freiheit et al., 2011).

CAHs have a role in providing skilled nursing home care in rural communities without an adequate supply of nursing home beds. These hospitals are certified by CMS (Centers for Medicare & Medicaid Services) to provide Medicare "swing beds," which provide Medicare-paid postacute skilled nursing care for qualifying hospital stays in the CAH (Centers for Medicare & Medicaid Services, n.d.).

Bolin, Phillips, and Hawes (2006) looked at a national sample and the differences between nursing home admissions for rural versus urban facilities. A higher percentage of new admissions to rural facilities were non-Medicare payers. These newly admitted residents were also older, had fewer ADL deficits, and were less likely to be transferred from an acute care setting. They were also more likely to have cognitive impairments and related behavior problems. The quality of rural nursing homes has also come into question. Lutfiyya et al. (2013) noted that rural nursing homes were less likely to achieve 4-star or higher quality ratings from the CMS Nursing Home Compare website compared to facilities in urban centers. Kang, Meng, and Miller (2011) noted that rural facilities were more likely to be unaccredited and lack special care units; also, residents of rural facilities were 1.5 times more likely to experience a hospitalization compared to residents in urban nursing homes.

Bowblis, Meng, and Hyer (2013) analyzed national survey inspection data discovering contractures were more common in facilities that were farther away from urban areas. Staffing levels were also lower in these facilities. Rural facilities were also more likely to be government-owned and had fewer residents on Medicare—both factors that have been associated with higher facility-acquired contracture rates. These homes were also smaller and more dependent on Medicaid funding. Another major difference found was that rural facilities had a higher percentage of residents with mental health problems, whereas urban facilities had residents who were more physically dependent. Kang and colleagues (2011) also compared quality between rural and urban facilities. Rural residents were older and more likely to be long-stay, had fewer ADL needs, had more cognitive impairment, had a lower income, and were more likely to have Medicaid. These rural facilities were less likely to have special care programs like dementia care and were less apt to have The Joint Commission (www.jointcommission.org) and other accreditations.

Gessert, Haller, Kane, and Degenholtz's (2006) sample of cognitively impaired nursing home residents in two states also looked at the usage of medical services at the end of life. Although residents in rural nursing homes had more hospital admissions, they were less likely to have "intense" procedures and services, such as feeding tubes, longer stays, and admission to intensive care units.

Ida required a blood transfusion during her hip replacement surgery and an extended period of hospitalization before she was discharged to a skilled nursing facility in the next county over. Her advanced age and frailty made the physical and occupational therapy sessions difficult and recovery was slow. After a couple of months, Ida was able to ambulate short distances with the assistance of a two-wheeled walker; however, returning home was impossible because she was now too frail to negotiate the stairs. Assessments of her cognitive functioning completed as part of her rehabilitation indicated that she was now moving from the mild to moderate level of cognitive impairment. This combination of factors meant that she would need a significant amount of support in her future housing. The nursing home social services director, working with the faith community nurse and pastor, who continued to be interested in Ida, helped locate a grandniece of Ida's in another state and encouraged her to visit. The niece agreed to make regular contact, and Ida enjoyed these brief and infrequent telephone calls. Ida and Frank had a small amount of savings, enough to support Ida in a small family board and care home for at least 1 year. Because her rehabilitation goals had been achieved and her Medicare skilled nursing days were running out, plans were developed to transfer Ida to the board and care home. As part of the screening process, the board and care home required medical clearance. Ida had blood and urine samples drawn because she had a persistent low-grade pain when urinating. Unfortunately, it was discovered that Ida did not have a urinary tract infection but instead had bladder cancer. After the full workup with a CT (computed tomography) scan it was determined that the tumor had spread aggressively and was now in her liver. Sadly, Ida's physician indicated that the condition was terminal and Ida probably had less than 6 months to live. Unfortunately, no formal hospice services were available in the community where the nursing home was located; however, the nursing home staff members did their best to provide a quality end of life for Ida. Ida remained in the nursing home for most of the last 8 months of her life but had two brief hospital admissions during this time for a medical emergency. She received frequent visits from members of her church, which had played such an important role in her life.

END-OF-LIFE CARE

Hospice and Palliative Care

Hospice care involves a team of medical, social service, and other professionals and volunteers who provide palliative care, or care that focuses on pain and symptom relief as opposed to curative treatments. Emotional and spiritual needs are also addressed. To receive hospice services, a physician must certify that a patient is terminally ill. Hospice services are typically provided in the home of a patient but can be delivered in a variety of settings such as skilled nursing facilities and freestanding hospices. Hospice services are offered on an on-call basis 7 days a week, 24 hours a day to persons of all ages, with services being covered by Medicare, Medicaid, and other insurance (National Hospice and Palliative Care Organization, n.d.).

Although both traditional hospice organizations and home health organizations deliver end-of-life care in rural communities, they differ significantly in their admission criteria, the types of specialty services offered, and use of professional versus nonprofessional staff. Differing reimbursement requirements drive many of these distinctions (Waldrop & Kirkendall, 2010). As a result, geriatric practitioners working in both settings must be prepared to address end-of-life care issues with patients and families.

Robinson and coworkers (2009), in a review of the literature, found the area of palliative care in rural areas to be underdeveloped, being few in number and diverse in focus. As a result, the authors found that there is little to offer in terms of informing policy and practice. Virnig, Haijun, Hartman, Moscovice, and Carlin (2006) examined the differences between rural and urban areas in terms of hospice availability. The researchers found a strong correlation between urban area and the availability of Medicare-certified hospice services. Of the zip codes of the most urban areas, 100% (meaning a population of more than 1 million) had hospices available, whereas only 24% of rural areas not adjacent to an urban area had such services. This trend also held true with predominantly rural states having less access to services.

Ida could have benefited from receiving hospice services that have been found to be valued by patients and reduce general health care costs (Candy, Holman, Leurent, Davis, & Jones, 2011). The delivery of specialized hospice services within nursing homes is linked to receiving care for nondementia-related illnesses; more receipt of assistance with eating, drinking, and mouth care (Munn, Hanson, Zimmerman, Sloane, & Mitchell, 2006); reduced hospitalizations during the final month of life (Gozalo & Miller, 2007); and lower Medicare and Medicaid costs (Gozalo, Miller, Intrator, Barber, & Mor, 2008).

Temkin-Greener, Zheng, and Mukamel (2012) looked specifically at rural–urban differences in the delivery of a specialty service, end-of-life care, and in nursing homes finding disparities in access. Rural residents had higher prevalence of in-hospital deaths and were less likely to enroll in and have access to hospice services. Rural facilities also had lower staffing ratios with less skilled staff, more Medicaid patients, and were less likely to be for-profit or part of a large nursing home chain.

Carlson, Bradley, Qingling, and Morrison (2010) found in their analysis of geographic influences on hospice access that factors associated with being 30 minutes or less in driving distance from a hospice agency included (among other factors) areas with higher population density, a lower population of those age 65 or older, and higher median household income. Since the majority of hospice patients receive services in their homes, distance to and from these agencies is a significant factor in terms of access. The authors suggested that since many more hospices have opened and been certified by Medicare since 2000, access may have improved in rural areas. Carlson et al. (2010) stated, "specifically, 30% of the population in the most rural communities was closest to a hospice newly established in 2000 or later and 36% of the population in the most urban communities was closest to a hospice newly established in 2000 or later" (p. 1332). Campbell, Merwin, and Yan (2009) found in their analysis of 3,140 counties that more rural counties were less likely to have a Medicare-certified hospice. Having fewer physicians in rural areas may prevent communities from having such services because a physician is required to certify the service for a patient.

Waldrop and Kirkendall (2010) studied rural and urban differences in end-of-life care provided by home health and hospice in western New York State. Geography was a significant challenge identified by rural agency administrators. Driving long distances, in inclement weather, and having to use secondary or dirt roads to reach patients' homes were mentioned. These challenges often translated in fewer visits possible each day. In their qualitative study of end-of-life care in rural areas from the perspectives of rural patients and their caregivers, Hansen, Cartwright, and Craig (2011) found many benefits that may be unique to receiving palliative care in a rural setting. These benefits include organizational and staff flexibility; patients and caregivers often personally knowing the staff providing care; and having informal support persons such as family, neighbors, and church members to provide additional support. Challenges that were apparent involved a lack of qualified formal caregivers, gaps in the continuity of care, and the limited hours and availability of services.

CONCLUSION

Major unmet service needs and less service use relative to urban older adults (Hutchison, Hawes, & Williams, 2005; Li, 2006; Sun, 2011) among older adults in rural communities persist. Li (2006) analyzed rural barriers from the perspective of caregivers in a representative national sample, identifying lack of access to respite, transportation, and homemaker services as the most noted service shortages. In addition to a lack of available services, lack of awareness about services and lack of income to make use of available services were prominent. Related, Sun (2011) reinforced lack of awareness of services as a driver of service use, and also highlighted the importance of church attendance in determining rural older adults' use of services. In this study of Alabama rural older adults, church attendance interacted with service awareness to help determine the lower rate of service use for rural versus urban older adults. Faith communities remain a core source of support for rural older adults and, given the service barriers described for rural communities, are likely to remain so. Creation of innovative partnerships, such as the faith community nursing approach, between formal home and community-based providers offers one strategy to integrate churches with services provided by rural CAHs. Home visiting programs using professional health care workers, lay health advisors, and gatekeepers have a proven record of supporting frail older adults' preference for aging in place. Adapting these interventions to evolving models of the patient-centered medical home in rural communities should be a priority for rural services researchers.

The emergence of new communications and adaptive technologies also hold promise for meeting growing needs of frail rural older adults in the future. However, the current cohort of frail rural older adults is likely to be more challenged to make use of these technologies. This may be due to a generational digital divide compounded by disparities in income. One study noted that only 17% of homebound older adults age 60 or older made current use of the Internet (Choi & DiNitto, 2013).

Rural residence and poverty go together for many frail older adults. Lifetime cumulative disadvantage is compounded by frailty and functional impairments. Addressing disparities in home and community support services received by frail older adults who are eligible for both Medicare and Medicaid will be important to promote QOL and to also address health care costs associated with caring for our growing population of frail rural older adults.

As noted by Hutchinson et al. (2005), Objectives 1 to 15 of *Healthy People 2010* call to increase access for individuals to the continuum of long-term care services. Rural residents are older, poorer, and less healthy and have more restricted access to services, creating specific challenges for achieving the aims of population health. In addition to the model programs described within this chapter, numerous efforts are under way to evaluate the benefits and limitations of these approaches. There are several national organizations (listed in the following useful websites) that provide information on best practices, model programs, and policies related to frail older adults and other rural residents with chronic health and mental health conditions. Geriatric health professionals and agencies serving frail rural older adults should critically assess the evidence base to support efficacy and effectiveness of these interventions, their applicability and adaptability to different rural contexts, and their consistency with the values and preferences of rural older adults in their communities.

USEFUL WEBSITES

Aging and Disability Resource Centers
acl.gov/Programs/CDAP/OIP/ADRC/index.aspx
American Hospital Association–Rural Health Care
www.aha.org/advocacy-issues/rural/index.shtml
American Psychological Association–Rural Health
www.apa.org/practice/programs/rural/index.aspx
Department of Health and Human Resources–Eldercare Locator
www.eldercare.gov/Eldercare.NET/Public/Index.aspx
Health IT.gov–Rural Health Resources
www.healthit.gov/ruralhealth
HRSA Office of Rural Health Policy
www.hrsa.gov/ruralhealth

National Association for Rural Mental Health
www.narmh.org
National Association of Rural Health Clinics
narhc.org
National Council on Aging
www.ncoa.org
National Hospice and Palliative Care Organization–Caring Connections
www.caringinfo.org
National PACE Association
www.npaonline.org
USDA Rural Information Center
www.nal.usda.gov
Veterans Administration Office of Rural Health
www.ruralhealth.va.gov

REFERENCES

Andren Kitchen, K. A., McKibbin, C. L., Wykes, T. L., Lee, A. A., Carrico, C. P., & Bourassa, K. A. (2013). Depression treatment among rural older adults: Preferences and factors influencing future service use. *Clinical Gerontologist, 36*(3), 241–259.

Averill, J. B. (2012). Priorities for action in a rural older adults study. *Family & Community Health, 35*(4), 358.

Bakola, I., Bellos, C., Tripoliti, E. E., Bibas, A., Koutsouris, D., & Fotiadis, D. I. (2014, January). An adaptive home environment supporting people with balance disorders. In *XIII Mediterranean Conference on Medical and Biological Engineering and Computing 2013* (pp. 1213–1216). Cham, Switzerland: Springer International Publishing Company. Retrieved from http://link.springer.com/chapter/10.1007/978-3-319-00846-2_300#page-1

Bartsch, D. A., Rodgers, V. K., & Strong, D. (2013). Outcomes of senior reach gatekeeper referrals: Comparison of the Spokane gatekeeper program, Colorado senior reach, and mid-Kansas senior outreach. *Care Management Journals, 14*(1), 11–20.

Behr, R., Sciegaj, M., Walters, R., Bertoty, J., & Dungan, R. (2011). Addressing the housing challenges of an aging population: Initiatives by Blueroof Technologies in McKeesport, Pennsylvania. *Journal of Architectural Engineering, 17*(4), 162–169.

Bolin, J., Phillips, C. D., & Hawes, C. (2006). Differences between newly admitted nursing home residents in rural and nonrural areas in a national sample. *The Gerontologist, 46*(1), 33–41.

Bowblis, J. R., Meng, H., & Hyer, K. (2013). The urban-rural disparity in nursing home quality indicators: The case of facility-acquired contractures. *Health Services Research, 48*(1), 47–69.

Buckwalter, K. C., Davis, L. L., Wakefield, B. J., Kienzle, M. G., & Murray, M. A. (2002). Telehealth for elders and their caregivers in rural communities. *Family Community Health, 25*(3), 31–40.

Buckwalter, K. C., Smith, M., Zevenbergen, P., & Russell, D. (1991). Mental health services of the rural elderly outreach program. *The Gerontologist, 31*(3), 408–412.

Calvert, J. F., Kaye, J., Leahy, M., Hexem, K., & Carlson, N. (2009). Technology use by rural and urban oldest old. *Technology and Healthcare, 17(1)*, 1–11.

Campbell, C. L., Merwin, E., & Yan, G. (2009). Factors that influence the presence of a hospice in a rural community. *Journal of Nursing Scholarship, 41*(4), 420–428.

Candy, B., Holman, A., Leurent, B., Davis, S., & Jones, L. (2011). Hospice care delivered at home, in nursing homes and in dedicated hospice facilities: A systematic review of quantitative and qualitative evidence. *International Journal of Nursing Studies, 48*(1), 121–133.

Carlson, M. A., Bradley, E. H., Qingling, D., & Morrison, R. S. (2010). Geographic access to hospice in the United States. *Journal of Palliative Medicine, 13*(11), 1331–1338.

Centers for Medicare & Medicaid Services. (n.d.). Your Medicare coverage: Skilled nursing facility (SNF) care. Retrieved from http://www.medicare. gov/coverage/skilled-nursing-facility-care.html

Charness, N. (2014). Utilizing technology to improve older adult health. *Occupational Therapy in Healthcare, 28*(1), 21–30.

Choi, N. G., & DiNitto, D. M. (2013). The digital divide among low-income homebound older adults: Internet use patterns, ehealth literacy, and attitudes toward computer/internet use. *Journal of Medical Internet Research, 15*(5), e93.

Dellasega, C. A., & Fisher, K. M. (2001). Posthospital home care for frail older adults in rural locations. *Journal of Community Health Nursing, 18*(4), 247–260.

Fan, L., Shah, M. N., Veazie, P. J., & Friedman, B. (2011). Factors associated with emergency department use among the rural elderly. *The Journal of Rural Health, 27*(1), 39–49.

Fortney, J. C., Harman, J. S., Xu, S., & Dong, F. (2009). *Rural-urban difference in depression care.* Boulder, CO: The Western Interstate Commission for Higher Education Mental Health Program Center for Rural Mental Health Research.

Freiheit, E., Hogan, D., Strain, L., Schmaltz, H., Patten, S., Eliasziw, M., & Maxwell, C. (2011). Operationalizing frailty among older residents of assisted living facilities. *BMC Geriatrics, 11*(1), 23. doi:10.1186/1471-2318-11-23

Fried, L. P., Ferrucci, L., Darer, J., Williamson, J. D., & Anderson, G. (2004). Untangling the concepts of disability, frailty, and comorbidity: Implications for improved targeting and care. *Journals of Gerontology Series A: Biological Sciences & Medical Sciences, 59A*(3), 255–263.

Geriatric Mental Health Foundation. (2011). *Home-based mental health services for older adults: A preliminary report from an invitational conference October 2011.* Retrieved December 1, 2013, from http://www.gmhfonline.org/gmhf/prog_HMBasedConfRep.pdf

Gessert, C. E., Haller, I. V., Kane, R. L., & Degenholtz, H. (2006). Rural–urban differences in medical care for nursing home residents with severe dementia at the end of life. *Journal of the American Geriatrics Society, 54*(8), 1199–1205.

Gozalo, P. L., & Miller, S. C. (2007). Hospice enrollment and evaluation of its causal effect on hospitalization of dying nursing home patients. *Health Services Research, 42*(2), 587–610.

Gozalo, P. L., Miller, S. C., Intrator, O., Barber, J. P., & Mor, V. (2008). Hospice effect on government expenditures among nursing home residents. *Health Services Research, 43*(1), 134–153.

Hansen, L., Cartwright, J., & Craig, C. (2011). End-of-life care for rural-dwelling older adults and their primary family caregivers. *Research in Gerontological Nursing, 5*(1), 6–15.

Hartman, L., Jarosek, S., Virnig, B., & Durham, S. (2007). Medicare-certified home health care: Urban-rural differences in utilization. *Journal of Rural Health, 23*(3), 254–257.

Hawes, C., Phillips, C. D., Holan, S., Sherman M., and Hutchinson, L. (2005). Assisted living in rural America: Results from a national study. *Journal of Rural Health, 21*(2), 131–139.

Hayslip, B., Maiden, R. J., Thomison, N. L., & Temple, J. R. (2010). Mental health attitudes among rural and urban older adults. *Clinical Gerontologist, 33*(4), 316–331.

Hilty, D. M., Ferrer, D. C., Parish, M. B., Johnston, B., Callahan, E. J., & Yellowlees, P. M. (2013). The effectiveness of telemental health: A 2013 review. *Telemedicine and e-Health, 19*(6), 444–454.

Hirsch, J. K. (2006). A review of the literature on rural suicide: Risk and protective factors, incidence, and prevention. *Crisis, 27*(4), 189–199.

Holden, D., & Dew, E. (2008). Telemedicine in a rural gero-psychiatric inpatient unit: Comparison of perception/satisfaction to onsite psychiatric care. *Telemedicine and e-Health, 14*(4), 381–384.

Hutchison, L., Hawes, C., & Williams, L. M. (2005). Access to quality health service in rural areas—long-term care: A literature review. In L. Gamm & L. Hutchison (Eds.), *Rural healthy people 2010: A companion document to healthy people 2010* (pp. 1–28). College Station, TX: The Texas A&M University System Health Science Center, School of Rural Public Health, Southwest Rural Health Research Center.

Joynt, K. E., Orav, E., & Jha, A. K. (2013). Mortality rates for Medicare beneficiaries admitted to critical access and non-critical access hospitals, 2002–2010. *JAMA: Journal of the American Medical Association, 309*(13), 1379–1387.

Kang, Y., Meng, H., & Miller, N. A. (2011). Rurality and nursing home quality: Evidence from the 2004 National Nursing Home Survey. *The Gerontologist, 51*(6), 761–773.

Kaufman, A. V., Scogin, F. R., Burgio, L. D., Morthland, M. P., & Ford, B. K. (2007). Providing mental health services to older people living in rural communities. *Journal of Gerontological Social Work, 48*(3/4), 349–365.

Li, H. (2006). Rural older adults' access barriers to in-home and community-based services. *Social Work Research, 30*(2), 109–118.

Luptak, M., Dailey, N., Juretic, M., Rupper, R., Hill, R. D., Hicken, B. L., & Bair, B. D. (2010). The care coordination home telehealth (CCHT) rural demonstration project: A symptom-based approach for serving older veterans in remote geographical settings. *Rural and Remote Health, 10*(2), 1375. Retrieved from http://www.rrh.org.au

Lutfiyya, M. N., Gessert, C. E., & Lipsky, M. S. (2013). Nursing home quality: A comparative analysis using CMS nursing home compare data to examine differences between rural and nonrural facilities. *Journal of the American Medical Directors Association, 14*(8), 593–598.

Lynch, S. (2013). Hospice and palliative care access issues in rural areas. *American Journal of Hospice and Palliative Medicine, 30*(2), 172–177.

Magilvy, J. K., & Congdon, J. G. (2000). The crisis nature of health care transitions for rural older adults. *Public Health Nursing, 17*(5), 336–345.

Martin-Khan, M., Flicker, L., Wootton, R., Loh, P. K., Edwards, H., Varghese, P., . . . Gray, L. C. (2012). The diagnostic accuracy of telegeriatrics for the diagnosis of dementia via video conferencing. *Journal of the American Medical Directors Association, 13*(5), 487.e19–487.e24.

McAuley, W. J., Spector, W., & Van Nostrand, J. (2009). Formal home care utilization patterns by rural-urban community residence. *Journals of Gerontology: Series B: Psychological Sciences and Social Sciences, 64B*(2), 258–268.

Munn, J. C., Hanson, L. C., Zimmerman, S., Sloane, P. D., & Mitchell, C. M. (2006). Is hospice associated with improved end-of-life care in nursing homes and assisted living facilities? *Journal of the American Geriatrics Society, 54*(3), 490–495.

National Hospice and Palliative Care Association. (n.d.). What is hospice? Retrieved November 20, 2013, from http://www.nhpco.org/about/hospice-care

Nelson, J. A., & Gingerich, B. S. (2010). Rural health: Access to care and services. *Home Health Care Management & Practice, 22*(5), 339–343.

Probst, J. C., Laditka, S., Moore, C. G., Harun, N., & Powell, M. P. (2005). *Depression in rural populations: Prevalence, effects on life quality, and treatment-seeking behavior.* Lexington: South Carolina Rural Health Research Center, University of South Carolina.

Robinson, C. A., Pesut, B., Bottorff, J. L., Mowry, A., Broughton, S., & Fyles, G. (2009). Rural palliative care: A comprehensive review. *Journal of Palliative Medicine, 12*(3), 253–258.

Sanders, G. F., Fitzgerald, M. A., & Bratteli, M. (2008). Mental health services for older adults in rural areas: An ecological systems approach. *Journal of Applied Gerontology, 27*(3), 252–266.

Scogin, F., Morthland, M., Kaufman, A., Burgio, L., Chaplin, W., & Kong, G. (2007). Improving quality of life in diverse rural older adults: A randomized trial of a psychological treatment. *Psychology and Aging, 22*(4), 657–665.

Scogin, F. R., Moss, K., Harris, G. M., & Presnell, A. H. (2013). Treatment of depressive symptoms in diverse, rural, and vulnerable older adults. *International Journal of Geriatric Psychiatry.* Advance online publication. doi:10.1002/gps.4009

Shah, M. N., Caprio, T. V., Swanson, P., Rajasekaran, K., Ellison, J. H., Smith, K., . . . Katz, P. (2010). A novel emergency medical services–based program to identify and assist older adults in a rural community. *Journal of the American Geriatrics Society, 58*(11), 2205–2211.

Shah, M. N., Clarkson, L., Lerner, E. B., Fairbanks, R. J., McCann, R., & Schneider, S. M. (2006). An emergency medical services program to promote the health of older adults. *Journal of the American Geriatrics Society, 54*(6), 956–962.

Social Work Leadership Institute (SWLI), Older Adult Service Matrix. (n.d.). *Practicum partnership program (PPP).* Retrieved September 24, 2013, from http://www.hartfordpartnership.org/index.php?/downloads/document/get/D2_Older_Adult_Service_Matrix.pdf

Sorocco, K. H., Bratkovich, K. L., Wingo, R., Qureshi, S. M., & Mason, P. J. (2013). Integrating care coordination home telehealth and home based primary care in rural Oklahoma: A pilot study. *Psychological Services, 10*(3), 350–352.

Stevenson, D. G., & Grabowski, D. C. (2010). Sizing up the market for assisted living. *Health Affairs, 29*(1), 35–43.

Sun, F. (2011). Community service use by older adults: The roles of sociocultural factors in rural–urban differences. *Journal of Social Service Research, 37*(2), 124–135.

Temkin-Greener, H., Zheng, N., & Mukamel, D. B. (2012). Rural–urban differences in end-of-life nursing home care: Facility and environmental factors. *The Gerontologist, 52*(3), 335–344.

U.S. Department of Health and Human Services. (n.d.-a). What is long-term care? Retrieved November 20, 2013, from http://longtermcare.gov/the-basics/what-is-long-term-care/

U.S. Department of Health and Human Services. (n.d.-b). What are critical access hospitals (CAHs)? Retrieved November 20, 2013, from http://www.hrsa.gov/healthit/toolbox/RuralHealthITtoolbox/Introduction/critical.html

U.S. Department of Health and Human Services. (n.d.-c). Aging and disability resource centers. Retrieved November 20, 2013, from http://acl.gov/NewsRoom/Publications/docs/ADRC_Factsheet.pdf

Virnig, B. A., Haijun, M., Hartman, L. K., Moscovice, I., & Carlin, B. (2006). Access to home-based hospice care for rural populations: Identification of areas lacking service. *Journal of Palliative Medicine, 9*(6), 1292–1299.

Waldrop, D., & Kirkendall, A. M. (2010). Rural-urban differences in end-of-life care: Implications for practice. *Social Work in Health Care, 49*(3), 263–289.

Wang, C. J., Fetzer, S. J., Yang, Y. C., & Wang, J. J. (2013). The impacts of using community health volunteers to coach medication safety behaviors among rural elders with chronic illnesses. *Geriatric Nursing, 34*(2), 138–145.

Wolinsky, F. D., Liu, L., Miller, T. R., An, H., Geweke, J. F., Kaskie, B., . . . Wallace, R. B. (2008). Emergency department utilization patterns among older adults. *The Journals of Gerontology: Series A: Biological Sciences and Medical Sciences, 63A*(2), 204–209.

Wu, Y. H., Cristancho-Lacroix, V., Fassert, C., Faucounau, V., de Rotrou, J., & Rigaud, A. S. (2014). The attitudes and perceptions of older adults with mild cognitive impairment toward an assistive robot. *Journal of Applied Gerontology.* Advance online publication. doi:10.1177/0733464813515092

Zanjani, F., Kruger, T., & Murray, D. (2012). Evaluation of the mental healthiness aging initiative: Community program to promote awareness about mental health and aging issues. *Community Mental Health Journal, 48*(2), 193–201.

IV

Competent Practice in Rural Areas

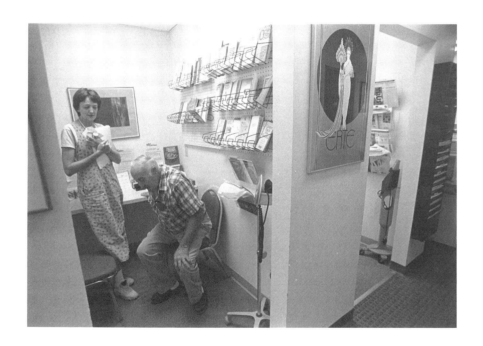

9

Interdisciplinary Teams Caring for Rural Older Adults

JANICE ELICH MONROE

After a series of falls, Anders Davies's primary care physician has requested in-home services from a local home health agency. As part of an initial assessment, a social worker is assigned to meet with Mr. Davies. The purpose of this assessment is to identify Mr. Davies's physical, social, and psychological strengths and needs. As needs are identified, available services in the community will be arranged to help meet these requirements.

Initial Assessment

Mr. Davies is an older White man who resides in a one-story house in a rural town outside the city of Ithaca, New York. He is currently 78 years old and has lived in the same town for most of his life. He has a high school education, and has worked throughout his life at a number of skilled labor jobs including masonry, lumberjacking, and blacksmithing. Mr. Davies speaks very proudly of his past working career and of his accomplishments.

The client struggles with a number of chronic medical conditions, including type 2 diabetes, coronary artery disease

(CAD), hypertension (HTN), and arthritis. He was hospitalized in the 1990s with intestinal surgery; recuperation included a 3-month stay in a nursing home. Over the past several months, Mr. Davies has been experiencing repeated falls that he blames on his "clumsiness."

Overall, Mr. Davies seems content and relatively outgoing. He was married for more than 40 years; his wife died approximately 2 years ago. He often speaks about how he misses her and feels quite lonely without her companionship. He lives alone; however, his neighbor Mildred, a 73-year-old woman, visits him at least three times per week to socialize and sometimes to have lunch. Occasionally, Mildred will drive Mr. Davies to the store to buy groceries and medications, if he is unable or not interested in driving. His hobbies include woodworking, which has decreased significantly since his arthritis has gotten worse, and writing poetry, which takes up much of some of his free time, but he has difficulty holding writing instruments.

He has a son, Jim, who works in construction and lives about 2 hours away from Mr. Davies. Jim is not married and has no children. Mr. Davies states that he sees his son every couple of weeks, but that he phones him at least twice a week.

Mr. Davies manages to take care of himself in regard to most activities of daily living (ADLs) and instrumental activities of daily living (IADLs), although he does have Meals on Wheels deliver lunch to him each day. He describes how proud he is to be able to cook his breakfast each morning. He mentions how he would like to go out of the house more often, but doesn't feel comfortable driving long distances. He did not seem concerned about falling, although there is a series of stairs and uneven surfaces that the client must maneuver to get to the sleeping, toileting, and laundry areas.

The client is currently managing six different prescription drugs. He says he occasionally forgets to take all of them, but that he probably doesn't need them all anyway. He also commented on the costs of these medications ($600 per month), which are not covered by insurance. Financially, the client lives on a small pension and Social Security (SS) benefit totaling about $16,000 per year. He receives health benefits from Medicare (HMO [health maintenance organization]/managed care plan). Mr. Davies continues to handle the finances and pays all of the monthly bills.

Mr. Davies and others with similar conditions and problems can often benefit from integrated care and services from a team of professionals. The role of interdisciplinary teams in the provision of health care service has been a topic of discussion for many years. One of the culminating results of this discussion is a series of recommendations delineated in a report, *Recreating Health Care Practice for the 21st Century* (O'Neil & the Pew Health Professions Commission, 1998). This report suggested that the provision of health care services has not kept up with the shifting landscape of health care in the 21st century. Recommendation three of this report suggested that interdisciplinary competence in all health professionals be required. The recommendation specifically states,

> Today's best-integrated health delivery systems are evolving toward a model of care in which interdisciplinary teams of providers manage the care of the sickest patients. This model, which involves physicians, nurses, and allied professionals, is proving its worth with both acutely and chronically ill patients. Resources are used in the most timely and efficient way; mistakes or duplication of services is avoided; and the expertise and instincts of a number of trained health practitioners are brought to bear in an environment that values brainstorming, consultation, and collaboration. This is not a value that has been inculcated in health professional training programs of the past. Medical and professional schools should fundamentally reassess their curricula to ensure that their programs embody and apply an interdisciplinary vision. (O'Neil & the Pew Health Professions Commission, 1998, p. iii)

There is, however, much confusion as to what interdisciplinary teamwork and collaboration means and how it is practiced most effectively in the health professions. The Committee on Quality of Health Care in America, Institute of Medicine (2001) issued a report, *Crossing the Quality Chasm: A New Health System for the 21st Century,* in which they discussed the importance of collaboration among health care team members. They noted, however, that collaboration is often found to be uncoordinated or sequential action rather than team members working together toward a common goal. This confusion is due in part to the education that health care professionals receive. Typically, each professional group is well trained in the principles and practices of its particular profession. It is, however, uncommon for educational institutions to provide adequate training in interdisciplinary collaboration or teamwork. As a result of utilizing the multidisciplinary approach to professional preparation, many professionals function in professional silos with little or no understanding of the practices of their team members. This lack of knowledge and collaborative effort often lead to duplication of services and profession-centered rather than client-centered provision of services.

The literature strongly supports the use of an interdisciplinary or a collaborative approach to the delivery of health care services to older adults (Interprofessional Education Collaborative Expert Panel, 2011). It is therefore important to understand the various collaborative approaches and to learn to apply them to specific environments that provide services to older adults in rural settings. This chapter provides an overview of the various models of interdisciplinary team collaboration and interprofessional education. In addition, it offers models of recruitment, training, and other considerations in rural, interdisciplinary practice. Further, Chapters 10 and 11 detail the specific roles of medical and human service professionals.

MODELS OF TEAMWORK

As noted in the previous section, there is significant confusion as to what the term interdisciplinary collaboration means. Often the words multidisciplinary, interdisciplinary, transdisciplinary, and interprofessional collaboration are used interchangeably. This leads to much confusion and misrepresentation of the knowledge skills and abilities that are requested for each type of service provision. This approach results in uncoordinated interventions that are often focused on the profession rather than coordinated, client-centered treatment. The following sections provide definitions of the various approaches to collaboration.

Multidisciplinary Team Approach

In the traditional model of collaboration, the multidisciplinary team approach (sometimes referred to as unidisciplinary), each professional works independently from other health care professionals. In this model, a client could be seen by a variety of health care professionals who independently complete assessments and develop treatment goals and interventions. For example, Mr. Davies would be seen and assessed by a physician, a nurse, a social worker, and occupational, physical, recreational, and speech therapists. In this model, a client could be asked the same demographic questions seven times. Due to the overlap in some allied health professionals' scope of practice, they may even be administering the same assessments. In the worst scenario, the client may be receiving interventions that have counter indications, due to the lack of communication among the health care professionals. It is clear from this example that the multidisciplinary approach often causes redundancy in the provision of services and is therefore not cost effective. More importantly, this approach is not client-centered (the client is not an active member of the team) and may therefore not be providing the best mix of rehabilitative services. Clients may feel overwhelmed by the mix of services they are receiving and may not understand how these services work together to benefit their quality of life (QOL). Communication among disciplines in the multidisciplinary team approach is limited to team meetings during which each discipline reports on individual goals, interventions, and client progress. The lack of frequent communication among team members can present problems in the effective and efficient provision of services to older adults who often have complex medical conditions that need reevaluation frequently.

Interdisciplinary Team Approach

The interdisciplinary team approach is client-centered. As with the multidisciplinary approach, the client may be seen by many health care providers. The difference between these approaches is that the outcome of interdisciplinary teams is the development of an integrated plan of services. Team members openly communicate about the problems and strengths of the clients, coordinate and share the results of their assessment data, and involve the clients and members of their families in treatment plan discussions.

In the interdisciplinary approach, there is less redundancy of services, and because the clients are involved in the planning process they tend to be less confused and at times more actively involved in the treatment process. Freshman, Rubino, and Chassiakos (2010) contended that with increasing health care costs, decreasing funding streams, and with many agencies competing for scarce dollars, it is imperative to utilize collaborative techniques and to avoid the silo approach to the provision of services. In addition, team members are more likely to understand the roles of their colleagues and are able to reinforce interdisciplinary treatment goals and/or strategies in their own work. For example, a physical therapist (PT) may recommend that Mr. Davies use a mobility device such as a walker to decrease his chance of falls. The rest of the interdisciplinary team members would encourage Mr. Davies to use the walker during their contact with him. This is a holistic, client-centered approach to service provision.

Another benefit of this approach is that it provides opportunities for co-treatments. Co-treatments are typically utilized in inpatient settings in which two therapists work with a client or client group on a specific goal(s) utilizing an activity/intervention that enables each therapist to meet a specific goal(s). For example, goals for Mr. Davies might include to increase independence in ADLs and to reduce social isolation. To address these problem areas, an occupational therapist (OT) and recreational therapist (RT) could plan a co-treatment involving having Mr. Davies prepare a meal for friends and/or family. The OT would focus on introducing adaptive cooking equipment to Mr. Davies (because he has difficulty grasping things due to arthritis), and the RT would focus on providing opportunities for social interaction among the participants of the meal.

The obstacles to this interdisciplinary approach are that it may take more meetings to develop an integrated plan of services and to educate members of the group on profession-specific interventions. Some members of the team may feel that they are losing professional autonomy. It takes time to gain understanding of the scope of practice of other professionals and to develop a sense of trust. According to Grant, Finocchio, and Primary Care Consortium Subcommittee on Interdisciplinary Collaboration (1995), the interdisciplinary approach may also increase professional satisfaction, facilitate the emphasis from acute care to long-term preventative care, enable the health care professional to learn about new skills and approaches, encourage innovation, and allow the health care professionals to focus on individual areas of expertise. For the health care delivery system, this approach holds potential for more efficient delivery of care, maximizes resources and facilities, decreases the burden on acute care facilities, and facilitates continuous quality improvement (CQI) efforts (Grant et al., 1995).

Transdisciplinary Model

The transdisciplinary model is designed to provide the highest level of integrative care. Rothberg (1992) stated that the essence of this model is that members cross disciplinary lines to provide reinforcement to client-centered treatment goals. In this model, team members are trained to provide services for clients under the supervision of other professionals. Halper (1993) stated:

> Representatives of various disciplines work together in the initial evaluation and care plan, but only one or two team members actually provide the services. . . . It should be noted that regardless of who is providing the service, professionals are still accountable for the areas related to their specific discipline and for training the team member who is delivering the service. (p. 2)

For example, in the case study of Mr. Davies, the first person to make a home visit and complete a formal assessment was the social worker. Since Mr. Davies seemed to show possible symptoms of depression, the Geriatric Depression Scale (GDS; short form)[1] was conducted. Mr. Davies scored an 8 out of 15; a score greater than 5 suggests depression. Upon completing a financial assessment, it appeared that the client would qualify for Medicaid assistance as well as other state and local health care discount programs. The social worker would then share a report of the initial visit and assessment results with the transdisciplinary team members.

Mr. Davies's transdisciplinary team would include the primary care physician, a nurse, a social worker, an OT, a PT, and an RT. In this case, it was determined that additional assessment needed to be completed by a PT and/or an OT. The purpose of these assessments would be to do a home assessment to determine if modifications could be made in the home to enhance mobility and to decrease the risk of falls. In addition, these therapists would be able to recommend adaptive equipment that would enable Mr. Davies to maintain independence and be able to continue to write poetry. After the PT and OT assessments are completed, another team meeting would be held to discuss the results of the assessments and the team would develop a set of client-centered goals. Since Mr. Davies is not in a health care facility, the team would also need to determine which health care professional would be most able to meet his needs and provide necessary services. Mr. Davies needs help with monitoring his medication, food intake and alcohol consumption, and self-care and maintaining a safe environment. The team would most likely recommend that a visiting nurse be assigned to the case and be the individual responsible for implementing the treatment plan. The nurse would be trained by respective therapists to implement and/or reinforce interventions that would help this client reach the medical, PT, and

OT goals. The nurse would report back to team members on a regular basis, identifying the client's progress on his goals and identifying any additional intervention needs. If it is determined that the client requires other services, the team would discuss these needs and provide training to the visiting nurse as to how to implement the necessary interventions. In some cases, another therapist may be asked to visit the client to complete additional assessment or discipline-specific interventions. In the case of Mr. Davies, an RT may be asked to complete a community reintegration assessment and create or implement a community reintegration intervention. It is important to point out that a physician's referral must be in place for any of the services to be reimbursed by Medicare or other insurance companies.

Although this is perhaps the most controversial of the three models mentioned, it may be the most useful in providing services to home-based older adults in rural settings. Due to the distance between rural clients and the lack of centrally based services, it may be difficult for all members of an interdisciplinary team to meet individually with a client. This transdisciplinary model would enable the clinicians to complete their assessments, determine and prioritize the client's treatment needs, and identify the health professional who can provide the best mix of services for the client. This professional would have to be trained to implement the interventions recommended by other team members. This model requires that an effective method of communication be initiated and that the team members have opportunities to meet in person or utilize real-time technology to determine the client's progress on goals and to make modifications in the treatment plan. It is not unlikely that the point person in this scenario could change based on the client's needs.

Collaboration Among Disciplines

The models delineated in the preceding paragraphs all require that team members have skills in collaboration. For any team to be successful, members must not only understand the needs of the clients they are serving and have professional expertise, they must also be able to work as effective members of a team. Collaboration skills include the abilities to listen actively, communicate nondefensively, share expertise openly, trust and respect members of the interdisciplinary team, solve problems, and resolve conflicts. These skills are all practiced with the primary intent of providing the client with the best possible mix of services and in establishing a positive and productive work environment. In addition, it is important for team members to be willing to work across discipline-specific cultures to find common goals and ways to achieve them in cost-effective and collaborative manners (Freshman et al., 2010).

There are many benefits to collaboration among disciplines. Perhaps the most important benefit is to the recipients of services because they are receiving the best mix of services from the various health care providers maximizing client outcomes. Benefits to the health care institutions include increased efficiency of operation and increased cost effectiveness due to the decrease in redundancy or duplication of services. In addition, having multiple disciplines share their ideas and approaches can generate new and innovative ideas and/or approaches to address client issues and problems and new models of service provision. Interacting with other therapists can have the added benefit of increased employee satisfaction. Clients may also become more engaged in their treatment because they feel that have more locus of control and a greater understanding of the services they are receiving—they are active members of the team (Freshman et al., 2010).

There are also several barriers to effective collaboration. Administrators must recognize and allow for the time it takes to create collaborative models and relationships. In the beginning, this process may seem like a waste of staff time in meetings or result in reduced client contact hours, with implications such as reduced reimbursement for the delivery of services. The impact of this barrier is reduced as the team establishes efficient methods for the delivery of services. Effective teams require training in team development. This may also be considered a waste of time by administrators as it, too, takes away time from providing direct service to the client. It is therefore vital to secure agency buy-in to providing the necessary time and resources to develop a team approach structure. Other barriers include finding ways to involve all partners, monitoring the team building process, and keeping participants on track (Avery, 2001; Frattali & Lorendom, 1993; Freshman et al., 2010).

Members of an interdisciplinary team must accept responsibility for their actions and contributions to the treatment process. Christopher Avery (2001) developed what he refers to as The Responsibility Process. In this process, team members are encouraged to be self-reflective and to recognize what their individual contributions are to the effective functioning of the team. He argued that team members must rise above denial (ignoring the existence of something), laying blame (holding others at fault for causing something), justifying (using excuses for things being the way they are), shame (laying blame onto oneself, often felt as guilt), obligation (doing what you have to instead of what you want to), and quitting (giving up to avoid the pain of shame and obligation) to the level of *responsibility*. Responsibility also means being "response able." This means that every individual team member must recognize that they are each responsible for the effective functioning of the team. In his TeamWisdom Model, Avery placed personal responsibility at the center with concentric circles moving outward with the central circle representing partnership, the second circle representing shared purpose, the third circle trust, and the final circle a collaborative mind-set.

TeamWisdom refers to all the individual mental skills and behaviors that lead to highly responsible and productive relationships at work. The idea is based on Avery's (2001) definition of team:

> A team is a group of individuals responding successfully to the opportunity presented by shared responsibility. Someone with TeamWisdom takes responsibility for ensuring that the group rises to the occasion and, in the process, makes sure his own work gets done and done well. (p. 3)

Interprofessional Collaborative Practice

The Interprofessional Education Collaborative Expert Panel (2011)—representing the American Association of Colleges of Nursing, American Association of Colleges of Osteopathic Medicine, American Association of Colleges of Pharmacy, American Dental Education Association; Association of American Medical Colleges, and the Association of Schools of Public Health—has worked together to create the report *Core Competencies for Interprofessional Collaborative Practice*. This report represents the most recent work on interdisciplinary collaboration. The report suggested the use of the terminology interprofessional teamwork. The definitions that the panel proposed are the following:

> *Interprofessional teamwork:* The levels of cooperation, coordination, and collaboration characterizing the relationships between professions in delivering patient-centered care.
> *Interprofessional team-based care:* Care delivered by intentionally created, usually relatively small work groups in health care, who are recognized by others as well as by themselves as having a collective identity and shared responsibility for a

patient or group of patients (e.g., rapid response team, palliative care team, primary care team, operating room team; Interprofessional Education Collaborative Expert Panel, 2011, p. 2).

These definitions reflect the same meaning and intent of the interdisciplinary teamwork model but place an emphasis on the importance of
recognizing the scope of practice and contributions of various health
care professions to client-centered care. They focus on the development
of a collective identity that will in turn enable more cost-effective and
efficient services to older adults.

Another approach to competency development, also with a national
consensus base, is found in the Partnership for Health in Aging (PHA)
led by the American Geriatrics Society (AGS). In response to the Institute
of Medicine (IOM) report (2008), a coalition of professional organizations was formed to work toward the development of core competencies
across the health professions by the completion of the entry-level health
professional degrees in the disciplines of: dentistry, medicine, nursing,
nutrition, occupational therapy, pharmacy, physical therapy, physician
assistants, psychology, and social work. The six domains of multidisciplinary, foundation competencies (Table 9.1) are health promotion
and safety, evaluation and assessment, care planning and coordination
across the care spectrum, interdisciplinary and team care, caregiver support, and health care systems and benefits.

Interdisciplinary collaboration is mentioned in Domain III: care
planning and coordination across the care spectrum (including end-of-
life care), and Domain IV: interdisciplinary and team care. Under the
theme of care planning, the recommendations focus on patient-centered
care and directed care results that are evidence-based and in which
older adults' preferences are taken into consideration when developing
a plan. These recommendations are complementary to the interdisciplinary team approach that is client-centered.

Domain IV focuses directly on interdisciplinary and team care. These
recommendations include the ability to distinguish among, refer to, and/
or consult with any of the multiple health care professionals who work
with older adults. This is necessary to achieve positive outcomes and to
communicate and collaborate with older adults, their caregivers, health
care professionals, and direct-care workers to incorporate discipline-
specific information into overall team care planning and implementation
(Partnership for Health in Aging, 2010). These competencies are also discussed in Chapter 10 with regard to the role of the medical professional.

TABLE 9.1 Multidisciplinary Competencies in the Care of Older Adults at the Completion of the Entry-Level Health Professional Degree

Domain I. Health Promotion and Safety

1. Advocate to older adults and their caregivers interventions and behaviors that promote physical and mental health, nutrition, function, safety, social interactions, independence, and quality of life (QOL).

2. Identify and inform older adults and their caregivers about evidence-based approaches to screening, immunizations, health promotion, and disease prevention.

3. Assess specific risks and barriers to older adult safety, including falls, mistreatment of older adults, and other risks in community, home, and care environments.

4. Recognize the principles and practices of safe, appropriate, and effective medication use in older adults.

5. Apply knowledge of the indications and contraindications for risks of and alternatives to the use of physical and pharmacological restraints with older adults.

Domain II. Evaluation and Assessment

1. Define the purpose and components of an interdisciplinary, comprehensive geriatric assessment and the roles individual disciplines play in conducting and interpreting a comprehensive geriatric assessment.

2. Apply knowledge of the biological, physical, cognitive, psychological, and social changes commonly associated with aging.

3. Choose, administer, and interpret a validated and reliable tool/instrument appropriate to use with a given older adult to assess: (a) cognition, (b) mood, (c) physical function, (d) nutrition, and (e) pain.

4. Demonstrate knowledge of the signs and symptoms of delirium and whom to notify if an older adult exhibits these signs and symptoms.

5. Develop verbal and nonverbal communication strategies to overcome potential sensory, language, and cognitive limitations in older adults.

Domain III. Care Planning and Coordination Across the Care Spectrum (including End-of-Life Care)

1. Develop treatment plans based on best evidence and on person-centered and directed care goals.

2. Evaluate clinical situations where standard treatment recommendations, based on best evidence, should be modified with regard to older adults' preferences and treatment/care goals, life expectancy, comorbid conditions, and/or functional status.

3. Develop advanced care plans based on older adults' preferences and treatment/care goals, and their physical, psychological, social, and spiritual needs.

4. Recognize the need for continuity of treatment and communication across the spectrum of services and during transitions between care settings, utilizing information technology where appropriate and available.

(continued)

TABLE 9.1 Multidisciplinary Competencies in the Care of Older Adults at the Completion of the Entry-Level Health Professional Degree (*continued*)

Domain IV. Interdisciplinary and Team Care

1. Distinguish among, refer to, and/or consult with any of the multiple health care professionals who work with older adults, to achieve positive outcomes.

2. Communicate and collaborate with older adults, their caregivers, health care professionals, and direct-care workers to incorporate discipline-specific information into overall team care planning and implementation.

Domain V. Caregiver Support

1. Assess caregiver knowledge and expectations of the impact of advanced age and disease on health needs, risks, and the unique manifestations and treatment of health conditions.

2. Assist caregivers to identify, access, and utilize specialized products, professional services, and support groups that can assist with caregiving responsibilities and reduce caregiver burden.

3. Know how to access and explain the availability and effectiveness of resources for older adults and caregivers that help them meet personal goals, maximize function, maintain independence, and live in their preferred and/or least restrictive environment.

4. Evaluate the continued appropriateness of care plans and services based on older adults' and caregivers' changes in age, health status, and function; assist caregivers in altering plans and actions as needed.

Domain VI. Health Care Systems and Benefits

1. Serve as an advocate for older adults and caregivers within various health care systems and settings.

2. Know how to access, and share with older adults and their caregivers, information about the health care benefits of programs such as Medicare, Medicaid, Veterans' services, Social Security, and other public programs.

3. Provide information to older adults and their caregivers about the continuum of long-term care services and supports—such as community resources, home care, assisted-living facilities, hospitals, nursing facilities, subacute facilities, and hospice care.

Reprinted with permission of Partnership for Health in Aging. (n.d.). Multidisciplinary Competencies in the Care of Older Adults at the Completion of the Entry-Level Health Professional Degree. Available at www.americangeriatrics.org/about_us/partnership_ for_health_in_aging/multidisciplinary_competencies/multidisciplinary_competencies/ multidisciplinary_competencies778926

Interprofessional Model of Education

To enable this trend in interprofessional collaboration, workplace models of interprofessional education need to be developed. Freshman and colleagues (2010) define interprofessional collaboration as

A complex process through which relationships are developed among health care professionals so that they can effectively interact and work together for the mutual goals of safe and quality patient care. (p. 110)

This approach focuses more on professional training and curricular development than on the team models that are utilized in the provision of client-centered health care service. The concept of interprofessional education is important because it provides health care professionals with the knowledge and skills that they need to be effective interprofessional team members prior to entering the workforce.

The Center for Life Skills (CLS) at Ithaca College, in the state of New York, is a working example of an interprofessional education model. CLS is an interdisciplinary postrehabilitation stroke clinic that serves stroke survivors who have completed their formal rehabilitation process and are still in need of goals-oriented intervention. The CLS is staffed by Ithaca College faculty and students from the School of Health Sciences and Human Performance. Faculty and students from the Departments of Occupational Therapy, Physical Therapy, Speech-Language Pathology, and Therapeutic Recreation provide client-centered interventions to meet the individual needs of participants. These adults have experienced either a stroke or some other type of brain injury; they are provided with opportunities to enhance their QOL, independence, health, and personal growth.

The CLS program meets three times a week for 3 hours each day. The students from the four departments are responsible for assessment, treatment plan development, and documentation for their assigned clients. They meet once a week as an interdisciplinary team to develop client-centered treatment plans and/or to participate in family conferences with the participants and their families. They develop goal-directed interventions that are implemented as individual or group therapy. Several of the programs are designed as co-treatments so that the students can learn to work collaboratively with other disciplines utilizing an outcomes-oriented, client-centered approach.

The CLS has been very effective in helping students learn about other disciplines and their scope of practice, how to communicate effectively during a team meeting and/or family conference, and how to work collaboratively during co-treatments. It has also enabled faculty members to work collaboratively with colleagues in other disciplines.

HEALTH LITERACY

An important aspect of interprofessional education and practice is the development of a working knowledge of the principles and practices of health literacy. Health literacy is defined by the IOM and *Healthy People 2010* as, "the degree to which individuals have the capacity to obtain, process, and understand basic health information and services needed to make appropriate health decisions" (HHS 2000 and Institute of Medicine, 2004, in Kutner, Greenberg, Jin, & Paulsen, 2006, p. iii). The Patient Protection and Affordable Care Act (PPACA) of 2010, Title V, utilizes this same definition but adds the word *communicate* to the legislative definition. Consumers of health care services are frequently forced to make decisions about their health care needs and the services that are offered to them. Yet research shows that 9 out of 10 adults have difficulty making these decisions (Kutner et al., 2006; Rudd, Anderson, Oppenheimer, & Nath, 2007). The 2003 National Assessment of Adult Literacy (NAAL) also found that adults older than age 65, individuals who spoke more than one language or who had less than a high school education, and adults living below the poverty level had lower that average health literacy (Kutner et al., 2006; Rudd et al., 2007). It is evident from these statistics, and as mentioned in Chapter 2, that health literacy can be a significant problem in the provision of rural health services for older adults because they often have these demographic characteristics.

The role of interdisciplinary teams in helping to enhance health literacy is important. Interdisciplinary teams are client-centered. The communication among team members focuses on providing the best mix of services for their clients. It follows that part of this communication would be to assess and discuss the clients' levels of health literacy and to develop interventions that will enhance the clients' understanding of the services that they are being offered. Another part of this communication would be providing patients with the information that they will need to be able to make informed decisions about their health care. The paradox is, however, that although this is a service that could easily be addressed by interdisciplinary team members, practicing professionals may not have the training they need to understand health literacy and the ways through which it can be improved.

The Centers for Disease Control and Prevention (CDC) have addressed this problem by providing a training program, Health Literacy for Public Health Professionals. This training is 1.5 to 2 hours in length and provides continuing medical education (CME) credit for some health care providers. There is no cost for this training. It is a web-based program (www.cdc.gov/healthliteracy/training/index.html) that focuses on providing training about public health literacy and the professional's role in providing health information and services. Institutions of higher education must also be encouraged to integrate health literacy modules into professional preparation programs, and agencies that provide services for older adults in rural environments should develop policy that integrates health literacy into the treatment process as an integral part of intervention planning and implementation. Agencies should also provide team members with the opportunity to receive training so that they can best meet the health literacy needs of their clients.

RECRUITMENT AND TRAINING OF PROFESSIONALS IN RURAL AREAS

The primary need and challenge associated with the provision of interdisciplinary team service for older adults in rural areas revolve around the recruitment and training of allied professionals to be effective team members. Very few academic institutions have team training as an integral part of their professional training. This primary problem is accentuated by the lack of health care facilities and available resources in rural areas. Attempting to maintain active team involvement is very difficult when clients and facilities are geographically remote and resources (such as clinics) are limited. There are, however, several innovative approaches to providing quality services as described in the following paragraphs.

Krout and Kinner (2007) identified seven challenges that are faced by those who develop and provide service to rural older adults. These seven challenges include availability, accessibility, affordability, awareness, adequacy, acceptability, and assessment. Elements among these challenges that impact interdisciplinary team involvement are the lack of qualified and well-trained human service providers who have an understanding of the particular needs and barriers presented by this population. Included in this lack of training is an understanding of the role and purpose of interdisciplinary team practices.

The literature strongly supports the lack of interdisciplinary training for allied health professionals during their educational preparation and even less once they are in the workforce (Krout & Kinner, 2007). This dearth of training, along with the scarcity of resources, distance between recipients of service, and professional isolation, makes it difficult to attract and retain health care professionals in rural environments (Krout, 1993). One successful attempt to provide interdisciplinary training in rural environments was developed and implemented by the Ithaca College Gerontology Institute (Krout & Kinner, 2007). This project, *Training Rural Health Professionals: Building Capacity Through a Community Team Approach*, focused on training frontline workers. The project received support from the Finger Lakes Geriatric Education Center (FLGEC) and a grant from the Central New York Area Health Education Center (CNYAHEC). The authors described the purpose of the project:

> This project taps existing networks, offices for the aging, rural health networks, public health departments, departments of social services and others who have a vested interest in geriatric training such as skilled nursing facilities, home health care agencies, and adult homes. It also incorporates knowledge and credibility of local professionals into the process and facilitates a geriatric training approach, which strengthens the community pool of professional and paraprofessional workers. In addition, the team model builds capacity for ongoing training initiated by local providers. (Krout & Kinner, 2007, p. 70)

To implement this project, county level teams with representatives from skilled nursing facilities, home health care agencies, departments of public health, offices of the aging, rural health networks, adult homes, the Veterans Administration (VA) medical centers, and departments of social services were formed to identify and prioritize the geriatric training needs of the county. As a team, they determined the best day, time, location, and format for training sessions. In 2003, 14 workshops, on a variety of topics, were held in 11 counties with 719 participants. The response to this program was determined to be very positive, based on a usefulness survey that was conducted 2 months after the training (Krout & Kinner, 2007).

Another effective method of providing training for rural health practitioners is distance learning. The Ithaca College Gerontology Institute has developed three free and successful web modules that are available online (www.ithaca.edu/aging/training) as well as on CD-ROM. This approach enables practitioners to gain training at their own convenience.

More than one fourth of veterans live in rural areas, whereas Veterans Administration Medical Centers (VAMCs) are in metropolitan areas. This translates to approximately 28% or 6.1 million veterans living in rural areas, of the total 22 million veterans. In 2007, the Veterans Health Administration (VHA) addressed the underserving of rural veterans by establishing the Office of Rural Health (ORH). Higher rates of chronic health conditions for rural veterans are compounded by the additional health problems associated with combat exposure including posttraumatic stress disorder (PTSD), depression, and traumatic brain injury.

The ORH's Rural Health Initiative addresses the need to build a system of care for veterans living in areas far from urban centers. Community-based outpatient clinics (CBOCs) form the foundation of this network of rural service. CBOCs aim to develop partnerships with non-VA rural providers. Technology plays an important role as well. Through the use of telemedicine and information technology including the computerized medical record, the goal is to increase access and promote continuity of care. ORH has provided support for more than 1,400 special rural veterans' projects. These projects include: transportation services, hospital-based home care, and mental health services.

An example of an ORH pilot project is Coordination and Advocacy for Rural Elders (CARE). CARE targeted older veterans who lived in rural counties within 50 miles to 100 miles from two host VHA medical centers. Through a telephone assessment, veterans age 75 and older who were at risk of repeated hospital admission were targeted for a comprehensive health geriatric assessment and home visit by a health professional. The outcome was the finding that the majority of rural older veterans had several identified geriatric conditions, including health problems/syndromes (falls, pain, and cardiorespiratory), mental health issues (social function), functional performance (IADLs and health performance), sensory (visual function and communication disorders), and service oversight (medication management). Evidence-based practices (EBPs) were applied by the nurse–social worker teams to develop individual veteran-specific care plans and resource mobilization working with family, community, and the VHA (Ritchie et al., 2002).

Based on this VA needs assessment, the Geriatric Scholars Program (GSP) was designed to educate health care providers working in rural VA CBOCs to manage the care of medically complex geriatric patients. The program includes intensive educational courses, ongoing coaching and mentoring opportunities, and a choice of self-directed learning activities. The clinical practicum is strongly encouraged and limited to 40 hours of training experience. The program has been funded since 2008 through generous grants from the VA ORH. Physicians, nurse practitioners, physician assistants, clinical pharmacists, and, more recently, social workers have participated in the program. The goals of the GSP are for rural health professionals to: gain the knowledge and skills to develop evidence-based care plans for medically complex older patients; assess and address functional health status; implement interdisciplinary care strategies; incorporate VA and community resources in care planning; and apply quality improvement (QI) methods for measurable improvements in care of older veterans. GSP has enrolled more than 140 participants from 20 VA regions and 109 CBOCs since 2008 (Veterans Health Administration [VHA] Office of Rural Health [ORH], 2011).

CONCLUSION

It is obvious that there is a significant need to design and implement interprofessional models of teamwork and education to enhance health care services. This need is particularly important for older adults living in rural environments who, as has been detailed in previous chapters, are often faced with barriers to accessing services including transportation, distance to or lack of available services, and the dearth of trained health care providers. Although there has been a trend toward the development of team-based services for many years, educational institutions have not integrated interdisciplinary or interprofessional team training units as part of the education process. In addition, there is a lack of interprofessional training programs for practicing professionals. To meet the recommendations of the Pew Foundation, the Committee on Quality of Health Care in America, and the Interprofessional Education Collaborative Expert Panel, institutions of higher education that prepare health care professionals must begin to recognize the importance of these initiatives and start integrating these recommendations into their professional development curriculums. Model curricular development programs need to be developed and disseminated so that there is mutual understanding of interprofessional practice across disciplines. Students should also have the opportunity to work on interprofessional teams prior to graduation for health service professions.

USEFUL WEBSITES

American Geriatrics Society
www.americangeriatrics.org
Geriatric Research Education and Clinical Centers (GRECC)
www.va.gov/grecc
Gerontological Society of America (GSA) Rural Aging Interest Group
www.geron.org/Membership/interest-groups#rural
National Association for Geriatric Education
www.n-age.org
Rural Geriatric Interdisciplinary Case Study
www.ithaca.edu/ahgitt/rochester/index.html
www.ithaca.edu/aging/training
VHA Office of Rural Health
www.ruralhealth.va.gov

NOTE

1. Ithaca College Gerontology Institute. (n.d.). *The Case of Mr. Davies*. From grant #29392, Finger Lakes Geriatric Education Center (FLGEC). Reprinted with permission.

REFERENCES

Avery, C. (2001). *Team is an individual skill*. San Francisco, CA: Berrett-Koehler.

Committee on Quality of Health Care in America, Institute of Medicine, National Academy of Sciences. (2001). *Crossing the quality chasm: A new health system for the 21st century*. Washington, DC: National Academy Press.

Frattali, C. M., & Lorendom L. C. (1993). *Professional collaboration: A team approach to health care*. Rockville, MD: National Student Speech Language Hearing Association.

Freshman, B., Rubino, L., & Chassiakos, Y. R. (2010). *Collaboration across the disciplines in health care*. Boston, MA: Jones and Bartlett.

Grant, R. W., Finocchio, L. J., & Primary Care Consortium Subcommittee on Interdisciplinary Collaboration. (1995). *Interdisciplinary collaborative teams in primary care: A model curriculum and resource guide*. San Francisco, CA: Pew Health Professions Commission.

Halper, A. S. (1993, June/July). Teams and teamwork: Health care settings. *American Speech-Language-Hearing Association*, pp. 34–35.

Institute of Medicine of the National Academies. (2008). *Retooling for an aging America*. Washington, DC: The National Academies.

Interprofessional Education Collaborative Expert Panel. (2011). *Core competencies for interprofessional collaborative practice: Report of an expert panel*. Washington, DC: Author.

Krout, J. A. (1993). *Providing community based services to the rural elderly*. Thousand Oaks, CA: Sage.

Krout, J. A., & Kinner, M. (2007). Sustaining geriatric rural populations. In L. L. Morgan & P. S. Stewart (Eds.), *Conversations in the disciplines: Sustaining rural populations* (pp. 63–74). Binghamton, NY: Global Academic.

Kutner, M., Greenberg, E., Jin, Y., & Paulsen, C. (2006). U.S. Department of Education. *The health literacy of America's adults: Results from the 2003 National Assessment of Adult Literacy* (NCES 2006–483). Washington, DC: National Center for Education Statistics.

O'Neil, E. H., & the PEW Health Professions Commission. (1998). *Recreating health care practice for the 21st century: The fourth report of the PEW Health Professions Commission*. San Francisco, CA: PEW Health Professions Commission.

Partnership for Health in Aging (PHA). (2010). *Multidisciplinary competencies in the care of older adults at the completion of the entry-level health professional degrees*. Retrieved September 10, 2013, from http://www.americangeriatrics.org/files/documents/health_care_pros/PHA_Multidisc_Competencies.pdf

Ritchie, C., Wieland, D., Tully, C., Rowe, J., Sims, R., & Bodner, E. (2002). Coordination and advocacy for rural elders (CARE): A model of rural case management with veterans. *The Gerontologist, 42*(3), 399–405.

Rothberg, J. S. (1992). Knowledge of disciplines: Roles and functions of team members. In American Congress of Rehabilitation Medicine (Ed.), *Guide to interdisciplinary practice in rehabilitation settings* (pp. 44–71). Stokie, IL: American Congress of Rehabilitation Medicine.

Rudd, R. E., Anderson, J. E., Oppenheimer, S., & Nath, C. (2007). Health literacy: An update of public health and medical literature. In J. P. Comings, B. Garner, & C. Smith (Eds.), *Review of adult learning and literacy* (Vol. 7, pp. 175–204). Mahwah, NJ: Lawrence Erlbaum.

Veterans Health Administration Office of Rural Health. (2011). *The geriatric scholars program*. Retrieved November 22, 2013, from http://www.ruralhealth.va.gov/docs/Geriatric_Scholars_Brochure_March_2011.pdf

10

Role of the Health Care Professional

SHIRLEY M. NEITCH

DAVID P. ELLIOTT

BARBARA L. NUNLEY

R. CONSTANCE WIENER

John Jefferson Marshall is a 72-year-old man retired for 6 years from his job as head of buildings and grounds for a community hospital. He quit school at the start of his senior year of high school and spent several years in the army, including a tour of duty in Vietnam. After Vietnam, he left the service and went to work at the hospital as a janitor. Over the years, he obtained his GED, then attended the regional technical/community college for courses in heating and air-conditioning technology and later in management; ultimately, he became the department manager. After several years in that position, he retired to spend time with his family. Mr. Marshall has been married to his wife, Joan, for 45 years. They have three children, James Edward (age 43), Thomas (age 42), and Sally (age 38), and they have five grandchildren.

Mr. Marshall's *history* includes

- Medical/Surgical
  - Hypertension (HTN) (high blood pressure) since age 48

- o Recurrent low back pain since a car accident 20 years ago
- o Surgical repair of an ankle fracture sustained in the car accident
- o Gall bladder surgery at age 50
- o Wife is complaining that he is "losing his memory"
- Dental
  - o Reports he has been diagnosed with "gum disease"
  - o Has had all his maxillary teeth extracted and has an "upper plate"
- Immunizations
  - o Had all immunizations required for school and military service
  - o Gets influenza vaccine yearly
  - o Had yearly TB (tuberculosis) tests and had Hepatitis B (HBV) immunization while employed at the hospital
- Medications
  - o Lisinopril 10 mg daily and hydrochlorothiazide 25 mg daily (for blood pressure)
  - o Occasional over-the-counter acetaminophen and multivitamins
  - o Over-the-counter sleeping pill (which contains diphenhydramine [Benadryl®])
- Social
  - o Lives in Springtown, population around 500
  - o Spent his career at Waterville Community Hospital, 30 miles from his home, requiring 60 miles of traveling daily over poor mountainous roads
  - o Smokes cigarettes, ½ pack/day for past 10 years; decreased from 1½ packs/day for the prior 30 years
  - o Substance Use—no alcohol since discharge from the service; no street drugs or excess use of prescription drugs
  - o Attends church on a semiregular basis and his hobbies are bowling and fishing
  - o Receives small pension from the hospital as well as Social Security (SS) and Medicare
- Family History
  - o HTN—mother and father (developed during their 40s)
  - o Coronary artery disease (CAD)—father had "fatal heart attack" at age 77

  o TB—father had in his teens
  o Dementia—father had some memory problems at the
     time of his death; mother had Alzheimer's disease (AD)
     when she died at age 85

A comprehensive picture of the roles and experiences of health care professionals in rural places, such as those who work with Mr. Marshall, fails to exist. They are ordinary professionals who are trained in the same schools and equipped with the same knowledge as their colleagues in urban/suburban practices. These professionals are unique in that they willingly perform in quite isolated and less than state-of-the-art surroundings compared to their urban counterparts, and they work longer hours for lower pay (Goetz, Musselman, Szecsenyi, & Joos, 2013). They have much in common with each other, including their love of their communities and their deep commitment to their patients, yet they are diverse in backgrounds, practice styles, and personalities. Some are local folks who have come home; however, many have come into their communities from quite far away, perhaps to repay a National Health Service Corps (NHSC) scholarship or to fulfill requirements for immigration (Faulkner, Wilson, Whitler, & Asher, 2012). This difficulty in defining their roles and experiences is one of the roots of the perpetual problem of attracting and retaining health care professionals in rural areas. Formulating a program to attract persons to practice in a certain area is difficult, when it cannot quite be determined what makes the area attractive to those who have already chosen to be there.

The term *health care professionals* covers a wide range of experts in specific fields, all of whom are concerned with maintaining or improving the health status of their patients or clients. This includes physicians and physicians' assistants; nurses, nurse practitioners, and other advanced-practice nurses; dentists and dental hygienists; pharmacists;

These enigmatic elements surrounding practice in a rural setting will always have to be dealt with by individuals who choose to be in rural places; however, the competencies needed for successful rural practice are more easily defined. This chapter reviews practice competencies for the care of *all* older patients and expands upon the general competencies to define needs of the rural population. As covered in Chapter 9, good geriatric care demands an interdisciplinary approach (also referred to as multidisciplinary or interprofessional); thus, rural practice is examined from the points of view of multiple health care professionals, as they work separately and together.

psychologists and other mental health professionals; dieticians; and various therapists (including—in addition to physical, occupational, and speech therapists—recreation, art, and music therapists). Social workers are discussed in Chapter 11 and are very valuable members of the health care professionals group, as are health care-based clergy, clinical laboratory and radiology technologists, and health informatics specialists. In this chapter, detailed discussion is limited to certain health care professionals who have perhaps the most prominent hands-on contact with rural older patients—physicians, nurse practitioners, dentists, and pharmacists. This does not diminish in any way the importance of the contributions of other health professionals in seeking to maximize the health status of rural older adults. This discussion examines current information about health care professionals who are practicing in rural settings and how their practices incorporate competencies and the rural culture.

HEALTH CARE PRACTICE WITH RURAL OLDER ADULTS

For each specific health profession, rural practice has challenges and rewards; nonetheless, certain themes recur when any health care practice in a rural setting is studied. Rural practice often connotes less time with each patient, since the few providers in the practice must see a community's worth of people seeking care. Because geriatric medicine usually calls for *more* time per patient, this places the rural practitioner at a potential disadvantage in lack of adequate time with the older patient. However, many providers feel that they overcome the time disadvantage because they know more about their patients by virtue of being acquainted with them outside the practice or by having been the only practitioners involved with them over a span of time (Ullman, 2012). Each provider must recognize this inherent time conflict in order to maximize the success of the encounter within the time available.

Quantity, and sometimes quality, of medical personnel are problematic in most rural sites. A patient's choice of physicians and/or other providers is usually limited, specialists are rarely present, and mental health resources are notoriously sparse in rural areas. In a 2010 study of rural health workforce issues, more than 1,000 rural hospital CEOs were surveyed, and 75% of them reported overall physician shortages; most indicated a need for more primary care practitioners, but they also had significant shortages of psychiatrists, surgeons, obstetrician-gynecologists, and others (MacDowell, Glasser, Fitts, Nielsen, & Hunsaker, 2010). Furthermore, not only physicians were found to be in short supply. This same study showed that 55% of these CEOs believed that their communities needed more pharmacists, 40% more dentists, 73% more nurses, and one third more dieticians and speech pathologists (MacDowell et al., 2010). The shortage of professionals and specialists can contribute to professional isolation in these areas. This situation can prove positive or negative for the professional, with some people thriving on the independence, but others feeling quite uncomfortable with a dearth of colleagues. Practitioners' families also have mixed responses to rural life and, if negative, may be the reason that some rural practices do not survive. For those that do thrive, however, rural practice and rural living can be rewarding and comfortable.

Not only is there a shortage of health professionals in rural areas, but the limited availability of various health-related resources is also an issue. This includes agency-based resources such as Home Health or Meals on Wheels, transportation, places to engage in exercise programs, and well-stocked grocery stores (Ziliak & Gunderson, 2009)—all of which have been discussed in depth in previous chapters. This may require practitioners trained in less rural settings to change their approaches to treating patients. For example, there would be little need to advise a patient requiring exercise to join a gym, if that patient lives in a community of a few hundred residents with the nearest commercial gym 40 miles away. Transportation is a significant contributor to the problem because it is often difficult to get patients to sites of more intense or specialized care when needed (Nachtmann & Pohl, 2009). Not only must patients be able to be transported in emergencies, but they also need everyday access to means of traveling to appointments with doctors, dentists, and therapists; to pick up prescriptions and groceries; and for a myriad of other activities of daily living (ADLs) and instrumental activities of daily living (IADLs). For most patients, this is a straightforward concern—the expense of having and maintaining a vehicle and the likelihood of poor roads, particularly in bad weather. With older patients, the issue may be much more convoluted. As many older patients acquire medical conditions that make it unwise to continue driving, the lack of other modes of transportation looms large. Public transportation is usually not even present and, if available at all, is likely to be limited in scope and scheduling. Physicians and other health professionals should be part of the process of determining when an older person should stop driving and, when so doing, must have knowledge of available family and community resources. Poverty in rural areas has also been discussed in earlier chapters and is another major contributor to access to care and services. In the setting of health care for older adults, poor rural areas may have more patients who will be "dual eligibles," meaning that they have Medicare and Medicaid as their co-payer, rather than a commercial insurance. This often indicates a disproportionately large number of chronic health concerns (Congressional Budget Office, 2013; Young, Garfield, Musumeci, Clemans-Cope, & Lawton, 2013). Medicaid eligibility also means the potential limitation of access to certain services and medications. Because each state has different benefits and medication lists available to Medicaid beneficiaries, practitioners must be alert to these limitations (Young et al., 2013).

PROFESSIONAL COMPETENCY

In spite of the potential pitfalls discussed, good interprofessional, geriatric practice in rural places *is possible*, albeit potentially more difficult to accomplish. Depending upon the degree of isolation, degree of poverty, and the actual number of people in the area, the opportunity to assemble a group of interested professionals will vary. As shown in Chapter 9, multidisciplinary teamwork is certainly possible. Chapter 9 also introduces the Partnership for Health in Aging's multidisciplinary competencies in the care of older adults (Partnership for Health in Aging [PHA], 2010). These competencies serve as guidelines for educators of health professionals, to provide an objective set of goals that students in various health fields should reach in the course of their training. The competencies are equally useful for professionals already in practice who seek a framework for the activities they are already doing. The PHA multidisciplinary competencies are reprinted in Chapter 9 and are referred to throughout this chapter in the context of practice in rural areas by physicians, dentists, nurse practitioners, and pharmacists. Attention by each of the disciplines to the case of Mr. Marshall highlights the special issues involved in and approaches to rural geriatric practice.

Physicians in Rural Practice

Of the U.S. population, 20% reside in rural areas but only 9% of physicians practice in rural settings (Rosenblatt, 2000); the demographic characteristics of those who are in rural practice differ in a few ways from those who practice in urban/suburban settings. One difference is that rural physicians are more likely to be men. Among older cohorts, those who graduated 30 or more years ago, rural doctors are men by an overwhelming majority of 20+ to 1. Although the ratio has gradually changed, especially among those who graduated 10 or fewer years ago, younger women medical graduates still choose urban practice by a 2 to 1 majority. This is in contrast to the men to women medical school graduates, which is approaching a 50/50 distribution. In 2011, women constituted 47% of matriculates in American medical schools (Association of American Medical Colleges [AAMC], 2012). Given that most patients who are now older are most likely familiar with the male physician model, this is not necessarily a significant issue in the medical care choices of rural older patients.

Predicting specifically who might choose a nonurban practice is surprising in other ways. Whereas it is somewhat counterintuitive, urban-raised physicians who go into rural practices remain in those practices longer than rural-raised physicians (American Academy of Family Physicians [AAFP], 2013). Additionally, young practitioners tend to choose practice locations near where they complete their residency training (more than they choose to locate near their medical schools or near their homes). Regardless of how a practitioner came to be in a rural practice, the PHA competencies outlined earlier point out the importance of such practitioners learning about their new communities in depth. This is especially true in the areas of health care systems and beliefs; those who are not life-long residents of a particular area need to appreciate community-specific issues early and come to respect the local mores. In the event that local customs or usual practices are seen to be detrimental to the provision of good medical care, savvy practitioners understand that they cannot change behaviors overnight and have nearly no chance of changing them at all if their "new ways" are perceived as disrespectful of local culture.

The physician who is successful in a rural setting is likely to be in a small or even a solo office. Those who are attracted by the advantages of solo practice are few (less than 20% of graduates); however, those who do consider the small office or solo route may look for and are even advised to look at rural areas (Alguire, n.d.). A solo or small practice provider, then, is often the first person to encounter an older patient with a new medical problem, such as case study patient Mr. Marshall:

> When Mr. Marshall comes to his primary care physician's office with his wife, she complains of his memory becoming a serious

concern for her. Over the past couple of years, and especially the last few months, he has become repetitive and short-tempered with the grandchildren, has begun refusing to go to church at all, and his personal hygiene has deteriorated.

Elements from all six of the PHA competency domains come into play in Mr. Marshall's case, first of all those related to evaluation and assessment (Domain II). His physician must differentiate among findings on his examination that are present due to changes of normal aging and those that are due to a disease process. If abnormalities are found, the physician must then complete a workup and will need to know if the full evaluation can be completed in the practitioner's locality. The physician should include a validated cognitive screening. If providers feel unable to do this, the PHA competencies indicate that this is a deficit in their practice, and thus a good place to concentrate continuing medical education (CME) learning efforts.

> Mr. Marshall's primary care physician, Dr. Morgan, recognizes that he is having difficulty taking his medications, and that he forgot an appointment last week; the doctor knows he needs to complete a cognitive screening. If that test shows deficits, he knows that the patient should have a brain-imaging test. The hospital where Mr. Marshall worked for many years, 30 miles away, can do CT (computerized tomography) scans; however, Dr. Morgan decides to order an MRI instead, and the nearest MRI scanner is in River City, 65 miles away. Mrs. Marshall says that they might not go for that because they don't like to drive in River City, population 100,000.

The physician at this point must decide if a CT scan is adequate for the evaluation, or if he needs to assist the family in finding transportation. This case demonstrates that even a common issue in an older patient may encompass multiple competencies. In Mr. Marshall's case, all of Domain II comes into play early in the evaluation and treatment process.

> Dr. Morgan was raised in River City, and he knows the traffic there is not a serious problem compared to certain other relatively close cities. He has practiced in this area for many years and he knows the Marshalls' concern is *real to them*, and so he chooses to do only the CT scan.

Like many rural doctors, Dr. Morgan was urban-raised but has settled into this community well over the years, and respects the patients' attitudes because he has a good understanding of the competencies, especially Domain III, Number 1.

As mentioned in Chapter 1, about 1 in 5 older adults live in a rural community and rural areas are typically older than those in more urban areas (Goins & Krout, 2006). Therefore, although practitioners in rural practice seldom have specialized training in geriatric medicine, they must care for *many* patients in the geriatric demographic group. Even if physicians *do* have special geriatric training, and especially if they lack it, the need to collaborate interprofessionally is clear and extends into virtually all aspects of patient care. For example, collaboration can be very helpful in improving the functional capacity of older patients. Whereas percentages of older persons rated as being "in fair or poor health" are not statistically different in rural versus metro counties, activity limitations are markedly more prevalent in rural older adults (Larson, Machlin, Nixon, & Zodet, 2004). These limitations cause the patients to have a significantly lower number of physician office visits. Thus, therapists, agencies, and various volunteer or quasi-governmental groups who can address the issues of remobilizing and remotivating older residents are of great value.

More than 91% of rural older adults have prescription medication expenses (Larson et al., 2004). Although this is not dramatically higher than the number of urban older adults taking prescription drugs, this fact does point out the importance of the pharmacist in the interprofessional care team. Pharmacists are trusted and respected in rural communities; in the past it was not uncommon for a town's pharmacist to also be known as "Doc." The role of the pharmacist in these areas is discussed in depth later in this chapter.

> Mr. Marshall returns to the office once his tests are completed, and he and his wife have an in-depth conversation with Dr. Morgan. They learn that John might have "the beginnings of dementia," and Dr. Morgan suggests a medication that might help. They take the prescription but decide that they want to talk to their family pharmacist, Amos Cline, before they fill it. Amos speaks with them for some time about the need to take the medicine regularly and reviews what Dr. Morgan told them about side effects.

The Marshalls decide that the medication is probably a good idea; however, John worries that he might not think to take it all the time. Joan Marshall has been volunteering with the Red Cross for many years, and sometimes she is out of town assisting in disaster areas for several days at a time.

They call Dr. Morgan's office about these concerns, and his nurse is able to advise them that she knows two retired nurses who volunteer at the local senior center every day. If he began attending that center, they would be able to remind him to take his medication whenever Joan is out of town. Joan also has a lot of concern about what might happen to John in the future because of his diagnosis of dementia. The nurse reminds Joan to talk with Dr. Morgan about that at the next visit and also tells her about the Alzheimer's Association website; she also suggests that a social worker at the hospital where John used to work would probably have some good advice.

Dentists in Rural Practice

It has been estimated that 47 million people, or nearly 15% of the U.S. population, live in *oral health underserved areas* that are primarily rural (Vargas & Arevalo, 2009). This is likely to increase because with the large population wave of people over age 55 there will be a surge of people retiring to rural areas (approaching 30% of new retirees; Skillman, Doescher, Mouradian, & Brunson, 2010). Rurality (the impact of rural life on various issues) is therefore an increasing oral health/public health concern because rural living has been shown to be associated with poor oral health (Kiyak & Reichmuth, 2005; Vargas & Arevalo, 2009), as well as with self-reports of fewer dental visits and greater tooth loss (Adut, Mann, & Sgan-Cohen, 2004; Vargas, Dye, & Hayes, 2003).

> Consider the case of John Marshall, the 72-year-old retiree who has been diagnosed with periodontal disease (which he refers to as "gum disease") and a maxillary denture (which he calls his "upper plate").

For the sake of his dental and his general health, Mr. Marshall needs to stop smoking. Not only has it contributed to his periodontal disease and tooth loss; it has also been associated with increased cardiovascular disease. He should be encouraged to remove his denture, clean it, soak it overnight, and let his tissue recover from being under the pressure of the denture during the day. His dentist should monitor Mr. Marshall for dry mouth and tissue breakdown via a patient-specific maintenance recall to follow up the care after treating the existing periodontal disease. All of Mr. Marshall's health care providers need to advocate smoking cessation and pay attention to his oral health. Because of the realities of rural practice, it is unlikely that all of his providers practice in the same community, much less in the same office complex, so telecommunication among his health care providers (with Mr. Marshall's approval, of course) will be an effective means for them to share care needs. As Mr. Marshall's memory declines, his oral health is likely to decline. The oral condition needs to be monitored by his nondental providers so that early referrals can be made. In a like manner, his dentist can observe Mr. Marshall's blood pressure, memory, activities, and interests and report changes to his other providers. The PHA competencies strongly emphasize the importance of health promotion, with all health care professionals working together. Nowhere can those goals be better put in action than in the oral care of a rural patient such as Mr. Marshall.

Although rural residents consider oral health as being important (Ahn, Biurdine, Smith, Ory, & Phillips, 2011), a paradox of dental need existed in research of rural older adults of North Carolina in which those most in need of dental care were not receiving it (Arcury et al., 2012). Edentulism (toothlessness) is high in rural counties (Mitchell, Bennett, & Brock-Martin, 2012) and rural residents were found to have more unmet dental needs than urban residents (Vargas et al., 2003). Oral health outcomes encompass not only routine oral health problems—caries, periodontal disease, oral pain, dry mouth, and tooth loss—but also craniofacial birth defects (such as cleft lip/palate, which may well have gone unattended when the current older rural resident was a child); head and neck cancers; temporomandibular disorders (problems in the joint of the jaw); tobacco, alcohol, and drug use; trauma; and oral health quality of life (QOL; ability to eat, engage in social activities without embarrassment due to one's teeth, etc.; National Institute of Dental and Craniofacial Research, 2000). Additionally, the mouth is a mirror for signs of nutritional deficiencies, several systemic diseases, and infections. Consequently, lack of good oral health care in rural areas has even more implications than appear on the surface.

Factors often cited for poor oral health in rural areas include (a) difficulties in accessing care due to distance or geography, (b) cost/lack of dental insurance, (c) socioeconomic status, and (d) less education (Ahn et al., 2011; Mitchell et al., 2012; Skillman et al., 2010; Vargas, Ronzio, & Hayes, 2003). However, the linkages are not necessarily straightforward. At least one study found that the most significant variables were delaying of dental care and lifestyle (Ahn et al., 2011), not the simple fact of rurality.

There are substantial differences between rural and urban areas in the prevalence of dentists. In rural counties in 2008 there were 22 dentists per 100,000 people, whereas in urban areas there were 30 dentists per 100,000 people; and dentists in the rural areas tended to be older as well (Skillman et al., 2010). An increase in clinical dental professionals and public health dental professionals in rural areas may be helpful in expanding rural residents' knowledge and appreciation for the influence of good oral health and may influence rural residents to maintain regular dental visits throughout life. However, such an increase in professionals would require a public health and policy commitment, and was one of the goals in addressing rural oral health disparities by the surgeon general in his 2000 assessment of oral health in America.

The roles of dental professionals are in transition in certain states that have vast rural/frontier areas. For example, in some states, dental hygienists may work without a supervising dentist on-site, providing dental prophylaxis in nursing homes, assisted-living facilities, or school settings. Alaska licenses dental health aid therapists who complete a 2-year, post–high school, competency-based primary care curriculum and are providing care in rural Alaska. Expanded-function dental assistants are certified in many states. They have privileges to complete certain procedures (sealant and restoration placement, etc.) that increase the efficiency of dental care.

Dentists themselves have also recognized the need for expanded services to older and more rural populations. Continuing education programs that emphasize working with older adults are becoming more common. Dental school curricula are addressing older adults early and often in courses including behavioral management, motivational interviewing, cultural sensitivity, communication, and dental literacy. Many states already monitor the dental health of school children; this practice needs to be expanded to include older adults, through programs such as annual screening at all senior citizen centers.

Nurse Practitioners in Rural Practice

Nurse practitioners (NPs) are more likely to practice in rural areas than are those in any other primary care disciplines. In fact, 18% of NPs work in communities with less than 25,000 residents. NPs also overwhelmingly treat patients ages 66 to 85 (93% of family nurse practitioners [FNPs] treat this age group, as do 97% of acute care nurse practitioners [ACNPs]). For patients over the age of 85, the percentages are similarly high (FNPs [79%] and ACNPs [84%]; American Academy of Nurse

Practitioners, n.d.). Although there are many challenges facing nursing practice in rural areas (professional isolation, weather-associated travel, limited job opportunities, outsider bias, maintaining confidentiality/ anonymity, and few resources, to name a few), nurses find practicing in this setting rewarding owing to the connectivity with the community, variety of experiences, providing needed services, and many other reasons for preferring to work in a rural setting (Bushy, 2006).

As part of the rural health care workforce, NPs, who are nurses with advanced degrees, have an active role in meeting patients' health care needs whether working independently or directly with doctors and hospitals. Many NPs are educated in a specialty area such as primary care or geriatrics that can be especially valuable in meeting rural older patients' health care needs. NPs can perform comprehensive health assessment including physical, functional, mental and psychoemotional assessments; diagnose and treat physical and mental illnesses; write prescriptions; order, conduct, and interpret select diagnostic tests; develop and implement plans of care; encourage/teach health promotion skills to patients and their families; refer patients to physicians; coordinate services to meet patient and family needs; and collaborate with other health professionals on the team involved with patient and family care (Florell, 2009; Yee, Boukus, Cross, & Samuel, 2013). NPs are also specifically prepared to focus on caring for patients holistically, in that the patient's physical, emotional, and behavioral aspects are integrated (Florell, 2009) with an emphasis on health promotion and disease prevention (American Association of Nurse Practitioners [AANP], n.d.).

NPs abide by the "scope of nursing practice" in the state where they are employed. State scope of practice laws determine NPs' array of services and the degree to which they can practice autonomously (Yee et al., 2013). Whether practicing solo or in a group with other health care professionals to meet the needs of rural older adults, RNs and NPs need to understand concepts associated with health literacy, be aware of disparities, be knowledgeable regarding vulnerable groups in rural areas (Stanton, 2009), and have an understanding of community standards and behaviors in order to make ethically sound and culturally appropriate nursing decisions (Bushy, 2006).

An NP working independently or with a team of health care professionals should approach cases such as Mr. Marshall's within a framework of competencies such as those from the PHA (Table 9.1; PHA, 2010). These provide the structure for NPs to ensure the delivery of optimal patient care. Studies have also identified nursing competencies specifically associated with delivery of care in rural settings. For example, for the rural hospital environment, Hurme (2009) employed a Delphi panel of rural directors of nursing in critical access hospitals (CAHs), and developed 102 competencies in four areas: clinical/technical (25 items), critical thinking (24 items), communication/interpersonal (27 items), and management/organizational (26 items). These findings were suggested to assist hospital nursing administration and education to plan for and advance competent nursing practice in rural hospital settings (Hurme, 2009).

Although there are many challenges and obstacles in the way of meeting the health care needs of rural patients and their caregivers, NPs working in partnership with other health care professionals or independently and adhering to the six domains of the PHA competencies can provide high-quality, competent, patient-centered care (Coalition for Patients' Rights, 2012; Martin, Ummenhofer, Manser, & Spirig, 2010). In the case of Mr. Marshall the following excerpt is an example of using the PHA competencies in an NP's practice.

> Since Mr. Marshall's wife is complaining about his loss of memory, and he has a family history of memory disturbance and AD, the NP must first screen for cognitive dysfunction and determine if his memory impairment is the result of dementia, depression, medication, a combination of any of these states, or any of several other conditions.

To screen Mr. Marshall's memory loss one needs to consider the validity and reliability of the instruments needed for screening (Mezey, Fulmer, Abraham, & Zwicker, 2003), and choose a solid and dependable tool such as the Mini-Cog (Doerflinger, 2007). If Mr. Marshall is assessed to have cognitive impairment in the early stage of dementia, he may require only monitoring with perhaps initiation of medication.

> Mr. Marshall and his family will need to be taught the range of dementia along with providing any educational materials and appropriate support resources such as the Alzheimer's Association and Area Agency on Aging (AAA).

Proper evaluation of cognitive decline requires that depression be considered. One of the best tools to use with older adults to screen for depression that is valid and reliable is the Geriatric Depression Scale: Short Form (GDS: SF). Because the GDS: SF is not a diagnostic test but a screening tool that suggests depression, a comprehensive assessment would be required if the screening is positive (Greenberg, 2007). Results of all screening tests and comprehensive assessment would be communicated to the interprofessional team for collaboration, to achieve positive outcomes through combining each member's expertise to jointly develop a plan of care (Doerflinger, 2007; Greenberg, 2007).

NPs can be invaluable in rural practice, especially in the care of older patients. By the nature of their training, NPs are often ideally suited to the positions and issues found in rural practices. When an NP is attracted to that type of practice, it can be a very positive experience for all concerned.

Pharmacists in Rural Practice

As is the case with other health professions, the practice of pharmacy is changing, particularly in community-based rural settings. Still, though, pharmacists most commonly interact with older adults in traditional community pharmacies (i.e., drugstores), which are either independently owned or part of a corporate chain. Pharmacists in these traditional community pharmacies see patients face to face, but have limited direct contact with other members of the interprofessional care team. In addition, these pharmacists do not have access to the health records maintained by the patient's primary and specialty care providers and are therefore dependent on the patient and caregiver to accurately report health-related information.

Pharmacies are also becoming more common in Federally Qualified Health Centers (FQHCs) that are present throughout the United States but are most heavily concentrated in the East, Midwest, and along the West Coast (U.S. Department of Health and Human Services [HHS], n.d.). The pharmacist whose practice is a part of an FQHC has many opportunities to collaborate with the other members of the interdisciplinary team and is able to view and contribute to the patient's electronic health record (EHR) or paper chart.

The type of pharmacists and their motivation for locating in a rural setting vary. Pharmacists who are employed in a chain pharmacy *may* be in a rural practice by choice; however, often they are less experienced pharmacists who are placed in the setting when another more senior pharmacist relocates to a larger community. On the other hand, a pharmacist who works in an independent pharmacy or FQHC is more likely to be in a rural community entirely by choice and is more likely to become involved in the community and its residents. Pharmacists who have chosen to remain in a rural community are able to overcome, at least in part, their dislocation from other members of the geriatric care team because they may be personally acquainted team members as well as with the patient.

Nonpharmacist members of the geriatric team can assist patients and caregivers by encouraging them to choose a pharmacy based on the level of professional service provided. Patients who have lengthy medication lists or have limited health literacy are best served by a pharmacist who sees them consistently in a local pharmacy, rather than by a mail-order facility or in a chain pharmacy with frequent staff turnover. Since almost all older adults have either private prescription drug insurance or are enrolled in Medicare Part D plans, their prescription medication costs will not vary significantly among local pharmacies. Once a person becomes eligible for Medicare, they may purchase Medicare Part D coverage that provides a partial payment for prescription drugs. Depending upon which specific Part D program a beneficiary chooses, different medications may be covered. Unfortunately, in the current economic environment, many prescription drug plans provide incentives or even require patients to obtain their chronic condition medications from a mail-order pharmacy. Pharmacists in mail-order pharmacies have essentially no opportunity for interaction with either the patient or the geriatric team. This is particularly problematic for older patients with multiple chronic medical problems.

Most pharmacists who practice in community settings have not completed advanced training programs to provide care to older adults. However, they may have demonstrated their interest in and knowledge of geriatric care by becoming members of the Commission for Certified Geriatric Pharmacists (CCGP; n.d.). Such pharmacists would be a particularly good choice for patients with complex medication regimens and care needs. The PHA multidisciplinary competencies discussed earlier are also beneficial, and were developed with pharmacist input and have been endorsed by major pharmacy organizations. Consider aspects of Mr. Marshall's case that could benefit from the input and viewpoint of a pharmacist in the context of the competencies.

A pharmacist can play an important role in the evaluation and assessment of Mr. Marshall's recent decline of memory and function by carefully documenting his medication regimen through a comprehensive history of all products that he has been taking (PHA Competency

Domains I and II). Patients and their caregivers often omit supplements and nonprescription medications when providing medication lists.

> Mr. Marshall has a short list that does include nonprescription medications and supplements. He has been taking a nonprescription sleep aid that contains diphenhydramine, which is also the active ingredient in the brand-name product called Benadryl®.

A pharmacist completing an assessment of Mr. Marshall's medications, who also has access to his medical record or who has been alerted by the physician, patient, or a family member, would also look especially closely to determine if any could be contributing to his current condition. Diphenhydramine, for example, is one of the medications on an often-cited list of drugs that should perhaps be avoided in older adults because they can worsen cognitive function, especially in patients with dementia (American Geriatrics Society, 2012 Beers Criteria Update Expert Panel, 2012). Another aspect of the pharmacist's role would be to collect information about any prescription drug coverage. Fortunately, most rural community pharmacists are interested in doing this for their clients.

> Mr. Marshall's medication regimen is remarkably simple, with only two prescription products. However, if his physician determines that Mr. Marshall has developed dementia and his condition deteriorates, new medications will probably be started.

As a result, the pharmacist should review Mr. Marshall's current and potential prescription insurance coverage in the context of predicted increased needs. Mr. Marshall may have VA benefits that would provide some coverage for prescriptions and he may also have retiree benefits from his previous employer. Medicare Part D plans are also an option for Mr. Marshall, if he does not already have credible coverage from a commercial plan. His current coverage should be documented in his medical record in anticipation of future care needs. The pharmacist can assist Mr. Marshall in reducing his potential out-of-pocket expenses by providing him, and those who assist in his care, information about prescription coverage, where to go to obtain more information, and how to communicate with his physician about prescription drug costs (PHA Domains V and VI). The pharmacist should participate as an interdisciplinary member of the care team by communicating both the information about the potential problems with the diphenhydramine and the information about Mr. Marshall's prescription coverage to the rest of the team, including Mr. Marshall, his caregiver, and his primary care physician (PHA Domain IV).

CONCLUSION

All health care professionals in rural practice share important challenges including high percentages of older adults in their practices (many of whom are living in poverty); potential professional and physical isolation; the dearth of certain facilities, agencies, and products; and the ubiquitous problem of transportation difficulties. Regardless of one's individual discipline, these issues are important on nearly a daily basis. Rural professionals also face cultural issues with their older adult patients; persons who grew up in a different era may have expectations of their medical care that differ greatly from younger populations. By incorporating the PHA competencies into their practices, health care professionals should be able to provide levels of care to their older patients that take all of these issues into account. Health profession schools should also increase their utilization of the competencies as a mechanism for ensuring better preparation of students for careers in rural practice. The competencies can serve as benchmarks, both for the progress of their students and for the eventual practice needs of their graduates.

Health profession schools in all disciplines have dealt actively for decades with the problem of rural areas being underserved, and still no unified model exists for attracting and training students for rural practice. Every state with a significant rural population has piloted programs for training and retaining rural practitioners, and there have of course been many individual successes. However as yet, no entity can claim to have designed a universally successful program. For example, in the very rural state of West Virginia the Higher Education Policy Commission has mandated for many years that students in all three of the state's medical schools have rural practice experience. The three medical schools comprise two allopathic schools and one osteopathic school. The rural health care experience provided by the schools include programs to recruit more potential students from rural and underserved groups (such as Upward Bound students), special events to increase interest among current students (such as a Rural Health Day), and summer programs and enhanced rotations in which students live in rural communities for an expanded period of time.

Some programs are now available in which the entirety of a residency training program may be undertaken in a smaller city hospital/rural clinic environment. In the commission's 2012 "report card" (Walker, 2012), the overall percentage of West Virginia medical school graduates choosing primary care was seen to be 57.02% over the preceding 5 years. The osteopathic school has regularly produced the highest percentage of primary care-bound graduates, with a 5-year average of 67.08%. Retention of those students in primary care and especially in rural care, however, is less successful for all the schools. Data are available for the period of 2002 through 2007 that show many fewer students who begin primary care residency training are practicing primary care over time. In 2012, an average of 23% of West Virginia medical school graduates from the 2002 through 2007 time frame were actively in primary care practice and only 9% were in rural practice, despite 57% having gone into a primary care field upon graduation from medical school.

The Office of Rural Health Policy (ORHP) within the HHS Health Resources and Services Administration (HRSA; www.hrsa.gov/rural-health/pdf/ruralhealthprofessionsguidance.pdf) has recently addressed this issue extensively in a publication titled *Rural Guide to Health Professions Funding* that can be accessed online. One of HRSA's programs in existence since 1970, the National Health Service Corps (NHSC), has as its goal the placement and retention of a variety of health care professionals in rural underserved sites. The model is that communities support the infrastructure needed to open or sustain a practice, and candidates may choose one of these rural communities to which to be assigned to repay their scholarship commitment or to achieve loan forgiveness. Retention of professionals in their chosen sites is reasonably high, up to 55% 10 years after their initial placement (HHS, 2012). One might speculate on reasons for the greater retention of professionals by the HRSA program than by the programs designed by a wide variety of health profession schools—perhaps it is the community support of infrastructure of the practice; perhaps it is because some remain in salaried (although not federally funded) positions; perhaps it is because recruits into the NHSC programs are not all fresh graduates of residency programs and thus are arguably more mature in their judgments regarding their site of practice. Some of the data may be skewed because some graduating students choose a primary care residency but change programs before they ever complete their training. Research to definitively answer this question is not available; however, exploration of the question remains important to health care planners.

Other model training programs for rural medical professionals and professional groups also exist. The National Rural Health Association (NRHA; www.ruralhealthweb.org) sponsors a Rural Health Fellows Program. This 1-year training program builds leadership and health policy and analysis skills among its participants. The NRHA also collects information on effective health service models in rural areas. Called Models that Work, the NRHA collects and lists programs from various U.S. rural areas, and focuses on a variety of population including Alaskan Natives and Navajo Native Americans. Several states also have rural health care associations that aim to improve health care delivery systems and to train and retain health care professionals.

In this chapter, important aspects of the practices of a selected few health care professionals in rural areas were reviewed. The authors clearly recognize that many more disciplines than those discussed here contribute to the health of rural older adults. Conditions and restrictions under which these practitioners carry out their jobs are often very different from the situations faced by those who practice in urban areas, yet public perceptions of their capabilities and accomplishments, and public policies that govern their practices, are too often based only on urban conditions. Ongoing research and continuing development of narratives of rural practice are invaluable as health care professionals go forward into new models and conditions of health care delivery.

USEFUL WEBSITES

American Association of Nurse Practitioners
www.aanp.org
American Dental Association
www.ada.org
American Geriatrics Society
www.americangeriatrics.org
Commission for Certification of Geriatric Pharmacists
www.ccgp.org
National Rural Health Association
www.ruralhealthweb.org

Rural and Remote Health Journal

www.rrh.org.au

U.S. Department of Health and Human Services,
Healthy People

www.HealthyPeople.gov

U.S. Department of Health and Human Services,
Health Resources and Services Administration

www.hrsa.gov

REFERENCES

Adut, R., Mann, J., & Sgan-Cohen, H. D. (2004). Past and present geographic location as oral health markers among older adults. *Journal of Public Health Dentistry, 64*(4), 240–243.

Ahn, S., Biurdine, J. N., Smith, M. L., Ory, M. G., & Phillips, C. D. (2011). Residential rurality and oral health disparities: Influences of contextual and individual factors. *Journal of Primary Prevention, 32*(1), 29–41.

Alguire, P. (n.d.). Types of practices. Retrieved June 15, 2013, from http://www.acponline.org/residents_fellows/career_counseling/types.html

American Academy of Family Physicians (AAFP). (2013). Keeping physicians in rural practice. Retrieved June 15, 2013, from http://www.aafp.org.online/about/policies/all/rural-practice-paper.html

American Academy of Nurse Practitioners. (n.d.). *Nurse practitioners in primary care.* Retrieved June 15, 2013, from http://www.aanp.org/images/documents/publications/primarycare.pdf

American Association of Nurse Practitioners. (n.d.). *Scope of practice for nurse practitioners.* Retrieved June 15, 2013, from http://www.aanp.org/images/documents/publications/scopeofpractice.pdf

American Geriatrics Society, 2012 Beers Criteria Update Expert Panel. (2012). American Geriatrics Society updated Beers criteria for potentially inappropriate medication use in older adults. *Journal of the American Geriatrics Society, 60*(4), 616–631.

Association of American Medical Colleges (AAMC). (2012, March). The changing gender composition of U.S. medical applicants and matriculants. *Analysis in Brief, 12*(1). Retrieved August 28, 2013, from https://www.aamc.org/download/277026/data/aibvol12_no1.pdf

Bushy, A. (2006). Nursing in rural and frontier areas: Issues, challenges and opportunities. *Harvard Health Policy Review, 7*(1), 17–27.

Coalition for Patients' Rights. (2012, April). Interprofessional care teams improve clinical outcomes, help address chronic health issues. Retrieved

August 28, 2013, from http://www.patientsrightscoalition.org/Media-Resources/News-Releases/Interprofessional-Care.aspx

Commission for Certification of Geriatric Pharmacists. (n.d.). *Commission for certification of geriatric pharmacists.* Retrieved July 24, 2013, from http://www.ccgp.org

Congressional Budget Office. (2013, June). *Dual-eligible beneficiaries of Medicare and Medicaid: Characteristics, health care spending, and evolving policies.* Retrieved September 25, 2013, from http://www.cbo.gov/publication/44308

Doerflinger, D. M. C. (2007). The mini-cog. *American Journal of Nursing, 107*(12), 62–72.

Faulkner, A., Wilson, E., Whitler, E., & Asher, L. (2012). Role of international medical graduates in Kentucky medicine: Implications for workforce planning and medical education. *Journal of the Kentucky Medical* Association, *110*, 417–421.

Florell, M. L. (2009, August). *Rural health care workforce: Opportunities to improve care delivery* (No. 6). Lyons, NE: Center for Rural Affairs. Retrieved May 15, 2013, from http://files.cfra.org/pdf/HealthCare_Workforce.pdf

Goetz, K., Musselman, B., Szecsenyi, J., & Joos, S. (2013). The influence of workload and health behavior on job satisfaction of general practitioners. *Family Medicine, 45*(2), 95–101.

Goins, R. T., & Krout, J. A. (2006). Aging in rural America. In R. T. Goins & J. A. Krout (Eds.), *Service delivery to rural older adults: Research, policy, and practice* (pp. 3–20). New York, NY: Springer Publishing Company.

Greenberg, S. A. (2007). How to try this: The geriatric depression scale: Short form. *American Journal of Nursing, 107*(10), 61–69.

Hurme, E. (2009). Competencies for nursing practice in a rural critical access hospital. *Online Journal of Rural Nursing and Health Care, 9*(2), 67–71.

Kiyak, H. A., & Reichmuth, M. (2005). Barriers to and enablers of older adults' use of dental services. *Journal of Dental Education, 69*(9), 975–986.

Larson, S., Machlin, S., Nixon, A., & Zodet, M. (2004, June). Chartbook #13: Health care in urban and rural areas, combined years 1998–2000. Retrieved from http://meps.ahrq.gov/mepsweb/data_files/publications/cb13/cb13.shtml

MacDowell, M., Glasser, M., Fitts, M., Nielsen, K., & Hunsaker, M. (2010). A national view of rural health workforce issues in the USA. *Rural and Remote Health, 10*(3), 1531. Retrieved June 24, 2013, from http://www.rrh.org.au

Martin, J. S., Ummenhofer, W., Manser, T., & Spirig, R. (2010, September). Interprofessional collaboration among nurses and physicians: Making a difference in patient outcome. *Swiss Medical Weekly, 140*, 1–7.

Mezey, M. D., Fulmer, T., Abraham, I., & Zwicker, D. (2003). *Geriatric nursing protocols for best practice* (2nd ed.). New York, NY: Springer Publishing Company.

Mitchell, J., Bennett, K., & Brock-Martin, A. (2012). Edentulism in high poverty rural counties. *Journal of Rural Health, 29*(1), 30–38.

Nachtmann, H., & Pohl, E. (2009, July). *Rural transportation emergency preparedness plans.* Fayetteville, AR: University of Arkansas Mack Blackwell Transportation Center. Retrieved September 24, 2013, from ww2.mackblackwell.org/

web/research/ALL_RESEARCH_PROJECTS/2000s/2091/MBTC_2091_Final_Report.pdf

National Institute of Dental and Craniofacial Research. (2000). *Oral health in America: A report of the surgeon general* [Executive Summary]. Retrieved September 24, 2013, from http://www.nidcr.nih.gov/datastatistics/surgeongeneral/report/executivesummary.html

Partnership for Health in Aging. (2010, March). *Multidisciplinary competencies in the care of older adults at the completion of the entry-level health professional degree.* Retrieved September 24, 2013, from http://www.americangeriatrics.org/files/documents/health_care_pros/PHA_multidisc_competencies.pdf

Rosenblatt, R. (2000). Physicians and rural America. *Western Journal of Medicine, 173*(5), 348–351.

Skillman, S. M., Doescher, M. P., Mouradian, W. E., & Brunson, D. K. (2010). The challenge to delivering oral health services in rural America. *Journal of Public Health Dentistry, 70*(1), S49–57.

Stanton, M. (2009, September 22). Rural nurse competencies: Experts, advocates and activists. *Online Journal of Rural Nursing and Health Care, 9*(2). Retrieved September 24, 2013, from http://www.thefreelibrary.com/Rural+nurse+competencies%3A+experts,+advocates+and+activists.-a0215842376

Ullman, K. (2012, November). Practicing in rural settings offers slower pace, personal satisfaction for many rheumatologists. *The Rheumatologist.* Retrieved June 24, 2013, from http://www.the-rheumatologist.org/details/article/3038931

U.S. Department of Health and Human Services. (2012, December). NHSC clinician retention: A story of dedication and commitment. Retrieved October 30, 2013, from http://nhsc.hrsa.gov/currentmembers/membersites/retain-providers/retentionbrief.pdf

U.S. Department of Health and Human Services. (n.d.). What are federally qualified health centers (FQHCs)? Retrieved July 24, 2013, from http://www.hrsa.gov/healthit/toolbox/RuralHealthITtoolbox/Introduction/qualified.html

Vargas, C. M., & Arevalo, O. (2009). How dental care can preserve and improve oral health. *Dental Clinics of North America, 53*(3), 399–420.

Vargas, C. M., Dye, B. A., & Hayes, K. L. (2003). Oral health status of rural adults in the United States. *Journal of the American Dental Association, 133*, 1672–1681.

Vargas, C. M., Ronzio, C. R., & Hayes, K. L. (2003). Oral health status of children and adolescents by rural residence, United States. *The Journal of Rural Health, 19*(3), 260–268.

Walker, R. (2012). *West Virginia health sciences and rural health report card 2012.* Retrieved October 30, 2013, from http://www.wvhepc.org/resources/Health_Report_2012_lr.pdf

Yee, T., Boukus, E. R., Cross, D., & Samuel, D. R. (2013, February). *Primary care workforce shortages: Nurse practitioner scope-of-practice laws and payment policies* (NIHCR Research Brief No. 13). Washington, DC: National Institute for Health Care Reform. Retrieved May 12, 2013, from http://www.nihcr.org/PCP-Workforce-NPs

Young, K., Garfield, R., Musumeci, M., Clemans-Cope, L., & Lawton, E. (2013, August). *Medicaid's role for dual eligible beneficiaries.* Menlo Park, CA: Kaiser Family Foundation. Retrieved September 24, 2013, from http://kff.org/medicaid/issue-brief/medicaids-role-for-dual-eligible-beneficiaries

Ziliak, J., & Gunderson, C. (2009, September). *Senior hunger in the United States: Differences across states and rural and urban areas.* Lexington, KY: University of Kentucky Center for Poverty Research in Special Populations. Retrieved September 24, 2013, from www.ukcpr.org/Publications/Senior-hunger followup.pdf

11

Role of the Human Service Professional

KRISTINA M. HASH

JOANN DAMRON-RODRIGUEZ

HANNA THURMAN

Jane Diller has lived in rural southeastern West Virginia for all of her 75 years. She would not consider living anywhere other than her "home in the hills," which is a winding 30-mile, 1.5-hour drive from the nearest metropolitan area. Her husband of almost 40 years, George, died last year at the age of 77 after being diagnosed with congestive heart failure (CHF) and end-stage renal disease (ESRD). Aside from having breast cancer 15 years ago, Mrs. Diller has not suffered from any chronic illnesses and remains very physically and socially active. Two months ago, she started caring for her 9-year-old-granddaughter, Lilly. She became Lilly's full-time caregiver when her daughter was mandated treatment for substance abuse at a rehabilitation facility 2 hours away. Mrs. Diller's daughter is her only child and is not expected to return home for at least another 11 months.

Jenny, an MSW (master of social work) student intern, worked with Mr. and Mrs. Diller at both of her field placement agencies. While interning at a small local hospital, Jenny helped to coordinate Mr. Diller's Veterans benefits. Six months later, Jenny provided end-of-life planning and counseling for the Dillers while interning at a regional hospice agency. In both of these settings, the Dillers reluctantly accepted assistance because Mrs. Diller prided herself on being able to take care of George in their home, remarking "We've always just done for ourselves." After George's passing, Jenny started and continues to make bereavement calls to Mrs. Diller.

Jenny also attends the same church where Mrs. Diller has worshipped most of her life. Last week, two of Mrs. Diller's longtime friends approached Jenny after the service and shared concerns that she had become very forgetful in the past few months. Mrs. Diller had missed several church events and planned outings with her friends. They also suspected that she had missed a scheduled doctor's appointment. Her response to them with regard to the absences had been "it just must've slipped my mind."

For rural older adults like the Dillers, health and well-being require a complement of both medical and social services, particularly in transitions between levels of care where health and human services are essential and yet difficult to arrange. These transitions are precarious for older persons and require skillful interventions (Coleman, Parry, Chalmers, & Min, 2006; Naylor et al., 2004). Part III of this book comprehensively describes programs and organizations that exist to serve older adults and their families residing in small towns and rural areas. This chapter further adds to this view a focus on the professionals who practice in rural settings linking medical and human or social services. These individuals are often deemed human service professionals. This designation can identify a person from any discipline with a focus not on a specific medical problem or disease, but on the whole of the human condition and the services that address these needs. The following is a comprehensive definition of human services:

The field of human services is broadly defined, uniquely approaching the objective of meeting human needs through an interdisciplinary knowledge base, focusing on prevention as well as remediation of problems, and maintaining a commitment to improving the overall quality of life of service populations. The human services profession is one that promotes improved service delivery systems by addressing not only the quality of direct services, but also by seeking to improve accessibility, accountability, and coordination among professionals and agencies in service delivery. (National Organization for Human Services, 2013)

As indicated by the definition, human services involve multiple disciplines. Social workers and nurses frequently work side by side and often supervise a variety of paraprofessionals in this human service realm. This requires interdisciplinary communication and practice as described in Chapter 9 of this book. It also demands teaching and collaboration competencies in order to assure community agencies and direct care workers have the necessary skills and resources to serve older adults effectively. Working within the interdisciplinary team, social workers are often identified as the professionals to meet the human service needs of older adults and their families. The goals of geriatric social work describe the domains of human services:

1. Enhance the developmental, problem-solving, and coping capacities of older people *and their families*
2. Promote the effective and humane operating of systems that provide resources and services to *older* people *and their familie*s
3. Link *older* people with systems that provide them with resources, services, and opportunities
4. Contribute to the development and improvement of social policies *that support persons throughout the life span* (Berkman, Dobrof, Harry, & Damron-Rodriguez, 1997)

This chapter presents the unique issues involved in rural practice and the emerging importance of a practitioner's competence in bridging health and human services to the advantage of the older adult. It emphasizes the human service practitioners' role in working with rural older adults and the strengths and challenges they encounter. The profession of social work is used to exemplify the role of the human service practitioner in the field of aging. Additionally, this chapter details the professional competencies developed for social work and related disciplines and examines these competencies in light of rural practice.

SOCIAL WORK PRACTICE WITH RURAL OLDER ADULTS

As Jenny is learning, the practice of social work with older adults residing in small towns and rural areas presents a multitude of challenges as well as opportunities. Guidance for rural social work (Ginsberg, 2011a; Lohmann & Lohmann, 2005) as well as for specific practice with older adults in these communities has been offered (Butler & Kaye, 2003). Principles for providing training and education in these areas have also been suggested (Bisman, 2003; Daley & Pierce, 2011; Kropf, 2003; N. Lohmann, 2005).

Guidance for Rural Practice

Locke and Winthrop (2005, p. 5) purported that social work educators agree about the "skills, attitudes, and knowledge" needed for rural practice and identified five major themes related to successful practice in these areas. To begin, social workers should be trained to function as *generalists,* meaning that the professional can effectively work at multiple levels, including intervention with individuals, groups, organizations, and communities. Given generalist knowledge and skills, social workers in rural communities can and should be involved in *community practice and development.* This often involves managing *external relations,* working with various community leaders and others with power to secure or initiate needed resources or programs. Ginsberg (2011b) noted that this often includes not only elected officials but also church leaders. R. A. Lohmann (2005) also stressed the importance of attending to and partnering with what is called the third sector (nonprofits) in rural areas that includes volunteers and church communities.

Locke and Winthrop (2005) also posited that successfully functioning within a rural community as a social worker involves an understanding of its *culture.* Knowledge of local customs, traditions, and social institutions is critical to the ability to establish helping relationships with residents. Similarly, the National Association of Social Workers (NASW; 2012) stressed the importance of understanding "rural people and culture" (p. 299), including the fact that rural communities place great value on community identity, family, and traditions. Understanding Mrs. Diller's strong sense of place and the pride she has in taking care of her family helped Jenny build rapport and trust in the case study at the beginning of this chapter. Additionally, it is important to realize that rural residents who relocate to urban areas often retain their rural influences and culture.

According to Locke and Winthrop (2005), there are also *personal and professional traits* that contribute to successful practice in rural areas. A rural social worker should be committed to the community, its issues, and its preservation. If this commitment is apparent, the social worker is viewed as an important community resource to link older adults' needs to both medical and social services in the community. According to Ginsberg (2011b), failure to integrate into the community can have especially detrimental effects on the ability to practice in these areas. Along with this commitment, professional social workers in rural areas must be prepared and able to deal with professional isolation; they may be the only social workers in certain agencies and areas (Locke & Winthrop, 2005). According to the NASW (2012), there is often a shortage of formally trained social workers in rural communities. Those that do practice in these areas tend to hold bachelor's degrees in social work or do not hold formal degrees in social work and are often employed in regionally focused agencies. As such, rural social workers should be able to function with little peer support and supervision and make an even greater effort in the areas of professional growth and development, including continuing education and membership and participation in professional groups and associations (Locke & Winthrop, 2005). Both Ginsberg (2011b) and N. Lohmann (2005) noted that technology does, however, hold promise in overcoming obstacles related to professional isolation. It also has the potential to form and strengthen interdisciplinary linkages.

Other rural researchers and educators add ethical issues, such as dual relationships, to the unique features of rural practice. The NASW (2008) identified dual or multiple relationships under the conflicts of interest section of the social worker's ethical responsibilities to clients. These relationships "occur when social workers relate to clients in more than one relationship, whether professional, social, or business" and "can occur simultaneously or consecutively" (1.06, c). These types of relationships in small rural communities may be unavoidable. Mrs. Diller's friends may have felt more comfortable sharing their concerns with Jenny because they all attended church together. In fact, Galbreath (2005) asserted that dual relationships are much more likely to occur because of smaller numbers of people in rural communities, and Bosch and Boisen (2011) suggested that practitioners should expect dual relationships in the very small communities where a professional may work and live.

Given the inevitability of dual relationships with clients in rural communities, several researchers have offered guidelines for managing such situations. There is consensus that social workers in these areas should prepare for these encounters and set very clear boundaries with clients (Bosch & Boisen, 2011; Galbreath, 2005; NASW, 2012). Along with setting boundaries, the practitioner should also carefully assess issues of potential harm, exploitation, and disempowerment of clients in various roles and relationships (Galbreath, 2005; Healy, 2003), and the potential risks involved in these relationships should be discussed with clients (Bosch & Boisen, 2011). Healy (2003) posited a "contextual ethical analysis" as a model for examining these issues. This involves multilevel analysis and self-reflection that consider relationships with and responsibilities to older clients and their families, organizations, and the community. In particular, the social worker should ensure that decisions do not disempower clients while favoring colleague, agency, or community interests. Bosch and Boisen (2011) also stressed that social workers in rural areas should be authentic in their relationships, meaning they are consistent in how they interact with individuals in their various roles and relationships and that the use of supervision can aid in identifying and managing dual relationships.

Principles for Training and Education

Although practice guidelines have been suggested for social work practice in rural communities, there is very little content in social work curricula on rural practice and a tendency to move toward specialization instead of generalist practice (NASW, 2012). A few educators have, however, offered solutions for educating students and professionals for rural practice. Daley and Pierce (2011) suggested that rural content can be offered as a stand-alone course or can be infused into a program curriculum. It can also be viewed within the context of diversity and cultural competence. Content about rurality can include definitions of rural, policy, and special ethical issues and challenges. Along with dual relationships, confidentiality and self-disclosure can be difficult in rural areas. In fact, practitioners may feel as though they live in a "fishbowl"; therefore, students should be educated to understand that their actions and self-disclosures can impact their practice. Jenny learned that in her rural social work practice she had to be very judicious in sharing anything about her personal life. Daley and Pierce (2011) also identified rural competency areas that included a generalist preparation, understanding the slower rate of change and acceptance of outsiders, ability to utilize informal networks, conducting community assessments, understanding the culture and engaging appropriately, attending to special social justice issues such as rural poverty, and dealing with professional isolation. N. Lohmann (2005) added that continuing professional education may be even more important for isolated rural practitioners. As mentioned, distance technology may be integral to delivering education in rural areas. Because the shortage of master's-prepared social workers can also result in limited supervision opportunities for students, N. Lohmann advises flexibility in this area.

Kropf (2003) went further by focusing on the difficulties of attracting students to rural areas and training them to work with older adults in these areas. According to Kropf, "In order to prepare students for practice roles, content on older adults (including those who reside in rural areas) needs to become more visible in the curriculum" (2003, p. 289). Methods for attracting students to practice in these communities include exposing them to the communities and their citizens; "home-growing" professionals who already reside in these areas; and developing curriculum, field experiences, and course content that focus on this population. Key issues for students to understand include the specific rural context, such as the diversity that exists among rural communities and whether older residents have aged in place or in-migrated from other areas. Accessibility of health care, economics, and available social supports are also key indicators to understand in a rural community. Students should be well trained in case management (or linking individuals and families to needed services). Content and skills in administration should be stressed, as should leadership skills. Kropf was also a proponent of using distance education (such as telemedicine) to bridge practice distances and in delivering educational content.

Bisman (2003) addressed providing social work education for practice with rural older adults as well as noting that social work's attention to the person in the environment, both micropractice and macropractice, advocacy, and social justice provide an exceptional basis from which to work with rural older adults. Further, the tools of assessment, biopsychosocial approach, and the professional use of oneself provide a good fit with this population. The concepts of social support and looking at family systems are key, and group work, case management, and community practice provide salient interventions for this population.

PROFESSIONAL COMPETENCY

Educating students and professionals for practice in rural communities and particularly with rural elders is imperative. Going beyond mere education to ensuring the competency of these students and professionals is critical for the delivery of effective services for this growing population. The Institute of Medicine (IOM; 2008) report *Retooling for an Aging America* asserted the need for all health care professionals (including social workers) to be competently trained to work with older adults. Competent gerontological or geriatric practice can broadly be defined as the state or quality of being adequately or well qualified in a specific range of knowledge, values, and skills to address the needs of older adults and their families (Damron-Rodriguez, 2008). Competency-based education and evaluation (CBE) is recognized as the foundation for professional education. CBE is the requirement for the measurement of practice outcomes of professional education. CBE requires the following elements: adoption of a *defined set of specific skills (competencies)* as a framework for education in a field of practice, and *assessment of student skill level* using the identified set of competencies (Bogo et al., 2004). Consensus-based geriatric competencies have been developed for medicine (American Geriatrics Society [AGS]), nursing (American Association of Colleges of Nurses [AACN]), and social work (Social Work Leadership Institute [SWLI]) supported by the John A. Hartford Foundation. The five major domains for the geriatric social work competencies are I. values, ethics, and theoretical perspectives; II. assessment; III. intervention; IV. aging services, programs, and policies; and V. leadership in the practice environment of aging (Damron-Rodriguez, Volland, Wright, & Hooyman, 2009). Table 11.1 lists the domains and their respective competencies.

The Partnership for Health in Aging (PHA) competencies discussed in Chapters 9 and 10 are also inclusive of the social work discipline.

Similar to competency-based education (CBE), evidence-based practice (EBP) works to assure quality and positive outcomes. CBE uses data to assess the impact of curricula and pedagogy on student competence and creating a competent workforce. EBP aims to assure positive patient or client outcomes from best practices and program design. Competent practitioners in both urban and rural areas must be prepared to enter the world of EBP. This model recognizes the impact of the environment on the application of any best practice. Rubin (2008) described the cycle of EBP illustrated as a Venn diagram with three major interrelated domains: research evidence, client preferences and actions, and clinical state and

TABLE 11.1 Geriatric Social Work Competency Scale II with Lifelong Leadership Skills: Social Work Practice Behaviors in the Field

Domain I. Values, Ethics, and Theoretical Perspectives (knowledge and value base, which are applied through skills/competencies)

1. Assess and address values and biases regarding aging.

2. Respect and promote older adult clients' right to dignity and self-determination.

3. Apply ethical principles to decisions on behalf of all older clients with special attention to those who have limited decisional capacity.

4. Respect diversity among older adult clients, families, and professionals (e.g., class, race, ethnicity, gender, and sexual orientation).

5. Address the cultural, spiritual, and ethnic values and beliefs of older adults and families.

6. Relate concepts and theories of aging to social work practice (e.g., cohorts, normal aging, and life-course perspective).

7. Relate social work perspectives and related theories to practice with older adults (e.g., person-in-environment, social justice).

8. Identify issues related to losses, changes, and transitions over their life cycles in designing interventions.

9. Support persons and families dealing with end-of-life issues related to dying, death, and bereavement.

10. Understand the perspective and values of social work in relation to working effectively with other disciplines in geriatric interdisciplinary practice.

Domain II. Assessment

1. Use empathy and sensitive interviewing skills to engage older clients in identifying their strengths and problems.

2. Adapt interviewing methods to potential sensory, language, and cognitive limitations of the older adult.

3. Conduct a comprehensive geriatric assessment (biopsychosocial evaluation).

4. Ascertain health status and assess physical functioning (e.g., ADLs and IADLs) of older clients.

5. Assess cognitive functioning and mental health status of older clients (e.g., depression, dementia).

6. Assess social functioning (e.g., social skills, social activity level) and social support of older clients.

7. Assess caregivers' needs and levels of stress.

8. Administer and interpret standardized assessment and diagnostic tools that are appropriate for use with older adults (e.g., depression scale, Mini-Mental Status Examination [MMSE]).

9. Develop clear, timely, and appropriate service plans with measurable objectives for older adults.

(continued)

TABLE 11.1 Geriatric Social Work Competency Scale II with Lifelong Leadership Skills: Social Work Practice Behaviors in the Field (*continued*)

10. Reevaluate and adjust service plans for older adults on a continuing basis.

Domain III. Intervention

1. Establish rapport and maintain an effective working relationship with older adults and family members.

2. Enhance the coping capacities and mental health of older persons through a variety of therapy modalities (e.g., supportive, psychodynamic).

3. Utilize group interventions with older adults and their families (e.g., bereavement groups, reminiscence groups).

4. Mediate situations with angry or hostile older adults and/or family members.

5. Assist caregivers to reduce their stress levels and maintain their own mental and physical health.

6. Provide social work case management to link older adults and their families to resources and services.

7. Use educational strategies to provide older persons and their families with information related to wellness and disease management (e.g., Alzheimer's disease (AD), end-of-life care).

8. Apply skills in termination in work with older adults and their families.

9. Advocate on behalf of clients with agencies and other professionals to help older adults obtain quality services.

10. Adhere to laws and public policies related to older adults (e.g., older adult abuse reporting, legal guardianship, advance directives).

Domain IV. Aging Services, Programs, and Policies

1. Provide outreach to older adults and their families to ensure appropriate use of the service continuum.

2. Adapt organizational policies, procedures, and resources to facilitate the provision of services to diverse older adults and their family caregivers.

3. Identify and develop strategies to address service gaps, fragmentation, discrimination, and barriers that impact older persons.

4. Include older adults in planning and designing programs.

5. Develop program budgets that take into account diverse sources of financial support for the older population.

6. Evaluate the effectiveness of practices and programs in achieving intended outcomes for older adults.

7. Apply evaluation and research findings to improve practice and program outcomes.

8. Advocate and organize with the service providers, community organizations, policy makers, and the public to meet the needs and issues of a growing aging population.

(continued)

TABLE 11.1 Geriatric Social Work Competency Scale II with Lifelong Leadership Skills: Social Work Practice Behaviors in the Field (*continued*)

9. Identify the availability of resources and resource systems for older adults and their families.

10. Assess and address any negative impacts of social and health care policies on practice with historically disadvantaged populations.

Domain V. Leadership in the Practice Environment of Aging

Leadership skills are lifelong learning objectives for which a foundation is laid in social work education. Competence is built over years of practice and continuing education.

1. Assess "self-in-relation" in order to motivate yourself and others including trainees, students, and staff toward mutual, meaningful achievement of a focused goal or committed standard of practice.

2. Create a shared organizational mission, vision, values, and policies responding to ever-changing service systems in order to promote coordinated, optimal services for older persons.

3. Analyze historical and current local, state, national policies from a global human rights perspective in order to inform action related to an identified social problem and/or program for older adults for the purpose of creating change.

4. Plan strategically to reach measurable objectives in program, organizational, or community development for older adults.

5. Administer programs and organizations from a strength's perspective to maximize and sustain human resources (staff and volunteers) and fiscal resources for effectively serving older adults.

6. Build collaborations across disciplines and the service spectrum to assess access, continuity, and reduce gaps in services to older adults.

7. Manage individual (personal) and multi-stakeholder (interpersonal) processes at the community, interagency, and intra-agency levels in order to inspire, leverage power, and resources to optimize services for older adults.

8. Communicate to public audiences and policy makers through multiple media including writing synthesis reports and legislative statements and orally presenting the mission and outcomes of the services of an organization or for diverse client group(s).

9. Advocate with and for older adults and their families for building age friendly community capacity (including the use of technology) and enhance the contribution of older persons.

10. Promote use of research (including evidence based practice) to evaluate and enhance the effectiveness of social work practice and aging related services.

ADLs, activities of daily living; IADLs, instrumental activities of daily living.

Reprinted with permission of Social Work Leadership Institute. (n.d.). *Geriatric Social Work Competency Scale II with Lifelong Leadership Skills.* Available at www.cswe.org/File .aspx?id=25445 circumstances. Social work practice has long employed an environmental and contextual assessment of clinical states and circumstances, which makes it consistent with the EBP model.

COMPETENCY AND EVIDENCE-BASED PRACTICE FOR GERIATRIC SOCIAL WORK IN SMALL TOWNS AND RURAL AREAS

Geriatric Competencies

The geriatric social work competencies identified earlier apply to a wide range of social work roles and settings. Unfortunately, they have not been examined in light of the unique challenges and opportunities offered by rural communities. The John A. Hartford Foundation has developed a field-based, geriatric training model for social work students that integrates the geriatric competencies with rotations in various older adult service settings (such as hospital, home health, hospice, mental health clinics, skilled nursing facilities, and senior centers). West Virginia University is one of more than 60 schools of social work that follows the Hartford Partnership Program for Aging Education (HPPAE) model and adds a focus on practice and competency in small towns and rural areas. For this program, at least one field rotation is conducted in a rural setting and assignments and discussions for the HPPAE students relate to the special issues encountered in these areas. Many HPPAE students also complete the interdisciplinary course, rural gerontology. A particular online discussion asked students to identify the unique features of geriatric social work practice in this context. The specific discussion questions asked can be found in the companion Instructors Manual for the book. The resulting themes are from 3 years of online discussions with approximately 15 MSW students. These themes can be tied to the geriatric social work competencies as well as the literature on general and geriatric-specific rural practice and education.

Intervention Domain and Aging Services, Programs, and Policies Domain

Given the lack of medical and social services in many rural areas, the following competencies within the intervention domain and the aging services, programs, and policies domain become even more important as well as difficult to attain:

Intervention Domain

6. Provide social work case management to link older adults and their families to resources and services.

Aging Services, Programs, and Policies Domain

1. Provide outreach to older adults and their families to ensure appropriate use of the service continuum.
3. Identify and develop strategies to address service gaps, fragmentation, discrimination, and barriers that impact older persons.
8. Advocate and organize with the service providers, community organizations, policy makers, and the public to meet the needs and issues of a growing aging population.
9. Identify the availability of resources and resource systems for older adults and their families.
10. Assess and address any negative impacts of social and health care policies on practice with historically disadvantaged populations.

Related to these domains, students overwhelmingly noted a lack of access to needed health and human services for rural elders with whom they worked. Most frustrating was that "there are a number of services that they are entitled to but are unable to receive." These services include medical care, mental health services, older adult housing, and transportation. Services were mentioned as being either nonexistent or fragmented. As such, students noted the importance of "being creative and resourceful with what is available, and the older adults are even more so (creative and resourceful)." Advocating for additional services and trying to bridge gaps in services are often necessary. And, since services are sparse, students or professionals may find themselves with few opportunities for support, consultation, and supervision. This is compounded by a shortage of trained professionals in these areas. In addition, the rising cost of gas was mentioned as a major barrier to reliable transportation, as was geographic isolation and inclement weather conditions. These issues "add to the challenges of getting older . . . to those who are already suffering." The lack of services is also very difficult for the professionals who work with rural older adults. Lower income and poverty add to older people's inability to acquire needed services. Lack of Internet access and knowledge can also be barriers to services (such as enrolling in Medicare Part D programs). And, as one student explained, these problems are often interconnected:

There are places that I have visited where, to get to a patient's house, you have to park at the end of a dirt road and walk across a field. There are places that are not accessible during the winter because of the dangerous terrain you have to drive on to reach an older client. Also, many older people do not drive and they rely on family members or neighbors for transportation. If these people are not around, older persons do not get to go to their needed doctor appointments; for example . . . they may miss appointments and end up in the hospital.

Values, Ethics, and Theoretical Perspectives Domain

Three competencies in the values and ethics domain are important to explore and meet within a rural context:

2. Respect and promote older adult clients' right to dignity and self-determination.
3. Apply ethical principles to decisions on behalf of all older clients with special attention to those who have limited decisional capacity.
5. Address the cultural, spiritual, and ethnic values and beliefs of older adults and families.

Rural older adults can be quite proud and determined. As Mrs. Diller told Jenny, "We've always just done for ourselves." As such, their rights to dignity and self-determination are even more crucial. Rural communities often have their own cultures, with values and beliefs unique to those communities or regions. Ethnic groups within these areas may have unique cultures as well. Residents in these communities may be more involved in and rely more heavily on support from their churches and faith-based organizations. HPPAE students specifically noted the self-determination and resiliency of the rural older adults they encountered. In fact, the qualities of "independent, self-reliant, resilient, and resourceful" were frequently used to describe rural older people. Older adults in these areas may live alone and not in close proximity to neighbors. Additionally, family members may have moved to larger cities for employment. Students noted that many of these older individuals did not want to ask for help because they were used to doing things for themselves. The case study in this chapter shows the reluctance of the Dillers to accept assistance. Some do not want to trouble their friends and neighbors for help and some mistrust formal services (especially those affiliated with the government); for that reason, they will not seek help from these services and professionals. When rural older adults do ask for help, it is often from informal sources (such as friends, neighbors, and church members) and rural communities are experienced in providing care for their members. In fact, rural communities often have a "strong sense of community where favors are done and returned." A student explained this in the context of rural culture:

> As a part of traditional rural culture, family members take care of their loved ones in times of illness, birth, and death. It was not always possible to get a loved one to a doctor or have the doctor make home visits so it was up to the family. Tragedy can strike at any time in the form of weather, death, illness, and so forth. Rural communities banded together to face these tragedies head-on and together. Many are very accustomed to working as a community or neighborhood to help someone overcome a hardship.

This resilience often comes as a result of spiritual faith. For many, spirituality provides rural older adults with "faith, purpose, and a support system and a good sense of hope and faith." As one student commented, rural older adults "find strength in themselves to take each day one day at a time." It may also be due to growing up in a rural community; as a student noted, "they worked off of the land they were raised on. Farming, hunting, logging, coal mining, and so forth all helped to build self-sufficient individuals."

Dual relationships with clients and confidentiality were also mentioned as ethical challenges in rural practice. It is not uncommon to be working with clients who are related to each other or with clients who are known from other life roles, such as church. One student described these areas as places where "everyone knows everyone." Relationships, in general, can be challenging, when a student or practitioner is considered an "outsider" to a small community and it is often difficult to "fit in." This can make establishing rapport more difficult. It was recommended that an outsider take the time to learn the culture and history of a community and that acceptance by the community can take "time and competence." In this regard it may be even more important to become involved at the community level and in policies to help the community. This involvement can help make a difference in the community and provide opportunity for a social worker to be a leader.

Equally important but outside of the domains of competency, students also touted the benefits of working with rural older adults. This work was deemed as being "graciously rewarding" and a "blessing" to interact with such wonderful people. The relationships that are formed in rural communities were mentioned as a significant advantage, as one student shared:

> I think it provides a safe, homelike environment that we can get to know one another. Working with the same people in the same small town, you begin to get to really know the people, almost to the point that they become like family. Our clients become real people, not just another case number; and for the clients, we become familiar faces they can come to rely on and trust.

Another student added:

> The stories and the knowledge I have gained from the rural older adults I have worked with are priceless. I think I have learned more from them than any textbook could have provided.

Although not addressed in this particular student discussion, social workers practicing in rural areas have the opportunity to become leaders in those small communities. The geriatric social work competencies address this opportunity in the domain of leadership in the practice environment of aging. At this higher level of competency, the following skills can be honed in the rural environment:

6. Build collaborations across disciplines and the service spectrum to assess access, continuity, and reduce gaps in services to older adults.
7. Manage individual (personal) and multi-stakeholder (interpersonal) processes at the community, interagency, and intra-agency levels in order to inspire, leverage power, and resources to optimize services for older adults.

Evidence-Based Geriatric Practice

Few EBP models have been developed in rural areas. That does not necessarily render them irrelevant to a rural context; however, they may require adaptation and case-by-case or program-by-program reassessment. EBP is about using the best evidence available. If there is no large clinical trial for a rural population using a particular intervention, it is still better to use a proven approach and adapt and document modifications and measure outcomes than practice from no evidence (Reuben, 2007). The rural environment is a powerful context in which to examine and reflect on best practice potential.

The IOM report (2008) *Retooling for an Aging America* presented new models of care that are evidence based. Although none of the models focuses specifically on rural older adults and none is based in the most rural American states, three are founded in states that are more than average rural. These three programs from Indiana, 40.8% rural; Minnesota, 42% rural; and Wisconsin, 44.2% rural (Daily Yonder, 2013) are described because of their EBP implications for human service practitioners in rural contexts. These programs are best practice examples at a program level and address the rural environment with a complement of health and human services; they illustrate the direct practice, program development, and policy impact of addressing the multiple needs of rural older persons. Two elements that run across these EBP models are the use of interdisciplinary teams and the bundling of resources.

Geriatric Resources for Assessment and Care of Elders (GRACE) provides care for low-income older people in Indiana who have the distinctive needs that relate to many rural older adults: chronic illness, care access barriers, low health literacy, and social stressors. GRACE services are initiated with a home visit by a professional team of nurse and social worker. This assessment is followed up monthly following protocols developed for 12 geriatric symptoms. Additional visits are made whenever an emergency room or hospital stay occurs. A larger interdisciplinary consulting team supports the home visiting team. In a controlled clinical trial, Counsell and colleagues (2007) found improved quality of care and a reduction in acute care utilization. Other outcomes were mixed and may have required longer study duration (Reuben, 2007). In Minnesota, Senior Health Options (SHO) is a Medicaid demonstration project. It provides dual eligible (Medicare/Medicaid) enrollees a package of acute care and long-term care services. Evaluation indicated a reduction in acute care costs and increased use of preventative services, although the capitation costs were higher (Kane, Homyak, Bershadsky, Flood, & Zhang, 2004).

Wisconsin's Family Care program aims to improve client choices for type or residence and service supports, access, and quality of care while controlling for cost. There is a single point of entry at a service center led by a social worker and nurse team with volunteer support. A comprehensive care plan was developed with a consolidated reimbursement methodology for delivery by Care Management Organizations (CMOs). The social focus on choice and access has had positive outcomes in improving quality; however, it was not possible to determine cost-effectiveness at the time of the evaluation (Medstart, 2003). Demand for the services has been high.

The Veterans Health Administration (VHA) recognizes that geriatrically prepared social workers can play a key role in meeting the needs of older rural veterans within the context of the interdisciplinary team. In 2007, the VHA addressed the underserving of rural veterans by establishing the Office of Rural Health (ORH). One of the pilot projects from this office was Coordination and Advocacy for Rural Elders (CARE) that incorporated health and social service professionals to target interventions on older veterans in rural counties within 50 miles to 100 miles from two VHA medical centers. Those at risk for repeated hospital admission were targeted for a home visit and comprehensive geriatric health assessment by a health professional. As a result, the majority of the participants' physical and psychosocial problems were identified and EBPs were applied by nurse–social worker teams to develop care plans and mobilize community resources (Ritchie et al., 2002). The VHA recognizes that geriatric-prepared social workers can play a key role in meeting the needs of older rural veterans (www.ruralhealth.va.gov/docs/Geriatric_Scholars_Brochure_March_2011.pdf) within the context of the interdisciplinary team and has included them in the VA Geriatric Scholars Program.

The SWLI investigated EBP related to work with older adults that utilized social workers (Rizzo & Rowe, 2006), and the findings pointed to evidence of outcomes very relevant for practice with rural older adults. The following are some of the areas particularly relevant to rural practice, due to the previously mentioned issues of self-determination and resiliency among rural older adults, gaps in the continuum of care in terms of services, and the importance of considering the rural culture in work with this population:

- Promote self-determination through older person and family-centered solutions
  Social work enhances the developmental, problem-solving, and coping capacities of older people and their families.
- Develop linkages to appropriate, accessible, and acceptable services
  Social work promotes the effective, coordinated, and humane operating of systems that provide resources and services to older people and their families.
- Respect the diversity of the older population
  Social work recognizes the needs and strengths of persons who differ based on culture, race, class, gender, sexual orientation, and disability.

CONCLUSION

Guidance offered by researchers and educators, the competencies for geriatric social work, EBP models, as well as the experiences of students engaged in specialized geriatric training can provide practice principles for the role of the human services practitioners working with rural older adults and their families. They can also offer direction for educating students and professionals for this practice area. To begin, providing human services to older adults and their families in small towns and rural areas presents many challenges, including dual relationships and other ethical issues and difficulty accessing needed health care and social services (Galbreath, 2005; Kerschner, 2006; U.S. Department of Health and Human Services [HHS], 2008). Given these issues, *human service professionals must practice with the understanding of the unique service needs of older adults living in small towns and rural areas* including transportation, access and distance to health and human services, a narrow range of services offered, a preference for informal supports, and poverty. They must also *effectively manage the challenges of functioning in small towns and rural areas* such as dual relationships, living in a "fishbowl," and professional isolation (Daley & Pierce, 2011; Galbreath, 2005; Locke & Winthrop, 2005).

Within the rural environment and in the absence of a full continuum of care, human service practitioners can also benefit from encountering and engaging with the resilience and informal support systems that their older clients have built over a lifetime. Thus, *recognizing and utilizing the strengths of older adults living in small towns and rural areas*—including resilience, social support, life satisfaction, community involvement, and culture—are critical for successful practice (Howell & Cleary, 2007; Yoon & Lee, 2007).

Human service professionals in rural areas also require access to the most recent knowledge of EBP. They must not rely only on local practice wisdom. Information literacy allows practitioners to weigh the rural relevance of a wide range of research. Technology even as simple as telephone interventions (Ritchie et al., 2002) may prove beneficial. A team approach of nurse and social worker and providing bundled medical and social services to communities are proved to be effective (IOM, 2008). All these approaches are particularly important in times of transitions from levels of care when older adults are most vulnerable (Counsell et al., 2007).

Education and training can help students and professionals meet these challenges and embrace these opportunities with rural older adults. Specifically, *higher education and continuing education should focus on the geriatric competencies and EBPs, giving special attention to those that relate to the unique nature of rural practice*. These include competencies within the values and ethics; intervention; and aging services, programs, and policies domains (Damron-Rodriguez, 2006). Training and opportunities should also be offered for preparing professional leaders in these communities. In order to prepare human service professionals to successfully manage the roles and hone the skills of social workers practicing in small towns and rural areas, training should provide a generalist orientation that includes knowledge and skill building in direct practice, administration, and community work (Bisman, 2003; Kropf, 2003; Locke & Winthrop, 2005).

The importance of working with volunteer groups and churches, fund-raising and grant-writing, community-building and developing community partnerships, and functioning in independent/minimally supervised practice should also be stressed in such curricula (Locke & Winthrop, 2005; R. Lohmann, 2005). It is important to note that because older adults make up a substantial portion of many rural communities (Housing Assistance Council, 2013), education for rural geriatric practice should not be limited to students who declare an interest in aging. Similarly, because many rural older people receive specialty care from organizations in urban areas, students preparing for urban practice should also understand the rural older adult population. It follows that rural practice often involves work with older people and that, sometimes, urban practice can be rural. Thus, educational programs should work to competently train all students in this area through course content and practicum experiences. Offering distance education and "home-growing" professionals are important considerations in educating these current and future professionals (Kropf, 2003; N. Lohmann, 2005).

Researchers, educators, and practitioners should continue to explore the unique features of and best practices for providing human services in rural areas to older adults. More specifically, the development and dissemination of EBPs and service delivery models are desperately needed (IOM, 2008). In addition, continuing education and higher education programs that specifically focus on competently training students and practitioners to enter work with rural older adults are necessary. Although the training itself is important, strategies to effectively recruit and retain students and professionals in geriatric practice in rural communities are critical.

USEFUL WEBSITES

Association for Gerontology Education in Social Work (AGE-SW)

www.agesw.org

Council on Social Work Education

www.cswe.org

Gero-Ed Center, The National Center for Gerontological Social Work Education

www.cswe.org/CentersInitiatives/GeroEdCenter.aspx

Hartford Partnership Program for Aging Education (HPPAE)

www.nyam.org/social-work-leadership-institute-v2/geriatric-social-work/hppae

National Association of Social Workers (NASW)

www.socialworkers.org

National Rural Social Work Caucus

www.ruralsocialwork.org

Veterans Health Administration Office of Rural Health

www.ruralhealth.va.gov

REFERENCES

Berkman, B., Dobrof, R., Harry, L., & Damron-Rodriguez, J. A. (1997). White paper: Social work. In S. M. Klein (Ed.), *A national agenda for geriatric education: White papers* (pp. 53–85). New York, NY: Springer Publishing Company. (Original work published as a monograph: U.S. Bureau of Health Professions)

Bisman, C. D. (2003). Rural aging: Social work practice models and intervention dynamics. In S. S. Butler & L. W. Kaye (Eds.), *Gerontological social work in small towns and rural communities* (pp. 37–58). Binghamton, NY: Haworth.

Bogo, M., Regehr, C., Power, R., Hughes, J., Woodford, M., & Regehr, G. (2004). Toward new approaches for evaluating student field performance: Tapping the implicit criteria used by experienced field instructors. *Journal of Social Work Education, 40*(3), 417–426.

Bosch, L. A., & Boisen, L. S. (2011). Dual relationships in rural areas. In L. Ginsberg (Ed.), *Social work in rural communities* (5th ed., pp. 111–123). Alexandria, VA: CSWE Press.

Butler, S. S., & Kaye, L. W. (Eds.). (2003). *Gerontological social work in small towns and rural communities*. Binghamton, NY: The Haworth Social Work Press.

Coleman, E. A., Parry, C., Chalmers, S., & Min, S. J. (2006). The care transitions intervention: Results of a randomized controlled trial. *Archives of Internal Medicine, 166*(17), 1822–1828.

Counsell, S. R., Callahan, C. M., Clark, D. O., Tu, W., Buttar, A. B., Stump, T. E., & Ricketts, G. D. (2007). Geriatric care management for low-income seniors: A randomized controlled trial. *Journal of the American Medical Association, 298*(22), 2623–2633.

Daily Yonder. (2012, April 3). How rural are the states? Retrieved May 2, 2013, from http://www.dailyyonder.com/how-rural-are-states/2012/04/02/3847

Daley, M. R., & Pierce, B. (2011). Educating for rural competence: Curriculum concepts, models, and course content. In L. Ginsberg (Ed.), *Social work in rural communities* (5th ed., pp. 125– 140). Alexandria, VA: CSWE Press.

Damron-Rodriguez, J. A. (2006). Moving ahead: Developing geriatric social work competencies. In B. Berkman (Ed.), *Handbook of social work in health and aging* (pp. 1051–1068). Oxford, UK: Oxford University Press.

Damron-Rodriguez, J. A. (2008). Developing competence for nurses and social workers: Evidence-based approaches to education. *American Journal of Nursing, 108*(9), 40–46.

Damron-Rodriguez, J. A., Volland, P. J., Wright, M. E., & Hooyman, N. R. (2009). Competency-based education: Implications of the Hartford geriatric social work approach. In N. R. Hooyman (Ed.), *Transforming social work education: The first decade of the Hartford geriatric social work initiative* (pp. 21–50). Arlington, VA: CSWE Press.

Galbreath, W. B. (2005). Dual relationships in rural communities. In N. Lohmann & R. A. Lohmann (Eds.), *Rural social work practice* (pp. 105–123). New York, NY: Columbia University Press.

Ginsberg, L. (Ed.). (2011a). *Social work in rural communities* (5th ed.). Alexandria, VA: CSWE Press.

Ginsberg, L. (2011b). Introduction to basic concepts of rural social work. In L. Ginsberg (Ed.), *Social work in rural communities* (5th ed., pp. 1–20). Alexandria, VA: CSWE Press.

Healy, T. C. (2003). Ethical practice issues in rural perspective. In S. S. Butler & L. W. Kaye (Eds.), *Gerontological social work in small towns and rural communities* (pp. 265–285). Binghamton, NY: The Haworth Social Work Press.

Housing Assistance Council. (2013, December). Taking stock: Rural people, poverty, and housing in the 21st century. Retrieved August 27, 2013, from http://www.ruralhome.org/component/content/article/587-taking-stock-2010

Howell, D., & Cleary, K. K. (2007). Rural seniors' perceptions of quality of life. *Physical & Occupational Therapy in Geriatrics, 25*(4), 55–71.

Institute of Medicine. (2008). *Retooling for an aging America: Building the health care workforce committee on the future health care workforce for older Americans.* Washington, DC: The National Academies Press.

Kane, R. L., Homyak, P., Bershadsky, B., Flood, S., & Zhang, H. (2004). Patterns of utilization for the Minnesota senior health options program. *Journal of the American Geriatrics Society, 52*(12), 2039–2044.

Kerschner, H. (2006). *Transportation innovations for seniors: A synopsis of findings in rural America.* Pasadena, CA: Beverly Foundation; Washington, DC: Community Transportation Association of America.

Kropf, N. P. (2003). Future training and education recommendations for rural gerontological social workers. In S. S. Butler & L. W. Kaye (Eds.), *Gerontological social work in small towns and rural communities* (pp. 287–299). Binghamton, NY: The Haworth Social Work Press.

Locke, B. L., & Winthrop, J. (2005). Social work in rural America: Lessons from the past and trends for the future. In N. Lohmann & R. A. Lohmann (Eds.), *Rural social work practice* (pp. 3–24). New York, NY: Columbia University Press.

Lohmann, N. (2005). Social work education for rural practice. In N. Lohmann & R. A. Lohmann (Eds.), *Rural social work practice* (pp. 293–311). New York, NY: Columbia University Press.

Lohmann, N., & Lohmann, R. A. (2005). *Rural social work practice.* New York, NY: Columbia University Press.

Lohmann, R. A. (2005). The third sector in rural America. In N. Lohmann & R. A. Lohmann (Eds.), *Rural social work practice* (pp. 86–102). New York, NY: Columbia University Press.

Medstart. (2003). *Wisconsin—resource centers offering access to services and comprehensive information.* Retrieved March 11, 2008, from http://www.sms.hhs.gov/PromisingPractices?downloads/wioss.pdf

National Association of Social Workers. (2008). *Code of ethics of the National Association of Social Workers.* Washington, DC: Author.

National Association of Social Workers. (2012). Rural social work. In *Social work speaks* (9th ed., pp. 297–302). Washington, DC: Author.

National Organization for Human Services. (2013). What is human services? Retrieved June 20, 2013, from http://www.nationalhumanservices.org/what-is-human-services

Naylor, M. D., Brooten, D. A., Campbell, R. L., Maislin, G., McCauley, K. M., & Schwartz, J. S. (2004). Transitional care of older adults hospitalized with heart failure: A randomized, controlled trial. *Journal of the American Geriatrics Society, 52*(5), 675–684.

Reuben, D. (2007). Better care for older people with chronic diseases: An emerging vision. *Journal of the American Medical Association, 298*(22), 2673–2674.

Ritchie, C., Wieland, D., Tully, C., Rowe, J., Sims, R., & Bodner, E. (2002). Coordination and advocacy for rural elders (CARE): A model of rural case management for veterans. *The Gerontologist, 42*(3), 399–405.

Rizzo, V. M., & Rowe, J. M. (2006). Studies of the cost-effectiveness of social work services in aging: A review of the literature. *Research on Social Work Practice, 16*, 67–73.

Rubin, A. (2008). *Practitioner's guide to using research for evidence-based practice.* Hoboken, NJ: Wiley.

U.S. Department of Health and Human Services, National Advisory Committee on Rural Health and Human Services. (2008). *The 2008 report to the secretary: Rural health and human services issues.* Rockville, MD: Author. Retrieved March 30, 2013, from ftp://ftp.hrsa.gov/ruralhealth/committee/nacreport2008.pdf

Yoon, D., & Lee, E. (2007). Impact of religiousness, spirituality, and social support on psychological well-being among older adults in rural areas. *Journal of Gerontological Social Work, 48*(3/4), 281–298.

Conclusions and Future Directions

Policies Impacting Rural Aging

ELAINE T. JURKOWSKI

Vernita Simonz is a 96-year-old woman who lives in her own home in a small community of about 850 people, in rural northern California. She is in fairly good health, and drives to a nearby community to access a senior center. There she is able to receive a hot meal when she attends, and she has the opportunity to socialize with others. The center provides blood pressure checks and opportunities for training and education on topics that impact older adults. When she goes to the center, she also makes a periodic visit to her primary care physician, who is located in the same town. Mrs. Simonz worked sporadically throughout her lifetime and is the widow of a veteran; thus, she did not work enough quarters to qualify for Medicare. Her primary care physician is one of the few providers in the area who accepts Medicaid from consumers.

Fortunately, Mrs. Simonz has her own car and still drives. She enjoys her home, chickens, and fruit trees. Often she barters with other local residents in her town for favors by offering eggs and fruit.

While Mrs. Simonz is in the neighboring town, she meets her 88-year-old friend Georgina at a local Denny's restaurant. Georgina appears a bit disoriented and confused and, once again, seems to have difficulty remembering where she was the day before. Although Georgina lives alone, she fell and broke her arm within the last 6 months. Because her children all live out of town, they set up some in-home support and services for Georgina.

The two women are engaged in a discussion about their local lodge; Georgina becomes a bit more disoriented, continues some rambled speech, and faints. Vernita, concerned about her friend, asks the restaurant staff to contact the emergency dispatch through 911, when Georgina does not respond after several minutes. The town is relatively small. The local fire department responds to the 911 call and decides to drive Georgina to the nearest outpatient department at the local hospital—some 25 miles farther away from Vernita's home.

Throughout this case study, it appears that a variety of services specifically designed for older adults are utilized. These services, along with the myriad services discussed throughout this book, are the result of programs mandated or authorized through a variety of policies, most of which emanate from the federal government level. However, they are developed, delivered, and managed at state and local levels. Whereas a range of policies impact older adults living in rural communities, this chapter describes some of the more popular and prevalent policy mandates and issues that increasingly impact older adults living in rural communities. These include policies such as the Older Americans Act (OAA) and service-related areas such as mental health, health care and health care access, long-term care, caregiver support, housing, transportation, income maintenance, and the most recent policy dimension—the Affordable Care Act (ACA).

OLDER AMERICANS ACT

The OAA serves as a significant piece of legislation that is responsive to the needs of older adults in general but also, specifically, for older adults living in rural communities. The OAA was originally signed into legislation in 1965 (Pub. L. No. 89-73); however, it has expanded its mandate, programs, and services over the decades through reauthorization amendments. It serves adults age 60 and older, and covers grandparents (age 50 and older) raising grandchildren. The following 10 objectives undergird its mandate for services but include the following:

1. Older adults should be valued and given dignity.
2. Older adults should have an adequate income so as to live a specific standard of living in the United States.
3. Older adults are entitled to the most up-to-date, evidence-based physical and mental health care.
4. Older adults are entitled to affordable and suitable housing.
5. Complete rehabilitative and restorative care for those who are living in institutional settings
6. Retirement that offers dignity and self-worth
7. The option to contribute to the economy without age discrimination
8. Freedom for autonomy and independence
9. Sufficient and effective community care services that promote independence and participation in civic, cultural, and recreational activity
10. The opportunity to benefit from immediate research

Although the act was initially signed into legislation in the 1960s, amendments over the years have expanded the programs and services mandated through the OAA and now include a variety of community-based services available to older adults, whether located in urban or rural settings. Despite the intention that the mandate would cover all needs exhibited by older adults, the reality is that not all people within rural communities can be recipients of services because of the limitations imposed by the rural nature of the service delivery system and the lack of population base. At the current time, the service delivery system includes a variety of mandated services that can be delivered within rural settings, which cover frail older adults to well older adults across fields such as socialization, health care, mental health, employment, legal advocacy, and caregiving. In fact, throughout this book, in practically each chapter, a variety of programs and services are detailed that have some connection to programs and services authorized within the OAA.

Overall, the OAA is administered through the Department of Health and Human Services (HHS) through the Administration on Aging (AoA; 2013), at the federal government level. Funds flow from the AoA to each state across the United States, and generally are administered through state-based Departments on Aging. Each Department on Aging at the state-based level then works with Area Agencies on Aging (AAAs) to administer/oversee services at the local levels. Nationally, there is also an oversight group known as the National Association of Area Agencies on Aging that serves as a lobby and advocacy group to assure that AAAs' needs are represented.

At the federal government level, a series of programs are overseen by the AoA that include the Eldercare Locater service, the National Administration on Aging website, and the National Aging Information Center. In contrast, state AAAs deliver programs and services to include the following:

- Home and community-based case management
- Pension counseling
- Legal hotlines
- Aging information and assistance
- Health insurance counseling
- Medicare antifraud advocacy
- Senior center information programs
- Nutrition counseling
- Long-term care ombudsman programs

At the time of this writing, the OAA had been reauthorized in 2006 for 5 years; however, despite attempts to reauthorize the bill, the most recent amendments to the bill were still under committee review in 2014. The reauthorization process continues to protect older adults in communities (both rural and urban) through the variety of programs and services that are outlined in the next few sections (Wacker & Roberto, 2013; Yokum & Wagner, 2010).

Home and community-based programs—include in-home services to help frail older adults remain in their homes, as opposed to long-term care settings. Based upon the functional status of individuals, activities of daily living (ADLs; Katz, 1983) are assessed to determine their ability to independently eat, bathe, dress, transfer, and go to the bathroom; their ability to cognitively function is also assessed (generally through a Mini-Mental Status Examination [MMSE]). Georgina in the case study would have had a home-based assessment prior to the determination that she needed services to help her when she broke her arm. Note, sometimes AAAs contract this service with a local home health provider as opposed to delivering the services independently. In many rural areas this function can also be assumed by a local health department, rather than a local service provider.

Aging information and assistance—In response to the need for information about aging and resource availability to older adults, the AoA has partnered with the Centers for Medicare & Medicaid Services to help states develop a single coordinated system of care and long-term support known as the Aging and Disability Resource Centers (ADRCs; Jurkowski, 2008). These centers are available within rural communities, often as storefront operations at local shopping malls, or in the local public library. The ADRCs improve coordination with AAAs and other community-based entities in disseminating information regarding available home and community-based services for individuals who are at risk for, or currently residing in, institutional settings. The most recent amendments to the OAA will update the definition of ADRC to be consistent with current practice and current law, including an emphasis on independent living and home and community-based services.

> Georgina and Vernita regularly visit their public library to glean ideas about how to access resources within their rural community. The local ADRC, housed in the regional public library, provides resources on a variety of topics, including free medications, that both women regularly access.

Senior centers—were originally conceptualized to provide a regular, nutritionally sound, daily meal and offer a locale for older adults to congregate and socialize. The concept was based upon research that suggested older adults with some element of social support would do better than those left isolated and alone (Older Americans Act, Pub. L No. 89–73, 1965). Thus the centers, especially in rural communities, offer a place for people to meet, socialize, and achieve some of their daily nutritional needs. The concept of socialization is important, and helps reduce potential isolation for people living in rural communities (Krout, 1987). Many senior centers also provide health services and wellness services, and information/referrals to their participants. Chapter 7 provides a more thorough discussion about these programs and services. Future changes to the OAA will direct the assistant secretary to provide information and technical assistance to support best practices for the modernization of multipurpose senior centers. Over the last 5 years, there has been a dwindling of participants at local centers for a variety of reasons (Pardasani & Thompson, 2012). Baby boomers may not view the centers as attractive to them or relevant to their needs; thus, the proposed legislative amendments to the OAA should encourage efforts to modernize multipurpose senior centers and promote intergenerational models of care (Heritage Area Agency on Aging, 2013).

Senior centers also prepare home-delivered meal options that are supplied to housebound people. When feasible, it is encouraged to use locally grown foods in meal programs. The legislation also ensures that, as appropriate, supplemental foods may be part of a home-delivered meal at the option of a nutrition services provider. Although the provision of home-delivered meals is mandated within the OAA, the actual delivery of meals can at times be problematic in more rural and isolated areas. Shrinking budgets for mileage and increasing costs of transportation and liability insurance for vehicles have a strong impact for rural communities on the provision of home-delivered meals.

Another hallmark offered through senior centers has been computer training, also a program mandated through the OAA during the last set of amendments (2006). This training has proved invaluable to older adults in rural communities because registration for Medicare Part D, pharmaceutical assistance programs and health care programs now mandated through the ACA, all require registration and selection through computer-based approaches.

Finally, the OAA also promotes the delivery of evidence-based programs, such as falls prevention and chronic disease self-management programs, particularly through senior centers via the information assistance aspect of the program. A specific focus has become (and should continue to be) the delivery of evidence-based intervention programs for both health and mental (behavioral) health well-being. The present focus on the delivery of evidence-based programs should ensure that programs are provided that address current practices—engaged with the most up-to-date focus on what we know from science—disease prevention programs, and health promotion programs. This is particularly important in rural communities because resources to support mobility impairments may be limited, and access to rehabilitation services is not as plentiful as in urban settings.

Some senior centers within rural communities have addressed the dearth of education and resources that provide screening and assessment for oral health disease prevention and health promotion activities (Napoli & Coello, 2013). The proposed OAA amendments of 2014 include technical assistance to improve collaboration with health care entities, such as Federally Qualified Health Centers (FQHCs), to enhance care coordination for individuals with multiple chronic illnesses. This approach should improve access to oral health and health promotion activities in rural areas because FQHCs tend to be found in medically designated shortage areas/rural communities.

> Georgina and Vernita attend their community's senior center for daily noon hot meals. They enjoy dressing up; comparing notes on their outfits; and exchanging tips on wearing their hair, makeup, and jewelry. They also receive health information related to blood pressure, healthy cooking for one person, and community resources. Vernita feels this opportunity gives her a chance to get out of the house, meet new friends, and share her wisdom with others. She also enjoys the biweekly opportunity to read to the day care children who visit from a neighboring day care center, and brings her 5-year-old great-grandson, Elijah, when he comes to visit. Both women have also benefited from their computer training classes at the senior center. Vernita is now able to communicate with Elijah via Skype. She was also able to change her pharmaceutical assistance program offered through Medicare Part D during the last enrollment period.

Long-Term Care Ombudsman Program, older adult protective services, and screening programs for older adults—The Long-Term Care Ombudsman Program serves as a watchdog for people living in long-term care residential facilities, and reports incidents of abuse or neglect by the caregiver. Some of the specific features of this program include the review and service to all residents of long-term care facilities, regardless of age. This OAA legislation also ensures private, unimpeded access to the ombudsman for all residents of long-term care facilities and provides for identification and resolution of potential individual and organizational conflicts of interest. The legislation also clarifies the role of the ombudsman program in advocating for residents unable to communicate their wishes. Through the mandate of the OAA an ombudsman may continue to serve residents transitioning from a long-term care facility to a home care setting. Finally, the ombudsman office is a "health oversight agency" for purposes of HIPAA (Health Insurance Portability and Accountability Act).

In terms of elder abuse, words used to describe elder abuse include definitions of "adult protective services," "abuse," "exploitation and financial exploitation," and "elder justice." The legislation also promotes best practices related to responding to elder abuse, neglect, and exploitation in long-term care facilities through the AoA. The OAA also mandates the states' submissions of data concerning elder abuse to a federal elder abuse repository, to help identify the incidence and prevalence of elder abuse. With the OAA mandate, there is also direction to the AoA to include, as appropriate, training for states, AAAs, and service providers on elder abuse prevention and screening. This streamlines federal-level administration of programs, promotes the efficient and effective use of transportation services, and improves coordination among programs at the federal, state, and local levels.

Transportation services—The Assistant Secretary is directed to provide information and technical assistance to states, AAAs, and service providers on supplying efficient, person-centered transportation services, including across geographic boundaries. The amendments of 2014 in OAA legislation also require the GAO (Government Accountability Office) to conduct a study of transportation services for older individuals that identifies challenges and barriers to providing and coordinating efficient and effective transportation services, including access to such services, for the aging network. The legislation also requires evaluation of the challenges and barriers in coordinating with other federal agencies.

Medicare antifraud advocacy—The OAA also has a provision to review Medicare billings through volunteers. This program is particularly important in rural communities because the myriad paperwork associated with Medicare billings and hospital stays can be overwhelming for some people, especially the oldest of the older, with limited education. It is also increasingly important for older adults with diminishing cognitive capacity. This initiative also provides training to volunteers whose mission is to identify health care fraud and abuse.

Pension counseling—The health and economic welfare dimensions of the OAA provide the opportunity to supply counseling related to pensions, pension reform, and advocacy pertaining to Social Security (SS). Despite this component of the legislation, this area is seldom utilized by AAAs in rural communities. Perhaps an overriding issue with pension counseling is the fact that many older adults from rural communities have limited incomes; thus, counseling is in the form of supplemental assistance—if person power resources allow for this within the AAAs' scope of activity.

Legal services—The OAA also authorizes legal services for people who have limited resources (generally living below the poverty line or a certain percentage near the poverty line). Usually older adults living in rural areas benefit from advice on power of attorney issues, wills, and guardianship ramifications (grandparents raising grandchildren). To some extent, issues related to financial abuse are also taken into consideration.

The OAA and AAAs' plans require advocacy on a routine basis by human service professionals working in rural communities for the benefit of older adults. One way to incorporate voice into the process is to assist a local AAA with its area plan, through operating focus groups or conducting data collection through service statistics. Other competencies that can be helpful in shaping an area plan include outreach to integrate the voices of older adults into the planning of service priorities within local communities.

MEDICARE: HEALTH CARE AND HEALTH CARE ACCESS

Earlier in this book, health care was discussed and some of the health issues facing older adults living in rural communities were examined. Medicare has been known as the health care provider for older adults for nearly half a century in the United States and, to a large extent, would be the response for addressing many of the health care concerns for older adults in rural communities. However, given that many rural-based older adults face a range of health disparities, one may question the efficacy of the Medicare program. First, many of the parameters of the Medicare program may not be able to be utilized within rural communities because of the lack of medical service providers. Depending upon the population size of a given town, it may not be financially viable to deliver long-term care services, rehabilitation services, diagnostic services, or preventative services within local communities; older adults living within a given community may be forced to visit a neighboring community to receive the services.

Medicare serves as an insurance program for health care to older adults who have a guaranteed source of financial resources to supply care, provided an individual has worked for 40 quarters over a lifetime (10 years of employment contributions to Medicare). The program, initially an amendment to the Social Security Act of 1965, provides hospital insurance, diagnostic care, and preventive services. The Medicare program is divided into four specific parts. Part A provides reimbursement for in-patient hospital stays, critical care hospital stays, rehabilitation, and long-term care bed stays. Table 12.1 provides an overview of some of the services and hospital stays covered.

Medicare Part B, a voluntary supplemental insurance, covers up to 80% of a range of services associated with diagnostic care, preventive

TABLE 12.1 Services Covered Under Medicare Part B

Service	Overview of what is covered
Ambulance	Transportation to a hospital or skilled nursing facility, when transportation by any other means would be considered a danger to one's health.
Ambulatory surgery	Facility fees covered for approved services.
Blood	Pints of blood received during outpatient services for Part B-covered services.
Bone mass measurement	Covered once every 24 months for patients at risk for bone fractures. Certain medical conditions qualify for assessment more frequently than once every 24 months.
Cardiovascular screenings	Cholesterol, lipid, and triglyceride levels tested once every 5 years for prevention of stroke or heart attack.
Chiropractic services	Limited services for manipulation of the spine to correct for subluxation (one or more of the bones out of position within the spine).
Clinical laboratory services	Blood tests, urinalysis, and some screening tests.
Clinical trials	Routine costs associated with qualifying clinical trials to test new regimens of medical care. Costs for the drugs or devices being tested within clinical trial may not be covered.
Colorectal cancer screenings	1. Fecal occult blood tests: Once every 12 months if age 50 or older. Although one does not pay for the test, a fee for the doctor's visit may be levied. 2. Flexible sigmoidoscopy: Once every 488 months if age 50 or older, or once every 120 months when used instead of a colonoscopy for those not at high risk. 3. Screening colonoscopy: Once every 120 months (high risk every 24 months). No minimum age. 4. Barium enema: Once every 48 months if age 50 or older (high risk every 24 months) when used instead of a sigmoidoscopy or colposcopy.
Diabetes screenings	Screenings up to two times per year based upon specific eligibility criteria including hypertension, dyslipidemia, history of abnormal cholesterol and triglyceride levels, obesity or a history of high blood sugar.
Diabetic self-management training	Provided for people with diabetes with a written physician's order.
Diabetic supplies	Supplies to include glucose testing monitors, blood glucose solutions, and, in some cases, therapeutic shoes. Syringes and insulin are covered if used with an insulin pump or if one has Medicare prescription drug coverage.
Durable medical equipment	Oxygen, wheelchairs, walkers, and hospital beds needed for use in one's home.

(continued)

TABLE 12.1 Services Covered Under Medicare Part B (*continued*)

Emergency room services	Coverage for visits when one's health is in serious danger, following a bad injury, sudden illness, or an illness that quickly causes physical deterioration.
Eyeglasses	Limited coverage for eyeglasses is available for one pair of eyeglasses with standard frames following cataract surgery that implants an intraocular lens.
Flu shots	Once per flu season.
Foot exams and treatment	For individuals with diabetes-related nerve damage.
Glaucoma tests	Tests to detect eye disease glaucoma, once per 12-month period for people with high risk for glaucoma (i.e., with a preexisting condition of diabetes or family history of glaucoma, or specific risk factors).
Hearing and balance exams	Coverage is based upon physicians' requests to determine if medical treatment is required for condition. Exams for the purpose of fitting hearing aids are not covered.
Home health services	Limited to reasonable and necessary services to include part-time or intermittent skilled nursing care, home health aide services, physical therapy, occupational therapy, and speech-language pathology ordered by a physician.
	These services must also be provided for through a Medicare-certified home health agency. Medical supplies for use within the home are also covered and include medical social services and durable medical equipment to include wheelchairs, hospital beds, oxygen, and walkers.
Kidney dialysis services	Covered within a facility setting or at home.
Kidney dialysis supplies	Covered within a facility setting or at home.
Mammograms (screening)	For women age 40 or older, preventative (screening) mammograms are covered once every 12 months.
Service	**Overview of what is covered**
Medical nutrition therapy	Individuals with diabetes or renal disease (prior to dialysis services or transplant), or for people up to 3 years postkidney transplant with a doctor's order. Mental health care (outpatient). Some limits and conditions will apply.
Occupational therapy (OT)	OT services to facilitate one's ability to resume activities of daily living (ADLs) following an illness episode.
Outpatient hospital services	Services provided as an outpatient, as part of a doctor's care.
Outpatient medical and surgical services and supplies	Based upon approved procedures.

(*continued*)

TABLE 12.1 Services Covered Under Medicare Part B (*continued*)

Pap test and pelvic exams	Women considered low risk are covered once every 24 months. Women considered high risk for cervical and vaginal cancer, and those past childbearing age who have had an exam that indicated cancer or other abnormalities in the past 3 years are covered once every 12 months.
Physical exams	A one-time physical exam within the first 6 months of enrollment in Medicare Part B.
Physical therapy	Treatment for injuries and disease through heat, light, exercise, and massage.
Pneumococcal shots	To aid in the prevention of pneumococcal infection. Currently shots last one's lifetime.
Practitioner services	Services provided for by clinical social workers, physician assistants, and nurse practitioners.
Prescription drugs	Limited at the current time to drug coverage through Medicare Part D.
Prostate cancer screening	Once every 12 months for all men over age 50. Exam includes preventative digital rectal exam and prostate-specific antigen (PSA) test.
Prosthetic/orthotic items	Arm, leg, and neck braces; artificial eyes; artificial limb and replacement parts; breast prostheses (following mastectomy); prosthetic devices needed to replace an internal body part or function (including ostomy supplies and parenteral and enteral nutrition therapy).
Smoking cessation	Up to eight face-to-face visits during a 12-month period, or if ordered by a physician, provided that one is diagnosed with a smoking-related illness or is using medications that may be affected by tobacco use.
Speech-language pathology services	Treatment to regain or strengthen speech skills.
Surgical dressings	Treatment of surgical or surgically treated wound.
Telemedicine	Services within some rural communities, provided within a practitioner's office, a hospital, or federally qualified health center.
Transplant services	Within a Medicare-certified facility, services for heart, lung, kidney, intestine, and liver, bone marrow, and some cornea transplants. If transplant was paid for by Medicare Part A or an employer/union group, and one is entitled to Medicare Part B, immunosuppressive drugs can be covered.
Travel services	Medical services provided for in Canada when one travels the most direct route to Canada between Alaska and another state.
Urgently needed care	Treatment for a sudden illness or injury not identified as a medical emergency.

Source: www.medicaid.gov

services, and services not covered under Part A that are medically necessary. Services deemed medically necessary also fall into this category. Although the list of services may appear to be comprehensive, in reality, many of the covered procedures may not be available through local primary care centers or critical care access hospitals (CAHs) that service older adults in small and rural communities. In addition, a range of services are not covered, including acupuncture, dentures and dental care, hearing tests not ordered by a physician, eye care, custodial care, cosmetic surgery, and long-term care. A detailed list of what is not covered under Medicare Parts A and B is found in Table 12.2.

Medicare Part C serves as a supplemental insurance program that helps cover the costs to the individual from Parts A and B. The insurance system combines coverage from one's hospital coverage (Part A) and medical coverage (Part B) through a health maintenance organization (HMO) or preferred provider organization (PPO).The intent of Medicare Part C is for private insurance companies to provide medical coverage to subscribers at a cost much lower than the original Medicare plan, with some enhanced benefits. Whereas Medicare Part C can be advantageous to the older adult, it can be problematic for older adults living in rural communities because the local providers may not be recognized providers by the supplemental insurance coverage plans.

Pharmaceutical or prescription drug coverage was initiated by the Medicare program through the Medicare Modernization Act (MMA) of 2003, and went into effect on January 1, 2006. This amendment, known as Medicare Part D, provides prescription drug coverage to Medicare enrollees. All too often, older adults living in rural communities may be limited to the range of possible coverage because they may not be technology savvy and able to utilize the computer to review choices in plans. In addition, primary care physicians may be limited in their understanding of what generic medications or substitute medications may be covered, in order to offer the best coverage possible for prescription drugs.

LONG-TERM CARE

Long-term care options run the range from assisted-living care to hospice care along the continuum of care. The cost of care for assisted living can be covered in two ways. The market share rate would be the going rate that covers the cost of doing business. Medicare Part A covers the first 100 days in a benefit period for skilled nursing care facilities. Hospice care can

TABLE 12.2 Services Not Covered by Medicare Parts A and B

Acupuncture
Chiropractic services*
Custodial care (help with activities of daily living [ADLs]—bathing, dressing, toileting, or eating) either at home or within a nursing home setting
Dental care, oral health screening, and dentures
Eye care (routine eye exams), eye refractions, and most eyeglasses
Foot care such as cutting corns or calluses
Hearing aids and hearing exams related to fitting a hearing aid
Hearing tests outside of physician's orders
Laboratory tests for screening purposes*
Long-term care and custodial care in a nursing home
Orthopedic shoes (with the exception of people who are diabetics, and under certain conditions)
Physical exams (routine or annual)
Preventative vaccinations*
Screening tests*
Travel (health care received outside of the United States, except Canada, under certain conditions)

*Outside of those listed in Table 12.1.

also be covered through Medicare at a point when a person has 6 months left to live and can no longer benefit from active rehabilitation services. Currently, regulations governing long-term care facilities include the Nursing Home Reform Act of 1987. This overhaul also led to the development of an innovation to long-term care facilities that focused upon the individual to have more decision-making ability, and be person-centered. This in turn gave rise to the Pioneer Movement in long-term care.

MENTAL HEALTH

Mental health care or behavioral health services for older adults was first addressed within the community during the 1960s, when a wellspring of agencies was developed to address mental health issues through the Community Mental Health Centers Construction Act of 1963 (Pub. L. No. 88-164). Although half a century has elapsed, unfortunately there still have not been tremendous strides in the development of policies and programs to address behavioral health issues for older adults, and specifically older adults living in rural communities. Community mental health centers do exist in rural communities; however, as has been shown in earlier chapters, stigma plays a large role in hindering older adults from receiving the help they may need for behavioral health concerns. This, coupled with limited behavioral health literacy, impacts older adults living in rural communities. Although Medicare does offer funding for the provision of mental health services and psychiatric hospitalizations, it does not provide adequate resources to meet some of the mental health counseling needs that older adults face.

The OAA amendments of 2006 introduced the notion of funding to support counseling services directed at the promotion of adequate mental health, which has been a tremendous boost for mental health care for older adults in rural communities. The Positive Aging Act of 2013 proposed to integrate behavioral health care for older adults into primary care practice settings. This approach would benefit older adults residing in rural settings.

CAREGIVER SUPPORT

The National Family Caregiver Support Program initiated through the OAA provides programs and supports to people who are caregivers. Initially conceptualized to support family members and caregivers of older adults, the amendments of 2006 to the OAA expanded the role of caregivers to include people age 50 and older who are also grandparents raising grandchildren. In addition, this program provides respite care for caregivers and the mandate for family leave. The OAA amendments of 2014 clarify and expand the current law that older adults caring for adult children with disabilities or raising children younger than age 18 are eligible to participate in the National Family Caregiver Support Program. Respite care is probably one of the most utilized components of this program. However, this aspect of the program can be problematic within rural communities because the funding for respite care is a part of the overall funding provided to local AAAs to administer the OAA programs and services. Respite care in many smaller rural communities for caregivers who may have been married to their spouses for years, living in isolated rural communities, may be nonexistent or available for very few hours per month. It is not uncommon to find users who receive about six hours per month of respite care. For the geographically isolated resident, this may mean an abbreviated shopping trip because it may take a few minutes to leave the house, another half an hour to get to the store in a neighboring town, a rush to get through and complete the weekly shopping, and then a rush back to the loved one.

> Vernita and Georgina were talking and sharing life experiences and memories about their respective spouses, while enjoying coffee and pie at the local Denny's. Vernita's husband had passed away nearly two years earlier from dementia. She recalled how challenging it was to leave her husband, Bernie, in order to do simple things like get her hair done monthly, or get a permanent. She remembered most vividly the rush and angst she would go through when a respite worker would be available to Bernie. She explained that she would worry about getting to the appointment on time, then worry that she would be delayed during the process of receiving her perm, and then have to rush home to relieve the respite worker from the 3-hour shift. Vernita shared with her friend her frustration when discussing the issue with the care coordinator from the local AAA, who indicated that the time allotted per month was all the agency could afford to provide.

TRANSPORTATION

Transportation within rural areas is direly needed, and quite inconsistently available across rural settings for a host of reasons, as described in Chapter 4 and various segments in this book. Attempts have been made to equalize the playing field through numerous pieces of legislation (National Rural Transportation Act, Rural Transportation Equity Act, and Consolidations Appropriations Equity Act of 2004); however, the funding appropriations do not follow with the legislation. The promotion of a rural transportation network system seems to be an uphill battle, but one worth the fight to assure that rural transportation networks are developed.

SOCIAL SECURITY ACT

In 1935, the Social Security Act was passed into legislation, and although most often it is thought of as a "retirement income" for our citizens, it also provides for a host of services that impact older adults who reside in rural communities. Supplemental Security Income (SSI) is a vastly important program for older adults who may live with limited incomes and resources, and provides a subsidy to one's SS pension benefits. Given that a higher proportion of older adults living in rural communities have limited incomes, this program becomes an important safety net. Food stamp programs, energy assistance programs, public health programs, benefits to World War II veterans, and benefits to people who are blind are also all covered by the Social Security Act.

AMERICANS WITH DISABILITIES ACT

Signed into legislation in 1990, the Americans with Disabilities Act (ADA; Pub. L. No. 101-336) has been a piece of legislation that impacts people across the life span, and has particular merit for older adults. Regardless of location (urban vs. rural), older adults all benefit from the service expectations outlined within this piece of legislation; thus, older adults in rural communities see a positive aspect to this legislation. The ADA covers a range of services and opportunities for community inclusion, defined by five specific titles of the act. Title I deals with employment; Title II with public services; Title III with public accommodations and services offered through private entities; Title IV with telecommunications; and Title V with miscellaneous provisions (Essex-Sorlie, 1994).

Employment—Title I of the ADA deals with employment and assures for accommodations within the employment setting, when a person with a disability qualifies for a position. It protects against discrimination or adverse treatment. Older adults living in rural communities who may become disabled due to medical or chronic health conditions thus are assured some measure of protection from employment discrimination.

Public entities and transportation—This applies to state and public housing, housing assistance, and housing referrals. It also includes paratransit services through public entities and national rail transportation.

Public accommodations and services offered through private entities—Title III of the ADA assures that people cannot be discriminated against from the enjoyment of public goods and services including hotels/inns, recreation, transportation, education, dining, shopping, receiving medical and social care, and using community resources. This has had a profound impact on older adults in rural communities because it assures that, despite ability, people will have access to their environments and the resources within them. Handicapped accessible parking at local stores and motorized shopping carts are two examples of how people can remain within their homes and home-based communities and still function.

Telecommunications—This title within the ADA assures that people who are deaf and hard of hearing or who have speech difficulties can receive communication services through relay services and closed captioning on television programs and in movie theaters. This benefits older adults in all communities, including rural communities.

Overall, the ADA was developed to protect people with disabilities from discrimination in and exclusion from their communities. The legislation has benefited older adults living in rural communities because the provisions of the ADA help assure older adults who become disabled that they can still remain in their homes, enjoy leisure activities, and engage in employment without discrimination or retribution (Jurkowski, 2008).

THE PATIENT PROTECTION AND AFFORDABLE CARE ACT

The Patient Protection and Affordable Care Act (ACA; Pub. L. No. 111-148, 2010) provides a variety of benefits to older adults without imposing additional health insurance coverage obligations. The ACA gives older people enhanced benefits in terms of wellness and preventive care and referrals to needed specialists. These are important for rural communities that have greater percentages of older residents than do urban centers. Rural residents also generally receive fewer medical screenings and preventive care procedures. The ACA also provides older adults with continuing benefits directed at paying the costs of their prescription drugs.

FOOD SUBSIDIES

Much hot debate about cutting nutritional benefits within the U.S. Congress and U.S. Senate over the past few years would impact older adults in rural communities who make use of nutritional subsidy programs. The Agricultural Act of 2014 (Pub. L. No. 113-79) protects the food stamp program and food insecurity programs for people in rural communities, including older adults.

COMPETENCIES TO IMPROVE POLICIES

Upon review of the competencies for practice within interdisciplinary and social work settings (Partnership for Health in Aging, 2010; Social Work Leadership Institute, n.d.), a number of specific practice competencies are relevant to facilitate the development of adequate policies, programs, and services. Some of these competencies include the following:

a. Provision of outreach to older adults and their families to ensure appropriate use of the service continuum

b. Identification and development of strategies to address service gaps, fragmentation, discrimination, and barriers that impact older adults

c. Inclusion of older adults in the process of planning and designing programs

d. Evaluation of policy outcomes through mandated programs and practices and the application of these findings to improve outcomes

e. Evaluation of negative impacts policies may have on the health and social well-being of older adults living in rural communities

f. Practice of organizing and advocating with service providers, community organizations, policy makers, and the public to meet the specialized needs and issues that impact the rural-based older adult population

CONCLUSION

The policy realm of practitioners' lives is intricately woven through how providers can exercise the practice of their disciplines. Without legislation and policy development, programs and services are nonexistent. This chapter examined a host of policies that impact older adults living in rural communities. Policies such as the OAA, Medicare, SS, the ADA, and the ACA were addressed. In addition, issues such as long-term care, mental health, caregiver support, transportation, income maintenance, and food subsidies were explored in terms of current legislation. Strategies to help support laws that impact older adults are also discussed. Finally, this chapter reviewed a series of competencies and strategies that would benefit from legislation, programs, and services. Although policy development is often perceived to be dry and unexciting by practitioners at the street level, in reality it is the lifeblood of the programs and services they deliver.

A series of issues require attention and action through research and policy development in order to assure that older adults living in rural communities have their needs addressed through social policies that currently exist or will be drafted in the future. These include the following:

a. Develop and maintain projects that help support rural communities identify and promote national policy issues and promising practices for rural health care providers focused on: quality of care, economic viability, access, workforce (recruitment and retention), and the changing health care environment as it relates to insurance coverage expansion

b. Promote available resources to communities for help in shaping their local health care systems to best meet the community needs of older adults

c. Promote promising practices to help older adults living in rural communities with quality initiatives

d. Identify and translate the key points from emerging policy issues to rural health care providers, researchers, and policy makers for the benefit of older adults living within those rural networks

e. Work with state-based entities such as State Offices of Rural Health (SORHs) and State Rural Health Associations (SRHAs) in identifying key rural health challenges that are faced by older adults within these regional areas

f. Provide technical assistance to small entities and rural communities for the purpose of improving access to quality rural health services for older adults living in these communities

g. Provide a forum for rural medical educators and students to share lessons learned to address recruitment and retention challenges

h. Foster the development of rural health systems that benefit and support older adults through the support of rural health networks and services

i. Expand public awareness of the importance of the economic impact of the health care sector and stress health care's critical role in rural development for older adults

j. Improve rural and underserved communities' access to quality health care through the development of national, state, and community-based linkages, particularly for older adults living within these communities

USEFUL WEBSITES

The official site for Medicare information

www.medicare.gov

Portal to governmental resources

www.thomas.gov

Social Security: The official government website

www.ssa.gov/pgm/reach.html

United States Government Accountability Office

www.gao.gov

United States legislative information

www.congress.gov

REFERENCES

Administration on Aging. (2013). *Historical evolution of programs and services for older adults.* Retrieved from http://www.aoa.gov/AoARoot/AoA_Programs/OAA/resources/History.aspx

Agricultural Act of 2014, Pub. L. No. 113-79. Retrieved January 29, 2014, from http://www.thomas.gov

Americans With Disabilities Act of 1990, Pub. L. No. 101-335. Retrieved January 29, 2014, from http://www.thomas.gov

Essex-Sorlie, D. (1994). The Americans With Disabilities Act: History, summary and key components. *Academic Medicine, 68*(7), 519–524.

Heritage Area Agency on Aging. The Legacy Foundation. (2013). *Older American act amendments act of 2013, a summary.* Retrieved from http://involvementonline.org/article/older-americans-reauthorization-act-2013-summary

Jurkowski, E. T. (2008). *Policy and program planning for older adults: Realities and visions.* New York, NY: Springer Publishing Company.

Katz, S. (1983). Assessing self-maintenance: Activities of daily living, mobility and instrumental activities of daily living. *JAGS, 31*(12), 721–726.

Krout, J. (1987). Rural-urban differences in senior center activities and services. *The Gerontologist, 29*(1), 92–97. doi:10-1093/geront/27.1.92

Medicare.gov. (2014). Retrieved February 10, 2014, from http://www.medicare.gov

Napoli, A., & Coello, K. (2013). *Funding for the older Americans act and other associated programs.* Retrieved from http://www.fas.org/sgp/crs/misc/RL33880.pdf

Older Americans Act, Pub. L. No. 89-73 (1965). Retrieved January 20, 2014, from http://www.thomas.gov

Older Americans Act Reauthorization of 2014, H.R. 3850, 113th Cong. (2014).

Pardasani, M., & Thompson, P. (2012). Senior centers: Innovative and emerging models. *Journal of Applied Gerontology, 31*(1), 52–77.

Partnership for Health in Aging. (2010). *Multidisciplinary competencies in the care of older adults at the completion of the entry-level health professional degrees.* Retrieved September 10, 2013, from http://www.americangeriatrics.org/files/documents/health_care_pros/PH A_Multidisc_Competencies.pdf

Rural Transportation Equity Act, Pub. L. No. 108-447. (2004). Retrieved January 20, 2014, from http://www.thomas.gov

Social Security Act of 1935. Pub. L. No. 74-271 (1935). Retrieved February 10, 2014, from http://www.thomas.gov

Social Work Leadership Institute. (n.d.). *Geriatric social work competency scale II with lifelong leadership skills.* Retrieved September 30, 2013, from http://www.cswe.org/File.aspx?id=25445

Wacker, R., & Roberto, K. (2013). *Community resources for older adults: Programs and services in an era of change.* Thousand Oaks, CA: Sage Publications.

Yokum, K. N., & Wagner, D. (2010). *The aging network: A guide to programs and services.* New York, NY: Springer Publishing Company.

Conclusions and Future Directions

KRISTINA M. HASH

ELAINE T. JURKOWSKI

JOHN A. KROUT

This purpose of this book was to respond to the lack of understanding and gaps in knowledge about individuals who are aging in rural places and the programs, policies, and professional practices that impact their well-being. This response has involved examining the problems faced by aging individuals and the professionals who work with them, as well as possible solutions to these problems in terms of effective programs and policies. This final chapter reviews key content, conclusions, and solutions from the book and provides next steps for research, policy and programs, and professional education.

PART I: INTRODUCTION

What Is Rural and Who Are Rural Older Adults?

An important issue that emerged early on in this book (Chapter 1) is how rural is defined. This definition question is important because it determines the data that are used in residential comparisons of older adults in terms of numbers and composition (i.e., age, gender, race, and ethnicity). The definition also impacts how data are collected and categorized for a large number of quality-of-life (QOL) indicators such as income, poverty, health, and housing. These data underlie discussions among researchers and policy makers of the advantages or disadvantages of living in rural versus urban areas and of what living in a rural place means. Equally important, and often overlooked, is that this definitional confusion/opaqueness complicates and compromises comparisons of rural places and people to other rural places and populations. Defining rural as not in a metropolitan county, or not in a metropolitan county but in a micropolitan area, or a place of fewer than 2,500 in population results in different findings on these questions. Over the years, a number of rural–urban continuums have been suggested by researchers that are seen as better than a dichotomous rural/urban distinction and as providing a more nuanced and accurate presentation of residential differences. However, few topics can be studied using these categories because the collection and reporting of variables in such a manner are often not available from primary data sources.

The lack of consensus and consistency on what constitutes a rural place geographically plague research on residential comparisons. Definitions of terms such as *metropolitan* have changed or been refined over time making longitudinal or trend comparisons difficult/misleading. Often, the exact measurement of rural or urban is not made clear in discussions of rural aging. Readers are either not given a definition or only given a very brief definition. Even more troublesome is the lack of any agreed-upon federal definition for data collection or presentation purposes. Different federal agencies use different criteria for what constitutes rural or urban and make statements about rural/urban differences according to this criteria. The U.S. Bureau of the Census 2007–2011 American Community Survey (ACS) has 64 residence categories on which data can be extracted. Ten of these categories are "not in metro." Although this level of specificity provides researchers with an opportunity to make very fine residential distinctions, it clearly is not very parsimonious and contributes to the confusion over residential differences because the exact ACS coding used for rural is often not specified by researchers. Much variation is also found in the definition of rural at the state level and these definitions are often used for state-level planning, funding allocations, and data reporting. This variation may make sense given the scale of population size and density in different states, but it complicates state comparisons.

For example, what is seen as rural in a high population and density state may be seen as much more urban in a low population and density state.

Often, the term *rural* is used to mean not in a metropolitan area. Metropolitan and nonmetropolitan categorizations are based on county boundaries. Rural as defined as a place of less than 2,500 people or open country is not county-based and almost always refers to a smaller geographic area than a county. As noted in Chapter 1, rural as defined by size of place and metropolitan as defined by county are not mutually exclusive. Rural places are often found in metropolitan counties. The important questions are if and how living in a small place in a metropolitan or nonmetropolitan county impacts the status and the experiences of older adults or, conversely, the impact of living in a larger place in a nonmetropolitan county. Unfortunately, most data are not presented or analyzed in a way that allows these questions to be examined. In addition, current cohorts of rural older adults (especially the old-old) may have lived in a rural place before moving to an urban area so teasing out the impact of residence on any number of variables can be very difficult. In-migration of urban older adults to rural retirement areas can create the same challenge. The bottom line is that the current residence of a population provides only a snapshot in fixed time and does not reveal the dynamic relationship between place and people or the changes that occur in a place even as its residents do not.

The impact of definitional muddiness extends to the discussion of what constitutes a rural experience or rural lifestyle, or as Chapter 2 asked, "Who are rural older adults?" For older people, residential comparisons are most often used in examinations of QOL and service or program needs. Health status and nutrition, income, education, housing, and use of services are typically included in rural/urban comparisons. Older adults categorized as rural, regardless of the definition, consistently compare unfavorably to older adults grouped as urban on many QOL measures. But various rural definitions do yield greater or lesser differences, and sometimes, as is the case with specific health conditions, a rural disadvantage disappears altogether.

Residential considerations of other topics such as lifestyle, values, and beliefs are rare and when done, typically involve small sample sizes and a limited number of communities. Thus, the knowledge of rural older people, their experiences and attitudes, and the strengths they and their communities bring to confront old age are not as robust as program planners, providers, and policy makers would hope for. Residential comparisons that clearly identify the indicator(s) used to define a place as rural or urban do contribute to our understanding of the relationship between rural residence and aging. However, much is not known about this relationship and greater definitional and conceptual clarity on what constitutes rural are needed. This conceptual clarity can assure that we accurately depict the experiences of and challenges faced by rural older adults and communities.

Next Steps

There appear to be a number of steps that could be taken to move beyond the current state of definitional inconsistency and confusion in rural aging research. These include the following:

1. More attention by researchers and government (state and federal) agencies to clearly explain how rural is defined and measured in their research and writing
2. More collection and reporting of data that are based on residential continuums as opposed to dichotomies
3. Establishing informal and formal interdisciplinary and interagency groups to explore the impact different definitions have on substantive research questions
4. Holding symposia at gerontology and demographic conferences to investigate the questions that emerge from these groups
5. Establishing an online rural aging research bank that would both help disseminate existing research findings and identify areas in need of more research
6. Encouraging research that highlights the positives and advantages of aging in rural communities, such as the informal supports and the strength and resilience of community older adults

PART II: HEALTH AND HUMAN SERVICE NEEDS OF RURAL OLDER ADULTS

The second part of this book addresses the health and human service needs of older people living in rural communities. Issues that impact the health and wellness among rural older persons are explored. The lifestyle realities that older adults living in rural communities are exposed to are discussed, within the context of housing options and opportunities, and transportation. Layered within these realities are the contexts of income and availability of fiscal resources; thus, socioeconomic factors play a central role in one's housing options and potential lifestyle. All too often a lack of financial resources and greater risk of poverty define the lifestyle, work opportunities, and leisure-time resources of rural older adults.

Chapter 3 explored health issues that are found within rural settings among older adults. The challenge that health disparities poses for rural communities includes the need to address the shortage of trained medical professionals working within rural communities to address the health care needs of older adults. Access to health care, health care professionals, primary care, specialty care, and critical care access all pose challenges that will impact the health outcomes of older adults. Chapter 4 immersed the reader in some of the realities of "aging in place" within rural communities. Housing options are often limited in scope and do not offer the range of options available for people who are in need of a transition from independent living within their own home to settings that provide more support to the individual and promote an enhanced level of security. Finally, transportation services within rural settings are complex systems that face multiple barriers to providing adequate services.

Chapter 5 addressed the realities of work, retirement, and leisure within rural settings, and deals with how people advancing in age transition from their livelihood to working for the opportunity to fill a community need/role and to promote general well-being. Although many view work, retirement, and leisure as three separate and distinct streams of activity, the reality for many older adults living in rural communities is that these three concepts may flow along a continuum. All too often, opportunities for meaningful employment have been limited in a rural community, which in turn leads to limited opportunities for older adults living in rural communities who may want to contribute to the labor force. Whereas agricultural opportunities may be more available in rural communities, these opportunities may leave women in an economically disadvantaged position if widowed or divorced due to the self-employment nature of the role. The agrarian nature of many rural communities may also leave people who are older adults underemployed, if they choose to maintain some employment in their later years. Conversely, the many opportunities for volunteerism and civic engagement within rural communities can be a definite strength of rural communities. People remain connected with their communities through community engagement and citizen participation.

The most striking reality throughout all chapters in this section is the paucity of research that focuses upon rural issues and outcomes. Research is also limited on the diversity of findings across rural settings. Policies tend to favor urban areas, and although social policies related to health, housing, transportation, and economic security definitely impact rural areas, the policies tend not to address the multifaceted needs that rural areas present. Consequently, policies may not facilitate ideal solutions for rural residents and older adults living within rural communities.

The chapters within this section also highlighted the need for specific practices and focus to address the needs of older adults living in rural communities, and attempts to help these individuals to optimize opportunities. As noted in Chapter 3, health disparities exist in rural communities, and health care access, availability, and affordability are issues that may impact one's health outcomes. Specialists available to local communities or accessible within driving distance are issues that impact rural communities. The idea that one must be "strong" and the stoicism that evolves because of the lack of resources also pose barriers for the development of reasonable access to care.

Next Steps

Some next steps that could help meet the needs older adults in rural areas include the following:

1. Convene a rural providers' summit that would bring together rural service providers who supply services to older adults from across the nation to discuss and prioritize how programs and services that result in service delivery to rural older adults could be adapted to better meet the uniqueness and challenges of rural settings
2. Collaborate with advocacy groups (such as the National Rural Health Association, Rural Social Work Caucus, etc.) to bring changes to existing legislation to address rural differences and challenges faced by older adults
3. Work with local health departments to identify some health disparities within local areas that impact older adults and assure that these challenges are integrated in local area plans for health intervention priorities

4. Identify local strategies to promote access to transportation services and a transportation network within rural communities, especially with the older adult in mind

5. Develop and disseminate models of best-practice service delivery options that will impact the lives of older adults within the areas of health, housing, employment, recreation, leisure, and transportation through state-based Departments of Aging and Area Agencies on Aging (AAAs)

PART III: PROVIDING HEALTH AND HUMAN SERVICES TO RURAL OLDER ADULTS

Part III of this book examined specific services to rural older adults through the venues of health and social/human services. A sobering reality demonstrated by this segment of the book is that not enough is known about rural areas, rural older people, and programs and policies that work for this population. Funding schemes to advance research and evidence-based practice within most fields have focused upon urban communities, with little funding to identify how these issues are impacted in rural communities, and few comparative research studies to identify how interventions yield similar or different outcomes in rural communities. Along with this issue is the need for more evidence-based practice models specific to outcomes for older adults residing in rural communities.

Chapter 6 explored the role that programs and services offer older adults who live in rural communities. The chapter provided a broad overview of service needs and challenges facing rural adults. It discussed the underlying causes of the rural service deficit and the factors that need to be addressed to ameliorate it. The chapter sensitized readers to the complexity of building and utilizing services in rural communities and aimed to help them become aware of the challenges and shortcomings that practitioners face when working in rural communities.

Chapter 7 focused on the range of services available to older adults to help maintain their mental vitality and wellness within rural communities and made the case that engagement is central to wellness and successful aging. Support systems intertwined with activities germane to one's community are strategies used by older adults living in rural communities who are successful in terms of the aging process and who are relatively healthy. As reviewed in this chapter, older adults stay connected through educational activities, volunteer activities, caregiving activities, and paid employment. Recreation, physical activity, gardening, group activities, and travel programming play key roles in the leisure realm for older adults living in rural communities. Opportunities for socialization include senior centers, programming at local religious institutions, and through taking advantage of technology. Each of these venues for socialization is changing within rural communities because cohort differences and expectations (i.e., old-old vs. baby boomers) are leading providers to be more responsive to the changing times, world, and technology. Civic engagement, leadership, and volunteerism, also facets that contribute to lifelong well-being, are described as increasingly essential ingredients for older adults who are thriving in rural communities. Education and lifelong learning are also addressed in the chapter as a venue for maintaining connections with others within one's community and social network, and contribute to overall cognitive and mental well-being. The trend toward later employment, although ideal to help with social engagement and some modest supplement to one's income, can pose a challenge to the older worker due to a shortage in viable employment options and the need for skill redevelopment to accommodate advances in the employment arena.

Chapter 8 dealt with the issue of providing services to frail older adults in rural communities. This chapter examined the range of services available for acute care such as hospitals and home health care and long-term care through in-home and community-based service. Behavioral health and dementia care, critical elements of any long-term care system, were addressed as well as were skilled and long-term residential care and assisted-living facilities. Last, end-of-life care is discussed in the chapter. This chapter showcased some of the challenges that practitioners face when working in rural communities and raised the realities of dual relationships, boundaries, and confidentiality—all possible problems as they strive to work with frail older persons in rural settings.

Next Steps

Some next steps that could greatly improve service delivery to older adults in rural areas include the following:

1. Work with local coalitions of providers to examine strategies to build in best-practice and evidence-based practice interventions within services constellation networks
2. Utilize new technologies (telemedicine, electronic and telephone applications) to help build upon opportunities for resources available to well and frail older adults living in rural communities
3. Advocate for the development of resources and services based upon evidence-based approaches, and evaluate the efficacy of these resources

PART IV: COMPETENT PRACTICE IN RURAL AREAS

In recent years, there has been a major movement toward competency-based practice (CBE) in geriatrics. This book presents such competencies, with the Partnership for Health in Aging (PHA; 2010) competencies discussed at length in Chapters 9 and 10, and the geriatric social work competencies (Social Work Leadership Institute, n.d.) detailed in Chapter 11. The book has also gone a step beyond and examined these competencies in light of the unique complexities of practice in rural areas.

The majority of health and human service providers may not have specialized training in geriatrics, but they do see many older adults in their practices. For this reason, practitioners must know the community in which they practice and its culture. These practitioners must also acknowledge the unique issues that they face in rural communities. In terms of professional ethics, these issues include the difficulty of maintaining confidentiality and managing boundaries and dual relationships. The realities of practice in these communities also include limited job opportunities, professional isolation, and the possibility of being considered an "outsider." In working with older patients and clients in these rural areas, providers can expect to face the challenges of limited health and community resources.

Despite these challenges, many prefer to practice in rural settings and find it rewarding because of their close connection with patients and the community and the ability to offer services in an underserved area. As mentioned, there may be personal qualities that make practitioners better suited for rural practice. In some cases, communities have the advantage of "home-growing" professionals who have grown up in their town, received a professional degree, and stayed or returned to the area to practice.

Institutions of higher education and continuing education programs provide the opportunities to attain necessary knowledge and skills for health and human service professionals to care for and assist rural older adults and their families. Many of these programs do not offer specific specializations or content in geriatrics, let alone rural geriatrics. And, although individuals may practice in urban areas, they often come into contact with rural residents who commute to urban organizations to receive care and assistance. Thus, "sometimes urban is rural" and the educational programs are not always preparing students and professionals for this reality. Professional organizations also offer sets of competencies for geriatric practice and these competencies are integrated into professional education. Unfortunately, these competencies do not always reflect the unique features and issues involved in rural practice. Technology plays a significant role in providing education to students and professionals.

Next Steps

A number of steps could be taken to more adequately train, recruit, and retain professionals to work with persons aging in rural communities, including the following:

1. Professional schools should include geriatric content and rural content, regardless of whether the program is urban or rural
2. Clinical practice rotations within rural settings should be considered as a component of training for professional health and human service providers as a strategy to expose providers to the uniqueness of rural practice and rural practice with older adults
3. Educators and practitioners should continue to investigate and disseminate ways interdisciplinary practice can work in rural areas
4. Professional associations should evaluate professional competencies in light of the realties of rural practice for health and human service professionals
5. Educators, continuing education providers, and organizations should continue to maximize use of technology in providing education to health and human service professionals
6. Marketing and incentives should be more widely utilized to attract health and human service professionals to live and work

in rural communities. These could include tax incentives, loan repayment opportunities, and housing/relocation allowances via tax deductions.

PART V: CONCLUSIONS AND FUTURE DIRECTIONS

Although many people would like to generalize that one type of rural community is the reality for all rural communities, hopefully the notions of individuality and difference emerged throughout this book. Whereas it would be easy to generalize across settings, regions, and geography, the reality is that each rural setting has its own personality and needs. With this reality, and as was apparent in Chapter 12, it is critical that policies and program development that pertain to rural communities facilitate the uniqueness of specific regional and geographic areas, rather than taking a "one size fits all" approach. Programs that emanate from the Older Americans Act (OAA), Medicare, Medicaid, and the Affordable Care Act (ACA) need to provide funding incentives to providers to assure that they are fairly compensated for the cost of providing services to older adults residing in rural communities. In addition, incentives should also be integrated into program development opportunities in efforts to make service provision an attractive opportunity for service providers in rural communities.

Next Steps

Policies and program planning initiatives that impact rural communities and their older adult populations would benefit from some of the following strategies targeting research, practice, and policy development, as follows:

1. Provide funds to support research initiatives monitored through the National Rural Health Policy and Community Development Program. Ideally this program would develop and maintain projects that should help support rural communities through a broad range of activities to include the promotion of national policy issues and promising practices for rural health care providers
2. Develop policies to facilitate forums for rural medical educators and students to share lessons learned to address recruitment and retention challenges

3. Convene policy discussions around emerging rural health access issues and rural leadership in hospitals, clinics, and communities vital to the survival of the rural health delivery systems

4. Ensure that policy development cultivates rural health systems through the support of rural health networks

5. Ensure policy development to improve rural and underserved communities' access to quality health care through the development of national, state, and community-based linkages, in support of recruitment and retention efforts

6. Consider the incidence and prevalence of health care conditions and issues and allocate resources accordingly through policies and program development. The traditional strategy of using "head count" for the allocation of resources consistently has disadvantaged rural-based communities and their residents. Professionals working within rural-based settings need to become advocates to argue for the need and importance of comparing rates of conditions (number of cases as the numerator ÷ the population × 100 or 1,000) rather than actual numbers or cases

7. Promote research initiatives through the National Institutes of Health (NIH) and HRSA (Health Resources and Services Administration) on the health outcomes of rural-based older adults versus health outcomes of urban adults involved in specific interdisciplinary practice

FINAL THOUGHTS

This is the conclusion of a journey into the lives and issues of older adults living in rural communities and settings. This journey has exposed readers to myriad issues, dimensions, and concerns that impact older adults nestled in rural communities; it has explored these concerns and identified policies, practices, and professional issues and needs. In addition, it has proposed potential solutions or "next steps" for addressing these issues and needs and improving the health and well-being of persons aging in rural communities. Immediate and widespread attention to these and other solutions are critical and rural communities and their older residents deserve nothing less.

REFERENCES

Partnership for Health in Aging. (2010). *Multidisciplinary competencies in the care of older adults at the completion of the entry-level health professional degrees.* Retrieved September 10, 2013, from A_Multidisc_Competencies.pdf

Social Work Leadership Institute. (n.d.). *Geriatric social work competency scale II with lifelong leadership skills.* Retrieved September 30, 2013, from http://www.cswe.org/File.aspx?id=25445

INDEX